Lovescapes

# Lovescapes
Mapping the Geography of Love

*An Invitation to the Love-Centered Life*

# Duncan S. Ferguson

CASCADE *Books* • Eugene, Oregon

LOVESCAPES, MAPPING THE GEOGRPAHY OF LOVE
An Invitation to the Love-Centered Life

Copyright © 2012 Duncan S. Ferguson. All rights reserved. Except for brief quotations in critical publications or reviews, no part of this book may be reproduced in any manner without prior written permission from the publisher. Write: Permissions, Wipf and Stock Publishers, 199 W. 8th Ave., Suite 3, Eugene, OR 97401.

Cascade Books
An Imprint of Wipf and Stock Publishers
199 W. 8th Ave., Suite 3
Eugene, OR 97401

www.wipfandstock.com

ISBN 13: 978-1-62032-133-1

*Cataloging-in-Publication data:*

Ferguson, Duncan S.

    Lovescapes, mapping the geography of love : an invitation to the love-centered life / Duncan S. Ferguson.

    xiv + 294 p. ; 23 cm. —Includes bibliographical references and index.

    ISBN 13: 978-1-62032-133-1

    1. Love—Religious Aspects. 2. Religion and science. I. Title.

BV4639 .F45 2012

Manufactured in the U.S.A.

To Dorothy and Brian whom I love with all of
"the depth and breadth and height my soul can reach."
—Robert Browning

"In the evening of life, we will be judged on love alone."
ST. JOHN OF THE CROSS

# Contents

*Preface*  ix

**Section I:** The Need for Love in Contemporary Life  1
  **1** Love in an Age of Crisis  3

**Section II:** The Geography of Love  29
  **2** The Understanding of Love Its Ground, Contours, and Dimensions  31
  **3** The Understanding of Love across History, Tradition, and Culture  53
  **4** The Understanding of Love within the World Religions  82

**Section III:** The Development of Love  109
  **5** The Nurturing Environment  111
  **6** Endowed for Love  138
  **7** Empowered to Love  163

**Section IV:** The Practice of Love  189
  **8** Love in Primary Relationships  191
  **9** Love and Compassion in Region and Society  217
  **10** Love in the Global Context: Creating a Culture of Compassion  244

*Bibliography*  271
*Index*  281

# Preface

ACROSS THE YEARS, I have gradually come to believe that the greatest human need is to love and be loved. Several experiences and exposures in my life have led me to this conviction, and because the insights gained from this reflection are so poignant for me, I want to briefly trace out the curve of my learning. I look back on my childhood, growing up in a somewhat dysfunctional family filled with alcohol abuse and all of its side effects, and I realize that I was deprived of the joy of living spontaneously and engaging in carefree play that blossom in a setting of love. My internal life was filled with strategy and calculation, believing that life was a bit risky and that the adults around me were driven by their own needs and could be angry and rejecting at any moment. As a boy and young adult, I spent a lot of time wondering if I was acceptable and worked hard in my studies and sports programs to demonstrate that I was a person of value, one that was "lovable." I focused on managing the conflicting and confusing array of emotions that swirled around me. My boyhood and young adult years were filled with a strong desire to be accepted, and I chose a way that was designed around pleasing others, feeling as I did that I was not truly loved although I may have been in a way that I was unable to recognize.

Gradually, as I became an adult, I began to understand the needs that were driving me, and I was able to become a more congruent person, true to myself and my values. But the need for love, which was not always conditional and driven by the needs of those around me, has not totally gone away. I find myself still wanting to be accepted, even respected by others. I do not sit in harsh judgment upon my parents for bequeathing me this psychic struggle. They did about as well as they could, given who they were. In fact, I have increasingly become a little sad that they did not have more rich and fulfilling lives and wish that I might have loved them better.

*Preface*

As the years have come and gone and I have developed committed primary relationships, established life-long friendships, and have associated with a wide variety of people in my work, I notice that I am not alone in needing and expressing love. Those around me struggle with the same issues, even if the pathways have been different. Gradually, pondering this reality, I have the growing conviction that love is the heart of life. Of course life is filled with a wide variety of activities and responsibilities that do not fit into the general category of love; they are important in their own right. But I have come to accept the logic of the Apostle Paul in his letter to the Corinthian church, "If I . . . [engage in a wide variety of activities, even noble ones], but have not love, I am nothing." Love is the cohering motivation for all that I do. Having been nurtured in the Christian faith, I have reflected on the saying attributed to Jesus drawn from the Hebrew Bible, "You shall love the Lord your God with all of your heart, and with all of your soul, and with all of your mind." This is the greatest and first commandment. And a second is like it: "You shall love your neighbor as yourself." On these two commandments hang all of the law and the prophets" (Matt 22:37–40). There is also the foundational statement by the author of 1 John 4:16b: "God is love, and those who abide in love abide in God, and God abides in them." These sayings serve to confirm my conviction that love is the ground of all of reality.

In addition, as I have had the privilege of traveling in many parts of the world to observe firsthand several of the religions of the human family, I have learned that these grand traditions teach their followers that love and compassion are central to their faith and ethical codes. I have also chosen a career that has invited me to study the world religions in some detail, and it has become clear to me that the ethic of love is integral to the beliefs and practices of the vast majority of the religions of humankind.

Given this exposure, I began several years ago to engage in a more systematic study of love. I have read many different kinds of literature, in religious studies, in the broad range of the humanities, in the social sciences, and in the physical sciences. I have read fiction, poetry, and gazed at the best expressions of the visual arts. Again, I was conscious that there was a wide variety of issues dealt with in these excellent products of the human mind and spirit, but I noticed that human relationships and the need for love were central themes. Growing out of this exposure, I was motivated to teach several courses in the context of the church and the academy that required a disciplined study of the literature of love.

*Preface*

I have become aware more recently of the emergence of a minor discipline on the study of love and in particular the study of altruism and compassion.[1] This movement has expanded and has encouraged some fine scholars to participate in this area of study.[2] A case might also be made that there is a new global consciousness emerging, given the current realities in the world (e.g., human hunger, natural disasters, violence, and global warming) and the ways that most of the people of the world can be immediately aware of them. Many of the people of the world can identify with human suffering, and so running concurrently with these global challenges is an increased empathy for human suffering and a genuine desire to reduce it.[3]

These factors and others have created in me a desire to explore the terrain of love in all its manifestations. I want to investigate how love and its cognates are crucial to human happiness and well-being, and how love and compassion will help in finding solutions to the problems we face in our time. It is a writing project that has been "bubbling up" inside me for years. I chose the title *Lovescapes, Mapping the Geography of Love: An Invitation to the Love-Centered Life* because the topography of love is so vast and diverse and because beautiful landscapes and lovescapes are life-giving and peaceful.

I begin in Section I by addressing the harsh realities of our global context and place a special emphasis on the need for an infusion of love and compassion at all levels of human life. Attention is given to the ways that love and compassion can serve to give perspective and motivation to those who address the international and regional problems that cause human suffering. I maintain that love can improve the quality of our individual lives, address their anxiety-filled character, and help reduce the ubiquity of loneliness.[4]

---

1. See the book by Post, *Unlimited Love: Altruism, Compassion, and Service*. Stephen Post has served as the President of the Institute for Research on Unlimited Love, an initiative funded by the Templeton Foundation. See as well the mission of the Fetzer Foundation which has the mission of "exploring and advancing the power of love, forgiveness and compassion." There are also some institutions of higher education that have introduced love and altruism into the curriculum.

2. See the essays in Post, et al., *Altruism and Altruistic Love: Science, Philosophy, and Religion in Dialogue*. See as well the volume edited by Sternberg and Weis, *The New Psychology of Love*, one that is an update of an earlier book entitled *The Psychology of Love*, edited by Sternberg and Barnes.

3. See Rifkin, *The Empathic Civilization: The Race to Global Consciousness in a World in Crisis*.

4. This point is integral to Cacioppo and Patrick, *Loneliness: Human Nature and*

## Preface

Section II, in three chapters, introduces the many ways that love is understood and offers a common universe of discourse. Love is described in all of its dimensions with care given to definitions of love and its many cognates. There is a description of the ways that love has been understood across history and in different traditions and cultures. Section II also traces the understanding of love within the teachings of the world religions.

Section III raises the question, where does love come from? How it is that we learn how to love and practice love more consistently in our lives? There are three chapters in this section as well, one speaking to the ways that our environment and the influences in our lives shape our capacity to love. It is the ecology of human development that enables us to love or diminishes our capacity to love.[5] The next chapter examines the ways that we are "wired" for love, that is, the ways that our physical nature has the need for love integral to it. Our "DNA" enables us to love or may prevent us from being a loving person. A third chapter in this section addresses the ways our beliefs and practices can encourage the practice of love and how we can be empowered to love.

Section IV, in three chapters, goes directly to the practice of love, looking first at love in primary relationships with a spouse or a committed partner, with family, and with those in the immediate context of one's life. The next chapter suggests ways of loving responsibly in the community where one lives and the surrounding region. The additional chapter in this section explores ways that the insights from the broad understanding of love might be applied in the national and global context.

Section V invites the reader to consider what it might mean to move toward a love-centered life. Perspectives, practices, and strategies are suggested for what might be called "love development."

I am indebted to the many friends who have lovingly counseled and advised me about this writing project. I am especially grateful to Vickie Drebing Crupi for her guidance in the use of information technology and her formatting skills, and to my wife, Dorothy, who assisted with the proof-reading. I am also grateful to Princeton Theological Seminary, which honored me as a Visiting Scholar in the fall of 2010, enabling dedicated time for writing and access to excellent resources for research.

---

*the Need for Social Connection.* See also Christakis and Fowler, *Connected: The Surprising Power of Our Social Networks and How They Shape Our Lives*, and Putnam, *Bowling Alone: The Collapse and Revival of American Community*.

5. Bronfenbrenner, *The Ecology of Human Development: Experiments by Nature and Design*.

*Preface*

Reading, writing, and teaching about love have been a great gift, one for which I will always be grateful. But that for which I am even more grateful has been the experience of loving and being loved. It is my wish as I offer to the reader my reflections on the love-centered life that those who read will also be those who love and are loved.

## SECTION I

# The Need for Love in Contemporary Life

PERHAPS EVERY AGE IS an age of crisis, although the judgment that is made about a period of time being in crisis may depend upon the conditions of one's life in a particular moment of history. It may be a crisis for some and not for others. The judgment about our age being a time of crisis is confirmed by most of us; the majority of us would say that we do live in a troubled time. Regardless of our circumstances, we who live in the early part of the twenty-first century find the problems we face daunting in character. Perhaps it is because our problems are staggering in complexity and stubbornly resist our efforts to solve them. Or it may be because they threaten our way of life and our earth habitat. In Section I we will briefly describe the range of these overwhelming problems, point out their size and difficulty, and propose that love and compassion, understood in their several meanings, have a critical role to play in solving them, or at least in gaining perspective about them and easing the pain and suffering which they cause.

> The world is a theatre of love.
> —KASHMIRI PROVERB

# 1

# Love in an Age of Crisis

## A PICTURE OF OUR CRISIS

THE POPULAR SONG OF a previous generation, which invited us to sing along, opened with the following words: "What the world needs now is love sweet love. It's the only thing that there's just too little of." These lyrics were true at an earlier time and certainly true today. We live in a difficult moment of history, one filled with vexing problems that have an enormous impact on individual lives. While there are signs of hope and encouragement, it is nevertheless accurate to say that we live in a volatile world, filled with global warming and a threatened physical environment, natural disasters, insoluble wars, international conflict, insurgency and violence, religious intolerance, cities rampant with crime, widespread poverty, devastating hunger, a threatened economy, failing states, and the list goes on and on. It would be easy to give up hope, especially if one is caught in the middle of one of these conditions. Perhaps Richard Cory was such a person, as described in the poem by Edward Arlington Robinson:

> Whenever Richard Cory went downtown
> We people on the pavement looked at him;
> He was a gentleman from sole to crown,
> Clean favored, and imperially slim.
> And he was always quietly arrayed,
> And he was always human when he talked;
> But still he fluttered pulses when he said,

# Section I — The Need for Love in Contemporary Life

> "Good morning," and he glittered when he walked.
> And he was rich—yes, richer than a king—
> And admirably schooled in every grace:
> In fine, we thought that he was everything
> To make us wish that we were in his place.
> So on he worked, and waited for the light,
> And went home without meat, and cursed the bread;
> And Richard Cory, one calm summer night,
> Went home and put a bullet through his head.

What Richard Cory needed was someone to give him "love sweet love." The fundamental purpose of this book is to add love and compassion in what I hope is a wise and realistic way as one part of the strategy as we seek to find solutions to the overwhelming problems we must face in the decades ahead. I am well aware that this rhetoric may be viewed as almost naïve, uninformed by a grasp of the complexity of the issues, real-world politics and uses of power, and the subtleties of human nature. In light of this point of view, I am reluctant to claim that love and compassion are *the* answer, but these qualities of the human spirit have the potential to provide an outlook and motivation for developing strategies to approach these staggering challenges. I am given guidance and encouraged by the Dalai Lama's determination to place love and compassion at the forefront of his life and leadership.[1]

The harsh realities which humankind must address in the first quarter of the twenty-first century are challenging, perplexing, and alarming. They are challenging in the sense that they demand solutions that require political will, international cooperation, and enormous costs. For example, to find solutions to the problem of global warming means challenging the vested interests of corporations whose profits depend upon the continuation of the use of fossil fuels. As we know, the extensive use of fossil fuels threatens the delicate ecological balance that sustains life. Questioning these vested interests requires political risk for elected officials. The same "inconvenient truth" about the environment requires international cooperation because global warming is indeed global, not exclusively regional, although some regions may feel its impact more profoundly than others.[2] Efforts to achieve international cooperation in solving the problems of the environment have been mixed at best. The costs of addressing the variety of problems caused by global warming are astronomical and require a

---

1. See for example the small book by the Dalai Lama, *The Compassionate Life*.
2. See Gore, *An Inconvenient Truth*.

fundamental shift of values and ways of life, not easy for any individual, society, or nation.

These harsh realities are also perplexing because the size and complexity of the problems are beyond the scope of what humankind has ever had to address before. New research and technologies are required for many of these disturbing problems. For example, new strategies and approaches are required in stabilizing the changing climate. It has been necessary to engineer a revolution in lighting technology and produce energy-efficient appliances that will reduce dependence on excessive uses of electricity. Cutting carbon emissions has meant a turn toward electrifying the transportation systems.[3] In a wide variety of ways, we have had to find new ways of generating energy that will stabilize the climate of the earth.

The tremendous changes that are occurring have caused alarm on many fronts. Again, to illustrate, there is the life and death issue of feeding over seven billion people well. It is not easy to learn about and watch children of the world suffer and die because of malnutrition and starvation. In fact it is so painful that we often switch channels or lay the paper aside in order to put it out of our minds. There may be enough food on the earth to feed all of the people of the world, but it is not easy to distribute food equitably across country and continental boundaries, and underlying equitable food distribution is the competition for water.[4] Equally alarming is the continuation of international conflict and the resort to violence to resolve conflict. At this point in time, we wonder if the violence in Iraq, Afghanistan, and the Middle East (and larger Arab world) will ever cease as others have wondered in the midst of their wars whether the violence would ever cease. We all suffer from the consequences of war, but it is especially the innocent who suffer the most. Finding solutions for world hunger and international conflict will require new strategies and shifts of outlook on the ways that we live together on the planet.

The purpose of this chapter is to provide a brief description of these critical concerns in order to see how love and compassion may be factors in addressing them. The description will be brief, providing only a glimpse of the current problems that must be faced by the human family. We divide these issues into two categories: (1) those that are global in character and deal with existing infrastructure and the macro systems that cause distress in nearly every corner of the planet; and (2) the ways that these conditions impact individuals, causing suffering, illness, and general dis-ease.

---

3. Brown, *Plan B 4.0: Mobilizing to Save Civilization*, 79–105.
4. Sachs, *Common Wealth: Economics for a Crowded World*, 115–37.

# Section I — The Need for Love in Contemporary Life

## THE EXPRESSION OF THE CRISIS IN THE WORLD WE INHABIT

I will group the global concerns in the following categories:[5]

1. The issues dealing with ecology.
2. The issues dealing with over-population.
3. The issues dealing with poverty, hunger, and disease.
4. The issues dealing with the global economy.
5. The issues dealing with war and conflict.

A central concern of all who dwell on the earth is whether it will remain a habitat that allows humans and all sentient beings to continue to flourish and live in an *environment* that will sustain a high quality of life. There are those who would argue that the earth continues to be relatively safe for all of life and that the changes we see and experience are just the natural rhythms of the earth which have within them some natural threat. Some knowledgeable scholars do not fully believe in what we have come to call global warming and deny that the slight change is caused by human practices.[6] But the scientific evidence would say otherwise; there is indeed a crisis that must be faced with a change in human behavior. It is a reality which if not dealt with in a timely and informed way will cause great suffering. The challenges are many.[7] There is the pressure of the increasing population that will tax the land and water resources of the earth. Already, a large percentage of the population does not have access to clean water and sanitation, causing disease and malnutrition with a devastating impact on children. Farmers who provide the food for the people of our cities and whose water tables are falling are in conflict with the cities for limited water supplies. There are political conflicts locally, regionally, and internationally about the use of land and access to water. Increasingly, there are "environmental refugees," vast numbers of people whose water supply has dwindled to little or nothing and whose land is no longer fertile. These

---

5. I am aware that there are many other issues and categories that might be listed, but would invite the reader to view this list as illustrative rather than exhaustive.

6. For example, Professor Fred Singer of the University of Virginia, a distinguished emeritus professor of environmental science, has serious questions about global warming.

7. Brown, *Plan B 4.0*. I am indebted to Lester Brown, the President of the Earth Policy Institute for his excellent research and clear and thoughtful publications. His book, *World on the Edge: How to Prevent Environmental and Economic Collapse* clearly states the challenges.

problems coupled with others are causing a number of failed states whose populations migrate to find ways of surviving.[8]

Equally alarming is the changing climate. Global warming is happening, temperatures are rising, ice is melting, floods are occurring, and populations are threatened, especially in the coastal areas of China, India, and Bangladesh with their large populations. We are reaching the time when we must act wisely and definitively or millions of people will suffer or die. As former Vice President Al Gore, in quoting Winston Churchill, writes, "The era of procrastination, of half measures, of soothing and baffling expedients, of delays, is coming to a close. In its place we are entering a period of consequences."[9] We must make an energy transition, moving away from fossil fuels and carbon emission to other sources of energy including wind farms, solar thermal power plants, and geothermal power plants.

Interwoven with the threat to the environment, as already implied, is the dramatic increase in the world's *population*. We are living on a crowded planet and with this condition has come the necessary economic activity to sustain this enormous growth.[10] The world's population has risen by more than 4 billion people since I finished my elementary education in the 1950s and is edging toward 8 billion, increasing each day. The world has changed dramatically in what feels like just a blink of time. The Sub-Saharan Africa population is 4 times larger than it was in 1950, going from 180 million to approximately 820 million. The same pace of growth has occurred in western Asia, a region that includes the Middle East, Turkey, and the Caucasus region, from 51 million in 1950 to approximately 220 million in 2007. Similar rates of growth have occurred in parts of Asia as well. Jeffrey Sachs lists six fundamental and challenging economic changes that have accompanied the steep increase in the population:[11]

1. First, the process of sustaining economic growth has now reached most of the world, so that humanity on average is rapidly getting richer in terms of income per person. Moreover, the gap in average income per persons between the rich world, centered in the North Atlantic (Europe and the United States), and much of the developing world is narrowing faster.

---

8. *Plan B 4.0*, 21.

9. *An Inconvenient Truth*, 100–1.

10. I am following the explanation of economist, Jeffrey D. Sachs, *Common Wealth: Economics for a Crowded Planet*, 17–53, and have been informed as well by his book, *The End of Poverty: Economic Possibilities for Our Time*.

11. *Common Wealth*, 17–18.

# Section I — The Need for Love in Contemporary Life

2. Second, the world's population will continue to rise, thereby amplifying the overall growth of the global economy. Not only are we each producing more output on average, but there will be many more of us by midcentury. The scale of the world's economic production is therefore likely to be several times that of today.

3. Third, the rise in income will be greatest in Asia, home to more than half of the world's population. As a result, the world will not only be much richer by 2050 but will have its economic center of gravity in Asia.

4. Fourth, the way people live is changing fundamentally as well, from rural roots that stretch back to the beginning of humanity to a global urban civilization. We crossed the midway point between urban and rural in 2008, on a one-way path to an urban-based economy.

5. Fifth, the overall impact of human activity on the physical environment is producing multiple environmental crises as never before in history. The environmental crises we face cannot be compared with the past because never before in history has the magnitude of human economic activity been large enough to change fundamental processes on a global scale, including the climate itself.

6. Sixth, the gap between the richest and the poorest is widening to proportions simply unimaginable for most people. This is not contradictory to the idea that on average the poor are getting richer. Most are, but the bottom billion on the planet are stuck in a poverty trap, which has prevented them from experiencing sustained economic growth. The center is in sub-Saharan Africa. This is also the site of the fastest population growth, meaning that the population bulge is occurring in the part of the world that at this point is least able to generate jobs.

The challenge of responding to this growth of population and its impact on the economy and way of life of the people on the planet creates an extraordinary challenge for those who shape global policy. At the heart of the challenge is how to create sustainable development in those regions facing extreme *poverty, hunger, and disease*. There are at least 1.3 billion people living below the poverty line. Approximately 850 million are malnourished, and as many as 880 million are without access to medical care. One billion lack adequate shelters. 1.3 billion have no access to safe drinking water. 113 million go without schooling, and most of them are girls. Another 2.6 billion go without sanitation, and about 30,000 die each day from preventable diseases. Life expectancy is quite low in several countries, many of them African, but some in Asia and Latin America as well.[12]

All of the global issues, the deteriorating environment, the inordinate growth of the population, and the increase in poverty, hunger, and diseases are interwoven with the ways that the human family must find to guide the *global economy*. This is necessary to insure that there is movement toward creating a world that is more just and peaceful and sustains a reasonable quality of life for all of the people of the earth. But in fact the current status of the global economy sustains the disproportionate differences between the wealthy and the poor. The assets of a few of the wealthiest people are more than the combined wealth of 600 million inhabitants of the least-developed countries. The extraordinary wealth of these few is shocking when placed alongside of the misery of the world's poor, starving, and diseased. What is emerging is the keen awareness that these stark contrasts in wealth cannot continue. The global economy must change in ways that encourage sustainable development in all parts of the world, ways that will protect the environment, stabilize the world's population, narrow the gap between the rich and the poor, and end extreme poverty. As noted economist Jeffrey Sachs says, "The defining challenge of the twenty-first century will be to face the reality that humanity shares a *common fate on a crowded planet*. The common fate will require new forms of global cooperation, a fundamental point of blinding simplicity that many world leaders have yet to understand or embrace."[13]

Finally, in this glance at the global challenges we face, I would mention the challenge of finding ways of resolving conflicts that do not resort to *violence and war*. War has become increasingly obsolete, if in fact it was ever the best solution for the resolution of conflicts. It is difficult for many people to see much value in the war in Iraq or the earlier one in Vietnam. Now, many are questioning whether there is wisdom in the continuing conflict in Afghanistan, especially as this war drains important resources for a struggling economy in the United States and its allies in NATO. The conflicts across the Middle East (and larger Arab world) pose still another baffling challenge. This is not to say that the conflicts are not very real, and there are those who do and will use violence to try to advance their cause. It is rather to say that the resort to violence, as a general rule, does not really make life better for those living in the regions where the wars

---

12. Jonathan Sachs, *The Dignity of Difference: How to Avoid the Clash of Civilizations*, 29.
13. *Common Wealth*, 3.

## Section I — The Need for Love in Contemporary Life

are taking place or after the wars have ceased. In fact, the violence has made life much more difficult for these populations that dwell in the war-torn regions. Nearly every country will have to assess its foreign policy in the twenty-first century and judge whether the resort to arms is a helpful strategy. It is certainly clear that violence does not assist in solving the global problems of the environment, the increasing population, and global poverty and hunger.

The United States is perhaps the best case in point as it continues to resort to violence in order to insure American security. There are changes in shades and tones as America moves from one President to another, but there is little evidence that the fundamental strategies of the United States are changing dramatically.[14] The current administration, under President Barack Obama, may not be acknowledging the limits of military power as a means of preserving American security and finding solutions to global problems. Also, the current power blocs on the American scene may not be fully utilizing our international partners as a primary means of advancing global stability. Military leaders in the United States continue to believe their own rhetoric about dominance and the role of the United States to preserve peace in the world, failing to recognize the limits of American power and the reluctance of other countries to have the United States interfere in their affairs. On occasion, there are those who demonize or at least caricature adversaries and reject dialogue and negotiation with them. At times, we feel frustrated because the government does not seem to function well and is not able to respond quickly or appropriately to international conflict. Our foreign policy, government structure, and our resort to dated strategies must change.

## THE EXPRESSION OF THE CRISIS IN OUR INDIVIDUAL LIVES

There are many other pressing global concerns, but perhaps the mention of these five—a threatened environment, the dramatic increase in the population, the collective problems of poverty, hunger and disease, a struggling economy, and war and violence—will be suggestive of what we face as a global community and as individuals who struggle to make life meaningful and fulfilling. I want to turn now to the profound challenges and problems which individuals in different parts of the world face daily and for which they struggle to find solutions in order to maintain

---

14. Sachs, *Common Wealth*, 272–89.

or improve the conditions of their lives. Again, I will bunch them in five categories as a way of illustrating, although not describing in detail, these challenges and concerns. I will tend to focus on the state of living in the United States in that it is what I face and observe on a daily basis, knowing it may not be representative of the conditions and realities that exist in other parts of the world. I will not utilize a simple cause-effect argument that the global problems cause the challenges for individuals, although the global issues do have a profound impact on the conditions that individuals deal with day to day. The five on which I want to focus are:

1. The challenge of receiving adequate health care.
2. The challenge of gaining access to high quality education.
3. The challenge of having an adequate income.
4. The challenge of adapting to rapid change in all aspects of life, and in particular with information technology.
5. The challenge of maintaining good mental health.

We begin with the challenge of receiving adequate *health care*. There has always been anxiety about maintaining one's health and being able to receive adequate health care when it is needed. We live with some fear that we will be injured or get ill, and when these conditions happen, we are put in touch with our mortality and realize that we will not live forever.[15] It is a subliminal fear that comes to the surface when our health is threatened. In recent years, there has been tremendous emphasis on the preservation of one's health. We have been made more aware of the risks to our health and been given guidance about how to live in a more healthy way. Everywhere we turn, we see suggestions about diet and exercise. Health clubs with personal trainers and nutritional experts are commonplace, and the internet, television, newspapers, health magazines, and other communications systems are filled with suggested programs to improve our health. Special attention is given to the health of children with a focus on diet and the risks of obesity. The first lady of the United States, Michelle Obama, has made the health of children and especially children's nutrition one of her primary concerns.

The growing numbers of seniors in our population who face the challenges of aging increase the attention on health. A recent study by the Stanford Center on Longevity suggests that America will continue to "age up" for decades. The over-65 sector will double, from 40 million today

---

15. There is a sensitive and insightful poem by John O' Donohue in his book, *To Bless the Space Between Us*, entitled "On the Arrival of Illness."

## Section I — The Need for Love in Contemporary Life

to 89 million by 2050 and move from 13 percent of the population to 20 percent of the population.

First world countries have generally given a high priority to the health care of their citizens. Different approaches have been used, with some countries providing access to health care with little or no cost, using the resources of government money. Others have asked that employers provide health care coverage with a modest contribution to be made by the employee. This option has been difficult for small businesses and does not always provide coverage for members of the family. Other countries have asked individuals, either through their employer or through individual coverage with insurance companies, to find ways of paying for health care. Combinations of these options are represented in the recent health care plan adopted by the United States Congress, an attempt by the Obama administration to increase health care coverage and make it available to the many who have no health insurance.

For the vast majority of the world's population, and especially in developing countries, health care is limited or non-existent. It has been especially tragic in those areas that have had natural disasters, such as the earthquake in Haiti or the floods in Pakistan. But the need for medical attention is profound even without the additional challenge of providing care for the victims of national disaster. Special attention has been given to the AIDS pandemic, and help has come from many different sources. Yet millions continue to suffer, and in many cases, the best medical care is simply not available. It remains true that health care is problematic in first world countries and coverage in third world counties is sketchy at best. Where poverty exists, the people may know what to do, but do not have the resources to do it. For example, with the illness of malaria, the people know that they can protect themselves with spraying, nets, and medicines, but they cannot afford the interventions.

Adequate health care is interwoven with the need for *access to adequate education*. The schools of the world will need to continue and even increase the emphasis on teaching basic hygiene, nutrition, sexual and reproductive health, and disease prevention and care. In many parts of the world, there are initiatives to teach all children, and especially girls, about these concerns. As the quality of education improves, it will enable these young people to navigate the complexities of latent cultural norms and a rapidly changing context; they will be helped to challenge these norms and to accommodate to new circumstances. Girls, for example, are beginning to postpone marriage and the demands of parenthood until they have completed a basic education. It has empowered them to negotiate changing roles with spouses and enter the market with the requisite skills for successful employment.

The means of delivering high quality education has sufficiently changed so that even those young people in more isolated areas of the world have access to distance learning, information technology, and study abroad programs which provide access to even the most advanced and subtle ideas, complex information, and advanced training for employment in the global economy. Education has become global, and children in every part of the world have more access than ever before, allowing them to enter fully into satisfying careers with sufficient compensation to provide a modest and livable income. I have personally observed these developments in Pakistan and Israel/Palestine, regions where marginal populations, non-Muslims in Pakistan and Arab Palestinians in the region of the Galilee, have access to high quality education that has given hope to young people seeking a meaningful and fulfilling life.[16]

These signs are encouraging, but high quality education remains out of reach for all too many for a variety of reasons. One of those reasons is that it is costly, and not every family has the resources to send their children to good schools and provide them with the school supplies that are required. It is especially problematic in post-secondary education whether it is vocational/professional or university level. The institutions themselves often have the difficulty of sustaining the quality of the faculty, the required laboratories, campus housing, and infrastructure. This generally means that institutions often have increasing levels of tuition to sustain the educational program. A second reason is that many children and young people have not been prepared adequately to take full advantage of the educational opportunities that are available. In some cases, the family does not value education, and in other cases the children and young people are not sufficiently mature and are distracted by the lure of harmful and self-destructive behavior. In other cases, the cultural norms even prohibit education, as for example, the prohibition placed on girls to get an education in Taliban-controlled areas. In addition, a third reason is the quality of the education itself; the schools are not adequately funded, are not managed in constructive ways, and the quality of the teaching is second rate.[17] The

---

16. Forman Christian College in Lahore, Pakistan and the Mar Elias Educational Institutions in the village of Ibillin in Northern Israel are good examples. It is encouraging as well to read Greg Mortenson and David Oliver Relin's book, *Three Cups of Tea*, although discouraging to learn about the financial difficulties of the organization.

17. For a more positive outlook on current change, see Ravitch, *The Death and*

## Section I — The Need for Love in Contemporary Life

stories of failing schools are numerous and discouraging in many places in the world, and remarkably so in the United States. New initiatives such as charter schools have been established as an alternative to public education. Many school systems, as is the case with many public services, are slow to change, filled with vested interests and lacking vision.

Education remains the way forward for the young people of the world, and there are signs of profound change in educational practices to meet the expectations of the new realities of a changing world. There is reason for hope, yet gaining access to high quality education in many parts of the world, even the most advanced countries, remains a challenge for far too many. It is a frustration and worry for many parents and students who seek to advance their careers and improve their lives through education.

Both the need for better health care and the quest for a quality education point to another concern that is common for a high percentage of the world's population, and that is the *need for an adequate income* to meet the demands of daily living and achieving a better quality of life. Poverty remains an intractable problem.[18] The comment attributed to Jesus in speaking to his disciples seems as true today as it was in his time, "For you will always have the poor with you . . ." (Matt 26:11). Experts on this issue argue about the definition of poverty, but agree in general that there are at least three levels: extreme poverty, moderate poverty, and relative poverty.[19] Extreme poverty describes those without adequate food, safe drinking water, sanitation and shelter, and little or no education. Moderate poverty describes those whose basic needs are just barely met, and relative poverty references those who incomes are below a certain level in a national income average.

The World Bank has a standard, although somewhat dated, of using the figure of $1 per day per person, based upon purchasing power, for the extremely poor with $2 measured in terms of purchasing power for those facing moderate poverty. The World Bank estimates that approximately 1.1 billion people were living in extreme poverty in 2001, down from 1.5 billion in 1981. The greatest number of the extreme poor live in the regions of East Asia, South Asia, and sub-Saharan Africa. The statistics indicate that the number of extreme poor has declined in East Asia and

*Life of the Great American School Systems: How Testing and Choice are Undermining Education.*

18. See Bassett and Winter-Nelson, *The Atlas of World Hunger* for the impact of poverty on people of the world.

19. Sachs, *The End of Poverty*, 20. I follow his account of the description of poverty in Chapter One, "A Global Family Portrait."

South Asia since 1981, but increased in sub-Saharan Africa. It is important to note that nearly half of Africa's population lives in poverty, while the number of extreme poor has been reduced in most of the other regions of the world. These numbers and the many other statistics provided by the World Bank have been debated, yet few would disagree that poverty is a profound problem for the world.

In the Western Hemisphere, we have been made aware by the devastating earthquake in Haiti about the number of people living in extreme poverty in that country, poverty that has been exacerbated by the earthquake. Many agencies, organizations, and countries have attempted to provide aid to the Haitians, but the nearly 1.3 million people continue to live in camps. They are forced to scrounge for food and suffer from poor nutrition, poor sanitation, and lack of safe drinking water. All of the problems of extreme poverty are there, especially in the camps. One tent (Tent J2, Block 7, and Section 3) placed a sign out front which says: "Please—do something!" and continued, "We don't want to die of hunger and also we want to send our children to school. I give glory to God that I am still alive—but I would like to stay that way."[20] A comparable story appeared in *The New Times* about poverty in Venezuela, describing human scavengers at the massive Cambalache dump on the edge of Ciudad Guauama. "I'm hungry, and my children are hungry," said Raisa Beria, 25, a Warao (indigenous tribe and language) who came to the dump to scavenge for clothes and food. In one outing, she found some rotting chicken still in a package and gave it to her 4-year-old daughter. "This is how we live," she said in accented Spanish.[21]

In mid-September, 2010, world leaders gathered to discuss what is to be done to meet the goals set in 2000 for reducing global poverty. This group was informed that part of the original UN strategy needs to be changed if services are to be provided to the world's poorest children. The conventional wisdom that maintains that more lives are saved—and the cost is cheaper—by focusing on the easiest people to reach, mostly in the cities where there is easy access and hospitals. A recent study by UNICEF indicates that helping the most deprived and vulnerable children in remote areas would reduce the death rate by 60 percent above the current approach of helping the poor in cities with better hospitals and

---

20. Deborah Sontag, "Haitians Cry in Letters: 'Please—Do Something,'" *The New York Times*, September 19, 2010.

21. Simon Romero, "Left Behind in Venezuela to Piece Lives Together," *The New York Times*, September 18, 2010.

## Section I — The Need for Love in Contemporary Life

transportation.[22] Love and compassion motivate all of us to do what we can to relieve that incredible suffering caused by poverty.

Another challenge for individuals in nearly every corner of the earth is how to cope with the *vast array and rapid pace of change* that intrudes into our lives. There are places in different regions of the world that have been able to maintain patterns of life that have existed for centuries, but these places are few and far between as new developments emerge, patterns of communication shift, and the demands of navigating in the contemporary world increase in complexity. Let me suggest some areas in which the nature and pace of change have been dramatic and allow them to be tell the story about the impact of change. The following list grows to some extent out of my own experience, and I am sure that each person might have suggestions to add to the list. Again, let me suggest five areas of change and challenge:

1. Information Technology.
2. Transportation.
3. Communication.
4. Knowledge.
5. Government.

One dimension of life that has introduced a substantial change in our way of life and continues to change daily is information technology. The digital age has arrived, and we scramble to keep up with its continuing development. It was just a few years ago, when I was teaching more regularly in a university setting, that students brought notebooks to class in which to take hand-written notes. Now, on nearly every student desk in most classrooms, there is a laptop computer. The material is presented in a variety of forms including Power Point, which can be accessed electronically. Learning is intimately connected to the digital age, as are many other human activities. We shop online, keep files online, speak with our family online, pay bills online, pay taxes online, access information online, find sexual stimulation online, read recipes for food preparation online, entertain ourselves online, play games online, and make reservations online. Some even "worship" online. What have I forgotten? A lot, I'm sure. The computer with its many applications is pivotal in our lives, and some have found it very difficult to keep up with the new programs and applications. For some, it is very stressful as they try to cope with this new world and

---

22. "Unicef's Idea," *The New York Times*, September 18, 2010.

they do not feel sufficiently skilled to fully enter it. For many it is a gift that has made life better, but for others, especially those who did not grow up with it, information technology can be a source of great anxiety.

Digital systems are an integral part of transportation, and we all travel. One does not easily repair the car in that its mechanical structures are controlled by digital systems and the repairs can only be done by a person with sophisticated training. One seldom picks up the phone to make a train, bus, or airplane reservation because these reservations are best made online, and there is additional cost if the reservations involve speaking with another human being. There is also the stress, as one travels, of accommodating the need for increased security especially in air travel, and it is not uncommon to hear a fellow traveler say, "Flying is no fun anymore; it is such a hassle." Nor is it all that easy to navigate through big cities using public transportation, and it is difficult to manage traffic and follow directions on the GPS if one drives alone. There is both anxiety and stress related to travel, and travel is an essential part of contemporary life for most people.

Our communication systems are equally complex as we move beyond the hand-written letter and the post office. We now use our computers and cell phones to communicate with family, friends, and business associates. All too often we feel virtually alone in that our connections with others are less frequently in person and more often electronic in character. A recent Harris Interactive poll found that the average Internet user spends 13 hours online each week, e-mailing not included. According to a report from the University of California at San Diego, the average American consumes a brain-expanding 34 gigabytes of content and either sees or hears 100,000 words each day from the Web to TV to text messages. It appears that we are entering some uncharted territory as phones and computers get smarter and tools like Facebook and Twitter become central to our social networking.[23] The debate continues about whether we are emotionally better off with all of our electronic ways of communicating and are able to stay more directly and more frequently in touch with others, or whether this kind of connection robs us of more life-giving and in-person relationships.

There has also been a tremendous expansion of knowledge with some calculations suggesting that the increase of knowledge doubles twice as fast each unit of time. For example from 1900 to 1920, it doubled, and then it doubled again in ten years, from 1920–1930 and so on. Regardless

---

23. Tyrone Beason, "Virtually Alone," *The Seattle Times*, March 14, 2010.

## Section I — The Need for Love in Contemporary Life

of how one calculates this expansion, we know that the increase in the pace of knowledge is staggering. The digital revolution has helped us to expand our access to this expansion of knowledge, but no one person can be a truly "renaissance person" given the extent and increasing amount of knowledge. It is true that we do not need to know everything, but we do face situations almost daily when we realize that we do not have the information necessary to manage adequately. The increase in knowledge has essentially forced us to become a specialist with the required skills and knowledge to be successful in at least one area. Even in our area of expertise, we find it difficult to keep up, a situation that carries with it a measure of insecurity and anxiety about the future and our ability to keep our job. Those who are unemployed almost universally need retraining in order to be competitive and find employment.

There is another challenge in reference to the expansion of knowledge, and it is related to the ways that new knowledge alters the way we understand the world. In different ages and different parts of the world, humans have found ways of understanding the world and describing it. They have used a range a categories, drawn from their environment and age, to frame the world and put words around its many dimensions and systems. It is possible to describe in the broadest terms the shift in understanding and categories of explanation across the ages from a pre-modern to a modern and now to what we sometimes call a postmodern or transmodern understanding of the world.[24] Admittedly, these categories do not fully describe the changes that have occurred in our outlooks, but may nevertheless be suggestive of patterns and ways of understanding and framing the world across history. So, we might maintain that pre-modern people often made sense of the world with such categories as spirits, miracles, and divine intervention into human affairs, categories of understanding that modern people would be less apt to use although many do. It is possible to suggest that people in modern times made sense of the world around them with a rational and scientific explanation of reality. Now, as the transmodern consciousness emerges, contemporary people,

---

24. The term "postmodern" has been in our vocabulary for several years and has different shades and tones of meaning, the most obvious being that we have moved beyond the modern outlook to a postmodern one. The movement, which began in literary criticism, moved to other areas of study including hermeneutics and philosophy and with these moves came "deconstruction," the attempt to see in our constructions of reality traces of personal interest in what was thought to be an objective description of reality. Another term that is now being used is transmodern, which implies some appreciation for the modern but recognizes that a new way of framing reality, beyond the modern is now necessary.

while often valuing the heritage of previous ways of understanding, might maintain that even the rational and scientific understanding needs to be deconstructed. The rise of quantum physics, a new appreciation for the non-linear, the ways that the learner's presuppositions participate in the formation of knowledge, and the counter-intuitive explanations of the swirl and swish around us have invited us to develop a new consciousness that goes beyond the modern consciousness based upon the enlightenment construct. We are putting the world together in different ways, and inevitably there is fear and threat about this new consciousness for those who are comfortable with older ways of understanding.

One final area of change that I will mention has to do with governance, the ways we design systems that enable us to live together in society. We are not sure that our current way of ordering and managing society is working for us. We look back into history, read philosophy, and study political science for guidance, and often we find systems and patterns that we hope will work. Some favor a more centralized governmental system and others favor less central governance. The categories of conservative and liberal are frequently used for these patterns. We ponder as well the patterns of governance in the twentieth century and see some that worked reasonably well such as the social democracies of Europe, but also see others that were tried and failed for a variety of reasons. We observed the rise of National Socialism in Germany, now described by the term fascism, and history has judged it as more than a failure, but an evil tyranny. We look back upon the rise of communism, the Russian experiment, and the communist governments in Eastern Europe, China, and Cuba. The communist regimes in Eastern Europe have either disappeared or radically changed, and certainly the Chinese government, while still centralized, has incorporated alternative economic systems in order to become a great economic power. Even Cuba, a hold-out for centralized government in order to insure fair and equitable distribution of wealth for all, is now realizing that it too must adjust to more private initiative and ownership in the economic system of the world.

Those of us who are used to more democratic forms of government as they exist, for example, in Europe and America, are now beginning to wonder if these patterns of governance can govern the affairs of their countries. Do they really insure security and provide for a just and equitable treatment of all of the citizens and a fair distribution of wealth? The increase in the diversity of the populations has added to the challenge of fair and equitable governance. As I write in the United States in the second

## Section I — The Need for Love in Contemporary Life

decade of the twenty-first century, there is a high proportion of people who do not trust our government, in large measure because they continue to suffer from the downturn of the economy and the loss of jobs. Governing our regional and national affairs remains a source of anxiety for many.

We do live in a rapidly changing and challenging time, anxious about not keeping up with the digital revolution, stressed by systems of transportation, feeling left behind and unconnected by new forms of communication, threatened by new understandings of the world and ways of framing reality, and lacking trust in our government's capacity to manage our common regional and national affairs. These factors and dozens of others mean that it is not easy to maintain good *emotional and mental health*. In fact a primary concern of public health is emotional and mental health, seen by many as a challenge of epidemic proportions. One of the fundamental challenges of our time is to achieve a high degree of integration and congruence as a person, a condition that empowers us to manage the complexities of contemporary life and achieve moderate levels of happiness and success in careers. While the circumstances of those in other countries and cultures may differ from ours, we all suffer from a range of emotional problems and mental pain, and we look for ways, often in our religious traditions and self-help literature and programs in order to achieve emotional equilibrium. Most likely, each person may have a list of the problems which they face, and my list is only an illustration of many kinds of emotional and mental struggles that we have. The following mental health challenges seem common, almost regardless of country or culture, though the cause and content may differ:

1. Stress.
2. Anxiety.
3. Depression.
4. Loneliness.

Let's look at each of them and try to understand how these mental and emotional health concerns may intersect with our lives, our family members, and those with whom we relate and associate with on a day-to-day basis. I often feel stress and see it in those with whom I interact with regularly. The word stress has several meanings, but I am using the term to describe an emotional state that causes us to feel tense because our life has conditions that feel overwhelming. Stress is a normal physical response to events that make us feel threatened or upset our balance in some way. The stress response is the body's way of protecting us, giving us the signal that we need to stay focused, energetic, and alert. The body does not distinguish between physical and psychological threats and if these threats are not managed well, it can lead to serious health problems.

When we perceive a threat, our nervous system responds by releasing a flood of stress hormones, including adrenaline and cortisol, arousing the body for emergency action. Our heart beats faster, muscles tighten, blood pressure rises, breath quickens, and our senses become sharper. Stress then can be positive as it telegraphs problems and increases our capacity to solve them. In emergency situations, stress can save our lives, giving us extra strength or quicker reflexes.[25]

But it becomes problematic when we feel a sense of external pressure that comes from the demands of others, perhaps a parent, a spouse, or a supervisor; or a sense of pressure that comes from feeling like we have too much to do and cannot get it all done in a prescribed period of time. Our use of the word has to do with excessive stress, often called distress, that creates feelings of being in trouble and of having more to do than is possible given one's abilities and time limits. It makes us feel like we are "in over our head." Stress is a fairly common feeling in the fast-paced world in which we live. It can create great discomfort and push us to the edge of genuine suffering and misery. As one in a caring, healing profession, I encounter overstressed people on a regular basis and try to help them gain perspective on their situation and solutions to the feeling of being burdened by having too much and too difficult work to accomplish.

The *Holmes-Rahe Life Stress* study, in the *Helpguide* publication lists the top ten stressful life events as spouse's death, divorce, marriage separation, jail term, death of a close relative, injury or illness, marriage, fired from job, marriage reconciliation, and retirement. The article lists several warning signs and symptoms:

1. Cognitive Symptoms: memory problems, inability to concentrate, poor judgment, seeing only the negative, anxious or racing thoughts, and constant worrying

2. Physical Symptoms: aches and pains, digestive problems, eating more or less, sleeping less or more

3. Emotional Symptoms: moodiness, irritability, agitation, feeling overwhelmed, sense of loneliness and isolation, depression or general unhappiness.

---

25. Smith and Segal in the article in *Helpguide*, available at www.helpguide.org.

## Section I — The Need for Love in Contemporary Life

Stress is our constant companion in contemporary life as we race to keep up with life's demands. It is closely related and often interwoven with anxiety, the feeling of apprehension about the future and the fear that something unfortunate might happen. Our time has often been called "the age of anxiety," one in which we constantly worry about what might happen.[26] As with stress, normal life does include a measure of anxiety and fear, and these signals can be helpful and protect us. In an anxious situation, our brain sends a flood of chemicals into our bloodstream, our hearts beat faster, and we become better equipped to handle an emergency. As we relax we may continue to worry about what caused the fear, and it may linger on and on. When this happens, these feeling may interfere with normal activities, and we may feel overwhelmed and become very afraid. These fears can easily become what doctors call an anxiety disorder. It is not just people in the fast-paced first world countries that feel anxious, but people in all parts of the world suffer from these feelings.[27]

The most common form of excessive anxiety experienced by many people is simply called by doctors a "generalized anxiety disorder" (GAD). Other forms of excessive anxiety are classified in the categories of obsessive-compulsive disorder (OCD), post-traumatic stress disorder (PTSD), panic disorder, and phobias. The person who worries excessively and unrealistically about a whole range of concerns and life-challenges for a period of time that exceeds six months with no letup is often diagnosed with GAD. The worries of a person who suffers from GAD may have some basis in reality, but generally the extent of the worry is excessive. For example, a parent may worry that her child is late getting home from school almost daily, a legitimate concern, but if it causes a sense of terror and the inability to find the reasons for the lateness, and these feelings continue day after day, then it becomes a genuine disorder.

For most of us, however, there is an ever-present low-level anxiety associated with the stressful nature of contemporary life. Unfortunate accidents, illness, job loss, and interpersonal conflicts may arise causing anxiety. It is possible to regain one's balance with support from others and taking time to pause, relax, and look for good solutions. But when

---

26. See for example, Tone, *The Age of Anxiety: A History of America's Turbulent Affair with Tranquilizers*. See also the excellent book by Scioli and Biller that offers guidance for those who experience excessive anxiety. It is entitled *Hope in the Age of Anxiety: A Guide to Understanding and Strengthening Our Most Important Virtue*.

27. See the review of several articles on anxiety by Amal Chakraburtty in *WebMD*, http://www.webmd.com/anxiety-panic/understanding-anxiety-basics, November 23, 2009.

these anxieties take over and control our lives, we suffer and life becomes a struggle. At this point, there is often the temptation and risk of resorting to self-medication, using over the counter drugs or alcohol to deaden our pain. But these false consolations in the long run only increase our anxiety.

Unfortunately, a certain measure of anxiety is another companion in life for most of us, one that can easily lead to depression. Depression, too, is a common mental health problem.[28] As with the other mental health challenges in contemporary life, depression can be an occasional visitor causing low levels of discomfort or it may be quite severe and debilitating. Essentially, depression is a state of feeling sad or melancholy. A distinction is occasionally made between depression and sadness, with sadness more related to specific occurrences in one's life, such as the loss of a loved one, whereas depression is not easily connected to specific events and is a general feeling of unrest, emptiness, or discomfort.

Depression is the leading cause of disability in the United States for people between the ages of fifteen and forty-four. It affects approximately 14.8 million adults or about 6.7 percent of the U.S. population age eighteen and older. Older adults are especially susceptible to depression as they face health problems, loss of a spouse, or feel as if their lives have no meaning in the retirement years. Depression is also been labeled a primary cause for the increase of suicides among military personnel and teenagers who have been victims of bullying and those seeking to find and be comfortable with their sexual identity.

Depression can affect anyone, even those who have good financial security, a job that is satisfying, a supportive and loving family, and good health. Often depression is related to physical causes, such as a chemical imbalance and it can be treated with anti-depressants, although in some cases, medicine taken for another ailment may have the side-effect of contributing to depression. The more severe form of depression, called Major Depressive Disorder (MDD), is a condition that interferes with the normal patterns of life. It may not be "just the blues" following a minor spat with one's spouse or teen-age child, but a severe state of despair that may have several of the following symptoms:[29]

- A feeling of sadness, emptiness, or moodiness
- Little interest in doing things that one ordinarily enjoys

---

28. A good introduction to the problem of depression in our time is Richard O'Connor's book, *Undoing Depression*.

29. From the Lexapro website about medicine for depression and other mental illnesses, www.frx.com/products/lexapro.aspx.

## Section I — The Need for Love in Contemporary Life

- A loss of weight or a gain of weight with fluctuations in appetite
- Trouble sleeping or sleeping too much
- A feeling of agitation
- A loss of energy
- A feeling or worthlessness and guilt
- Inability to concentrate, think clearly, and make good decisions
- Preoccupation with dying and thoughts about suicide

When these feelings are intense, it is time for professional consultation and treatment.

Most of us have had traces of stress, anxiety, and depression. Perhaps these conditions were as common in people who lived in previous eras, although they may have been less preoccupied with them than are contemporary people, or they may have simply used different language to describe them. But it does seem that the pace and the demands of contemporary life have increased these mental health risks for us. As we experience the discomfort of stress, anxiety, and depression, there is the additional risk of loneliness, the final mental and emotional health challenge that I will mention. In our emotional discomfort, we may find it hard to reach out to others, and other people may find us difficult to approach and find good ways to help us. Often we suffer alone, afraid and ashamed, and feeling that if we just had the will power to change, we could overcome our feelings. It is so painful to suffer alone, as King Lear says, "Who alone suffers, suffers most."

To be lonely is one of the worst experiences in life in that we do not meet our most basic human need which is to be socially connected, to love and to be loved.[30] Loneliness is the state of being disconnected from others and experiencing emotional and social isolation.[31] The causes of loneliness are many and complex, frequently related to our infancy and childhood, our family experience, our emotional well-being, our social circumstances, and our introverted or extroverted tendencies.[32] More specifically, our isolation and resulting loneliness may occur because of abuse and rejection by others, often a carryover from childhood. As a

---

30. See Cacioppo and Patrick, *Loneliness: Human Nature and the Need for Social Connection*. See as well the book by Christakis and Fowler, *Connected: The Surprising Power of Our Social Networks and How They Shape Our Lives*.

31. Weiss, *Loneliness: The Experience of Emotional and Social Isolation*.

32. I have been informed about the causes and patterns of loneliness in part by the contributors to the web site, sean@weboflonelines.com.

child or young person, with these feelings of rejection, we carry with us a certain amount of insecurity and find it difficult to fit in, especially if we are teased or bullied. Loneliness also comes our way if we lose a spouse, a parent, a sibling, or a best friend. It can also happen easily if and when we try to build a relationship and have our heart broken if the feelings are not returned.

As we try to find our way through loneliness, it is important that we distinguish between being alone and being lonely. It is healthy to be alone, to have time to reflect, and to gain balance and perspective. Loneliness is different; it is the pain that comes when we are not included and when we have no close personal friends. Unfortunately, loneliness too is often our companion in contemporary life.

## THE QUEST FOR SOLUTIONS AND A RAY OF HOPE

We have attempted in this opening chapter to describe the multitude of problems which exist, both at the macro level in the infrastructure of our countries and across the globe, and at the micro level in settings in which individuals attempt to find their way in a complex and rapidly changing world. We have tried to describe the need for love and compassion as we seek solutions to our problems and attempt to build lives that are happy, meaningful, and responsible. The context in which we search for personal and social transformation is complex and difficult, and it asks from international bodies, from countries, and all human associations a new vision for a sustainable and nurturing way of life. This new vision for an empathic civilization will require a greater degree of awareness, a new consciousness, and a higher level of commitment from individuals who will dedicate themselves to creating more just, humane, and caring settings in which to live.[33] We will need a new way of seeing and acting, a new lovescape, and it is this geography of love that we will explore in the succeeding chapters of this book. It will be a hopeful journey, and we begin our travel with an effort to describe the meanings of love and all of love's many cognates.

---

33. Rifkin, *The Empathic Civilization: The Race to Global Consciousness in a World in Crisis*. See also the hopeful book by Korten, *The Great Turning: From Empire to Earth Community*.

# Section I — The Need for Love in Contemporary Life

## STUDY RESOURCES

## Discussion Questions

1. What additional global problems would you add to the ones listed? Which of these challenges is the most threatening and the most difficult to solve?

2. In what ways might the presence of love and compassion contribute in finding solutions to these problems? What suggestions for programs would you make if you were in charge of UNICEF?

3. What additional challenges to individuals and families would you add to the ones listed? Which of these challenges is the most severe and why?

4. How might love and compassion assist in easing the suffering of so many people in the world? What steps would you propose if you were the mayor of New York? Of London? Of Mumbai?

5. Are you hopeful or despairing about the human future? Why?

## Key Terms and Concepts

- *Global warming:* an increase in the average temperature of the earth's atmosphere, especially sustained increases that cause climactic changes

- *Sustainable development:* development which seeks to produce sustainable economic growth while ensuring future generation's ability to do the same by not exceeding the regenerative capacity of nature; to develop while protecting the environment

- *Transmodern:* a term that is often used as a substitute for postmodern which describes a new way of framing and understanding reality

- *Anxiety:* the feeling of apprehension about the future and the fear that something unfortunate might happen

- *Depression:* state of feeling general sadness and discouragement about life over an extended period of time

- *Loneliness:* state of being disconnected from others and experiencing emotional and social isolation

## Suggestions for Reference and Reading

1. Brown, Lester, *Plan B 4.0: Mobilization to Save Civilization.* New York: W. W. Norton & Company, 2009.
2. Cacioppo, John T. and William Patrick, *Loneliness: Human Nature and the Need for Social Connection.* New York: W. W. Norton & Company, 2008.
3. Gore, Al, *An Inconvenient Truth: The Planetary Emergency of Global Warming and What We Can Do about It.* New York: Rodale, 2006.
4. Sachs, Jeffrey D., *Common Wealth: Economics for a Crowded Planet.* New York: The Penguin Press, 2008.
5. Rifkin, Jeremy, *The Empathic Civilization: The Race to Global Consciousness in a World of Crisis.* New York: Jeremy P. Tarcher/Penguin, 2009.
6. Scioli, Anthony and Biller, Henry B., *Hope in the Age of Anxiety.* New York: Oxford University Press, 2009.

## SECTION II

# The Geography of Love

IN SECTION II, WE explore the terrain of love, its mountains and valleys, its lakes and rivers, its trees and flowers, and its place under the blue and gray skies of life. The lovescape is vast and complex and forms the heart and home of human life. Although beautiful and comforting, the experience and topography of love can also be confusing, and it is easy to get lost as we travel. We begin in Chapter Two with an attempt to understand the ground, contours, and dimensions of love. We offer a metaphysical foundation, definitions and characteristics of the many forms of love, explore the shades of meanings of the cognates of love, and provide a common universe of discourse. In Chapter Three, we describe the ways that love has been understood over the course of history in different traditions and cultures, believing that being exposed to many sincere hearts and sets of eyes will deepen our understanding. In Chapter Four, we move to an examination of the ways that love and its cousins have been taught by sages and saints to the followers of the several religious traditions of the human family. By the end of this section, we hope to be able to join the poets and the scientists, the mystics and the philosophers and hike the trails of love with them. As we go, we desire to see, fully appreciate, and be enriched by the lovescapes of life.

> It is in the shelter of each other that people live.
> —IRISH PROVERB

# 2

# The Understanding of Love: Its Ground, Contours, and Dimensions

## THE CORRESPONDENCE OF LOVE AND HUMAN NEED

CHAPTER ONE IS ABOUT the crisis of our time and the need for love at all levels, macro and micro, global and individual. Chapter Two is the attempt to describe what love is and to begin to suggest how it can be applied to the problems that we face at this point in history. The method is simple; it is to begin to see the correspondence and connect the dots between human need and the ways that love and its cognates can contribute to a positive perspective on the problems and provide motivation for addressing them in constructive ways. In the succeeding chapters, I will continue to try to refine the understanding of love and compassion by exploring the way it has been understood in history and its foundational character in the religions of the world. I will then describe ways that love and compassion can become an essential part of who we are and what we do by exploring how love can be formed within us. My hope is that we will see how nurture and a life-giving environment can cultivate love in our lives. We will go on to explore how nature, that is, how we are wired, contributes to our capacity to love; and then suggest how the development of certain skills and the discipline of spiritual practices can empower us to love. We then turn in Section IV to the application of love and compassion to primary

## Section II — The Geography of Love

relationships, regional concerns, and global challenges. The conclusion will be an attempt to articulate the divine invitation and vocational call to the love-centered life.

As we go on this journey together through the lovescapes of life, we do so with some fear and trembling and with a great deal of humility, knowing that love and compassion are very complex human experiences. The admirable qualities that cluster around love tend to get hijacked by ulterior motives and filled with the clutter of our own deep needs, easy rationalizations, fearful defensive posturing, and formative influences that are both positive and negative. We journey as well with the knowledge that love has been variously understood over the centuries and that there are several starting points for understanding and describing it. For example, is it a transcendent ethic, universal in character and noble in purpose, or does it grow out of our evolutionary development and fundamentally serve humans well in the competitive game of survival of the fittest? Or is it both and much more? We know that love and compassion are as beautiful as a Celtic knot, but equally as hard to understand as we look for beginnings and endings. Let's explore together, starting with foundations.

## THE GROUND OF LOVE

Not infrequently, when a conversation or discussion turns to the topic of love and its many meanings and related cognates, the exchange is almost always about love as a value, a behavior, or an ethical code. It is all of these and more, but the prior question, not always asked, is whether love is the Logos of the macroverse.[1] Is it integral and foundational to reality? Should we explore the metaphysics of love as a way of better understanding the ethics of love? Is there an ontological question hidden in the background? I am persuaded that there is a question and possible answers, (including "no" or "I don't know") that should precede the development of our theories and ethical codes about love and compassion.[2]

So I begin with a partial inquiry regarding the metaphysics of love, and I do so out of my Christian convictions and commitments. It is my starting point, one that may be easily discounted as a leap of faith rather

---

1. The term, macroverse, is occasionally being used as substitute for universe in that it suggests the broad expanse of space rather than a single and unified galaxy.

2. I have been informed by several authors, but two in particular have been helpful to me in thinking about the metaphysics of love, Daniel Day Williams in *The Spirit and Forms of Love* and Paul Tillich, *Systematic Theology* in three volumes with Volume Three speaking directly to the metaphysics of love.

## The Understanding of Love: Its Ground, Contours, and Dimensions

than a scientific inquiry. Admittedly, the starting point is a theological exploration rather than an empirical one. It is not an inquiry that begins with biological theories about love. It is not about recent heart[3] or brain research,[4] the new psychology of love,[5] biological or evolutionary theory, or cultural theories of love. Nor is it an attempt to understand love from its rich expressions in literature and the arts. Many of these views are extremely helpful and cast abundant light on the origins and definitions of love, although the metaphysical inquiry is not generally present.[6] I have incorporated these points of view into my understanding of love, and I will include a description of them in succeeding chapters. But I get there first by probing the daunting question about whether love is integral to reality, forming the foundation of the world as we know it. Let me begin then with some theological affirmations, knowing full well that a careful discussion of the metaphysics of love is a book-length discussion.

The first affirmation is that *God is love*, one that assumes that God (however the divine is understood and whatever the tradition) exists and is personal. Late in the first century CE, John of Patmos writes to new Christians, "Beloved, let us love one another, because love is from God; everyone who loves is from God; everyone who loves is born of God and knows God. Whoever does not love does not know God, for God is love" (1 John 4:7–8). He continues, "So we have known and believe the love that God has for us. God is love, and those who abide in love abide in God, and God abides in them" (1 John 4:16). I believe that John is on to a great truth, not just because it appears in the New Testament, although its appearance there is not unimportant in that the New Testament became the *Scripture* of Christianity, but also because it has the ring of truth and may resonate with those from other religious traditions and worldviews. The sort of love about which John speaks, *agape,* is the essence of the divine being, understood in the Abrahamic monotheistic traditions as Creator and Sustainer of all that exists. The passage also implies that love is what puts human beings together and motivates them to care for the world and all that is in it. It is self-giving and unlimited, filled with altruism, compassion, and

---

3. Childre and Martin, *The Heartmath Solution.*
4. Amen, *Change Your Brain Change Your Life.*
5. Sternberg and Weis, eds., *The New Psychology of Love.*
6. There are notable exceptions not the least of which is Plato. There has been an interest in cosmology and ethics encouraged in part by the Templeton Foundation series on Theology and the Sciences. See, for example Murphy and Ellis, *On the Moral Nature of the Universe: Theology, Cosmology, and Ethics.*

## Section II — The Geography of Love

service.[7] Soren Kierkegaard, 19th century Danish philosopher, drawing upon this theological affirmation, underlines that love is the heart of human life, although often hidden. He writes, "To cheat oneself out of love is the most terrible deception; it is an eternal loss for which there is no reparation, either in time or in eternity."[8] Love is the core and meaning of the cosmos and of human beings who live in one corner of the cosmos.

A second theological affirmation is that *the God who is love created the world*,[9] filling it with the divine essence. As one nurtured in biblical stories, I turn to these stories in Genesis. They are just that, stories, and mythical stories[10] with a deep and abiding truth that God created all there is and "saw that it was good." The stories point to a process, not to total completion and perfection. The "days" of the creation story imply that the creation would develop across time, and we now understand this developmental process to be inherent in the order of creation. Some argue that the incomplete nature of creation is the result of a cosmic "Fall" which resulted in the imperfection we see all around us, a position that has been a part of orthodox Christian understanding from the early centuries, perhaps most closely connected with Augustine. I would argue that the creation is in process and continues to develop, explained in large part by theoretical physics and evolutionary theory.[11] It is in the context of theoretical physics and evolutionary theory that one places such troubling issues as disease and natural disaster. What is called sin or evil has been and is very real, and its presence remains the most perplexing and challenging intellectual problem if one affirms that God, who is loving and all-powerful, is the Creator.[12]

One possible direction in finding perspective on the so-called problem of evil is to suggest that God is present in the evolving process, but *kenotic* in style. God chooses to be self-limiting and self-emptying in

---

7. Post, *Unlimited Love: Altruism, Compassion, and Service*.

8. Kierkegaard, *Works of Love*, 23–24.

9. See Gen 1 and 2 for the biblical stories of creation.

10. Myth is understood here to mean a story that is not historical, but containing a profound truth.

11. Physicists date the origin of the macroverse (Big Bang) to be 13.7 billion years ago. The macroverse at its origin was referred to as being a "vast wasteland" by Dr. Frank Wilczek, theoretical physicist and Nobel laureate, in a lecture at Princeton University, November 12, 2010.

12. I will not try to deal with the problem of evil at this point, but only suggest directions that do not ultimately answer the questions, but provide some perspective on them.

## The Understanding of Love: Its Ground, Contours, and Dimensions

gracious action to move creation forward, inviting humankind to share in the creative process.[13] A secondary part of this perspective is that God is love and relates lovingly, inviting love in return. God chose not to design a system that is dictatorial or mechanical, wanting neither obedient slaves nor love machines. There is no love unless it is self-chosen and freely given. We are asked to love God with our whole being, and we give this love out of freedom or it would not be love. An additional part of this perspective has to do with sin and evil being defined, as Augustine does, as the absence of God. When God is not present, love is not present and sin and evil can emerge.

A third theological affirmation is that *God is triune, experiencing love within the divine being and expressing love for all of creation*. To say that God is triune is not to say that there are three gods, but to affirm that God knows and expresses love within, even as human beings may love themselves in healthy and life-giving ways. Self-love is linked to the Christian tradition, as in the saying of Jesus, "You shall love your neighbor as you love yourself" (Mark 12:31), and it is viewed as essential to human well-being in contemporary understandings of emotional health. To say that God is triune is also to affirm God's love for the creation: that God is Creator, Redeemer, and Sustainer. God is the designer, the builder, and the energy of all that is (the Creator); God has "spoken" a definitive Word in Jesus (the Redeemer), and is gracious in power and presence within the creation as Spirit (the Sustainer).

The argument of Christians with Jews, Muslims, and others about radical monotheism has been difficult, complex, and often the differences of understanding have limited important collaboration. It is the case that at times Christians have described their beliefs in ways that might imply tri-theism, both in reference to the Trinity and in Christology.[14] But in the effort to understand the fullness of God, Christians have spent centuries

---

13. See Phil 2:6-11 for a description of kenosis (self-emptying) and the work of Jesus.

14. Good progress is being made, and the document "A Common Word Between Us and You" prepared by notable Islamic scholars and leaders sent to the Christian community is a step in the right direction. Several Christian scholars and leaders have responded with both caution and hopefulness. See, for example, the several documents on the "Common Word" website. I have found the paper presented by Daniel Migliore, entitled "The Love Commandment: An Opening for Christian-Muslim Dialogue" to the American Theological Society, April 4, 2008 very helpful. At the heart of this discussion is the commitment of the three Abrahamic monotheistic religions to the double love commandment, to love God with one's whole being and one's neighbor as oneself.

## Section II — The Geography of Love

developing ways to articulate God's essence as personal being and used the concepts of the Trinity and Jesus as saving Word as means of pointing to a profound mystery. God the Creator is certainly present in Judaism and Islam, as is the guiding Word and sustaining Spirit, but it has been and continues to be difficult to get past the Trinitarian and Christological issues in the conversations between representatives of these traditions.

Christians affirm that God is person, and the expression of the personhood of God is both external (creation, redemption, and transformation) but also internal in the sense of a loving internal life. Augustine argues that love is integral to the being of God, Father, Son, and Holy Spirit. He explains that "this consubstantial and coeternal communion . . . is more aptly called *caritas*."[15] Less well known, but perceptively, Richard of St. Victor (d. 1173) extends Augustine's belief in the internal love of the Triune God and says that God has all perfection which includes perfect love, and no love can be expressed without a partner. Where a plurality of persons is lacking, true charity cannot exist. God does love the creation, but so as not to have this love be "disordered," God's ultimate and perfect love must have a divine object worthy of itself. God's love therefore is expressed within God's inner life between the divine persons.[16] It is sufficient to say at this point that God is filled with love and it flows freely toward the creation.

Regarding Christology, Christians fully acknowledge the human Jesus, a first-century Jew who lived in Palestine and became a great prophet. They believe he was called to bring the Word of God to the human family, not unlike the belief in both the Torah and the Quran about the specific role of the prophet. The prophet, whether Moses or Muhammad, received the Word from God, passed it on orally, and it became written as an expression of the will and way of God for the world. A comparable belief is expressed in the New Testament in the Gospel of John in an ontological way; John says that the eternal Word, Logos, became flesh in Jesus (John 1:14) so that we might understand God's love and be saved. Again, in the teaching of Paul, the belief is reaffirmed when he writes that "God was

---

15. Carmichael, *Friendship: Interpreting Christian Love*, 63. Carmichael quotes Augustine's *On the Trinity (De Trinitate)* in *The Works of St. Augustine: A Translation for the 21st Century*, edited by Rotelle, 6.vi, 7, PL42.928.

16. See the discussion of this issue in Carmichael's *Friendship: Interpreting Christian Love*, 86, 193–197. Ms. Carmichael draws upon the work of Elizabeth Johnson, *She Who Is: The Mystery of God in Feminist Perspective* and incorporates feminist insights that enhance the understanding of the loving inner life of God. See a fuller development of Richard of St. Victor's view of the love within the inner life of the Triune God in *The Twelve Patriarchs: The Mystical Ark, Book Three of the Trinity*.

## The Understanding of Love: Its Ground, Contours, and Dimensions

in Christ, reconciling the world to himself . . ." (2 Cor 5:19). The eternal Logos and love of God was in Jesus, a *person* who brings the human family into the loving arms of God. The revelation of God's love comes in person and word.

A fourth theological affirmation is that *human beings are created in the image of God.* It is clear that the classical categories used to describe God, such as eternal and unchanging, drawn in large measure from Greek philosophy, are not the categories we would select to describe human beings. More frequently, we have chosen to understand the image of God in humans as rationality, self-awareness, having a moral conscience, and having the capacity to love and be loved. It is these qualities that we discern in reading the stories and wise counsel in the Bible, the Quran, and indeed the sacred scripture of other religious traditions.

It may also be possible to reverse the process, saying that if human beings are created in the image of God, then to look carefully at how humans live and love might provide some clues about the character of God. If humans experience individuality, freedom of choice and intentionality, action and suffering, causality, and impartiality as they engage in loving activity, then it is possible to postulate that these same characteristics may be present in God.[17] In fact, we tend to do it (create God in our image) on a regular basis. There is great risk in the argument from analogy; not infrequently, it invites us to become overly anthropomorphic in our description of the divine. But the risk may be worth taking for the sake of understanding as long as it is prefaced by an acknowledgement that we are speaking in metaphors and approximations. It is also essential to acknowledge that our understanding is prefaced by the affirmation of God's self-chosen kenosis, the emptying of the full divine power and character for the sake of humankind and to communicate with humankind.[18] The larger insight remains, namely, that human beings participate in an ontological structure that has love as its essence.

I will mention one other theological affirmation as foundational, and it is that *the primary meaning of human life is to join God in the on-going*

---

17. Williams, *The Spirit and Forms of Love*, 114–122.

18. Martin Heidegger begins his search for "being" with an analysis of *Da-sein* or the human experience of *being-there* suggesting that the categories of care, anxiety, freedom, decision-making, and death may provide clues to ultimate being. Process philosophers such as Alfred North Whitehead and Charles Hartshorne, while differing in details, move in a similar direction by taking their departure from the human experience and using feeling as the major clue to being. See Whitehead, *Process and Reality*, Pt. I, Ch. 1, 5–21.

## Section II — The Geography of Love

*processes of creation with self-giving love as our motivation, empowerment, and strategy.* We go into the world in love, empowered by God's Spirit, to engage in wise and careful stewardship of the world and to create a more just and humane world. Human life is filled with a rich variety of experiences, many of which would not be called "duty." It is not just doing good deeds because God tells us to, but living responsibly, motivated by love; it is certainly part of what it means to be in harmony with the will and way of God. It is also to know and experience the richness of life; to flourish is part of being in a love-centered universe. Further, to join with God in the on-going processes of creation will not mean that we are free of pain and struggle. We will continue to be haunted by the ambiguities of life, with estrangement, conflict, and emptiness. We will know suffering, but we go with God, believing that in time our existential life filled with struggle will be gradually transformed to "transcendent union" with love.[19]

### DEFINITIONS OF LOVE AND ITS COGNATES

We have given only hints and clues about the metaphysics of love, in part because our purpose is less philosophical and more directed to understanding love and learning how to be those who practice love, and in part because the subject is quite complex and would demand an extensive treatment. We will continue to be aware of the metaphysics of love as we work toward a symbiosis of a theological understanding of love and the various definitions of love and approaches to understand and describe love. But at this point, we want to move toward finding clarity about the meaning of love and its many cousins; it is a large family! We will not meet all of the relatives, but to be introduced to a select group of them that typify the family characteristics will guide us as we attempt to apply love to the crisis of our age.

Let's begin our effort to find a common universe of discourse by examining the several meanings of the word *love*. It is interesting to note that the *Merriam Webster's Collegiate Dictionary* provides several meanings of the word as a noun and several as a verb. One of them, being "at love" in tennis or another sport is not germane to our discussion. Seven of the noun meanings give us several nuances of the word, the first being somewhat generic: (1) strong affection for another arising out of kinship or personal ties; attraction based on sexual desire; affection and tenderness felt by lovers; affection based on admiration, benevolence, or common

---

19. Tillich, *Systematic Theology, Volume Three*, 137–47.

interests; an assurance of love. (2) Warm attachment, enthusiasm, or devotion. (3) The object of attachment, devotion, or admiration; a beloved person. (4) Unselfish behavior, loyal and benevolent concern for the good of another; as the fatherly concern of God for humankind. (5) God or god as the personification of love. (6) An amorous episode as in "love affair." (7) The sexual embrace. The verb meanings amplify the noun definitions: (1) To hold dear (cherish). (2) To feel a lover's passion, devotion, tenderness for; to fondle amorously; to copulate. (3) To like or desire actively; to take pleasure in. (4) To feel affection or experience desire.[20]

As one sorts through these various definitions of love, it is possible to find at least three larger and more generic categories used in the in Greek language, ones often employed to speak about the different kinds of love.[21] Greek has other words that may be translated into English as love as well, and we will note these. But the three Greek words used most commonly to define love are *eros, philia,* and *agape,* and let's use these words as a way to clarify the shades of the meaning of love.

The word *eros* is most appropriately used to describe the feeling of attraction to that which is filled with goodness, truth, and beauty and which has the capacity to fulfill and complete us. The word is often used to describe our physical attraction for a possible lover, as in erotic feelings, but the meaning should not be limited to sexual feelings. While the word is generally used in reference to self-fulfillment, it should not be viewed exclusively as selfish or self-seeking. For example, it is possible to say that we love great literature or art; it inspires us, helps us to understand the human drama, and makes us better persons. Or we might say that we love the philanthropic work that we do, and we feel profoundly grateful for the privilege of helping others. We can say that we love, even cherish our children; they delight us like nothing else, unless it is the love we have for our spouse or life partner.[22]

The full-orbed meaning of *eros* comes to us in a profound and elegant way in the writings of Plato, and in particular in his book called the *Symposium.* The *Symposium* is structured like the other writings of Plato, as a dialogue with the philosopher Socrates as the main character. Socrates in the *Symposium* is in conversation with several others who put forth their arguments about the nature of goodness and the human love for the

---

20. Tenth Edition, Springfield, MA: Merriam-Webster, Inc. 1994, 690.

21. See for example Brander, *Love that Works,* 76–77.

22. A classic work that describes the romantic aspect of love, using the Tristan myth, is written by Denis De Rougemont, *Love in the Western World.*

## Section II — The Geography of Love

good. Systematically, Socrates fields their arguments, speaks of the persuasiveness of their positions, and then proceeds to point out the limitations of their views. The argument of Socrates has the following flow:

1. It is the ideal that is truly real and what we see in our everyday life and circumstances are but shadows of the real. Socrates points out that the arguments of some of those in the conversation are too circumstantial and contextual, speaking more about the shadow and not reflecting the ultimately real and good.

2. In that the subject is love, Socrates reminds his friends that love is the desire for the perpetual possession of the eternal good. He uses a wonderful image of a fire in a cave whose light casts a shadow and as we view the shadow, we mistakenly think of it as the ultimately real; we may see a mere shadow of love and passionately want it for our gratification.

3. Part of the human problem, Socrates explains, is that human beings are incomplete, partial and not all they ought to be; they are half persons seeking the other half in order to be whole. Love is our desire to be whole, and the supreme object of desire, the Good and the Beautiful, must be present in all aspects of our lives in order for us to be complete. This is what we truly seek and need, but few of us recognize it. We continue to live in ignorance, even with our striving. Our feeling of *eros* is misdirected.

4. So we need to find a method of clarifying our desire, a way of directing it toward its real objective. We need to go through the process of maturity, one that might have the following steps: we may see a beautiful body, be attracted, and feel a strong passion. But, as we reflect and become more mature, we move beyond external beauty, which will fade in time, and begin to see the beauty of the soul in the person. From there, as we continue to mature, we move on to the higher levels of social and moral beauty and goodness. Finally, we realize through our stages of education and development that we must go beyond the individual expression of goodness and beauty to that which is absolute beauty. "The beauty is first of all eternal; it neither comes into being nor passes away, neither waxes nor wanes." The earnest seeker "will see it as absolute, existing alone with itself, unique, eternal, and all other beautiful things partaking of it."[23]

---

23. In Plato's *Symposium, The Dialogues of Plato,* 2 volumes, Vol. 1. See the full discussion, 332–41.

## The Understanding of Love: Its Ground, Contours, and Dimensions

5. At the end of a discussion, Socrates sums up his argument: "To sum up then, love is the desire for the perpetual possession of the good." The others reply, "Very true."

6. So the highest love (*eros*) is really the search for beauty, truth, and goodness through mature reasoning.

The love we speak of as *eros* can be noble, but as Plato points out, it can also be mundane, and even turn harmful as the "shadows" limit our vision and behavior.

Other Greek words are often used to describe erotic feeling and behavior. *Storge* often connotes tenderness,[24] *pothos* has the meaning of desire, and *mania* points to unleashed passion. *Epithymia* is more a direct reference to strong desire and is often used to refer to sexual desire or passionate love. It may have a positive meaning, as in the New Testament when Jesus speaks of his strong desire to eat the Passover Meal with his disciples (Luke 22:15) or Paul's longing to depart this life and be with the Lord (Phil 1:23).[25]

Our second broad category of meaning for love is the Greek word *philia*, which is often translated as friendship (*amicitia* in Latin). At its best, friendship is both fulfilling, as is *eros*, but also giving in nature, focusing on the happiness and well-being of the other.[26] True happiness includes life-giving friendships, and these friendships are sustained by caring about the welfare of those who are our friends and being cared for by them. Friends, generally, are those with whom we have experiences in common and those who share common values and appreciate common experiences. Because we have so much in common, having participated together in life's sadness and joy and tend to view the world in similar ways, we find friendships very fulfilling.[27]

But true friendships are not as common as we assume and are difficult to sustain. C. S. Lewis rightly speaks about friendship as in integral part of love, but says that we seldom experience that which is so enriching because it is not a part of our nature-endowed needs; "we can live

---

24. Lewis in *The Four Loves* translates *storge* as affection and speaks of it as one of the four loves.

25. Morris, *Testaments of Love: A Study of Love in the Bible*, 114–28. See as well the volume edited by Sternberg and Weis, *The New Psychology of Love* for several taxonomies of love, 149–221.

26. Other Greek words that have some similarity to *philia* and nuance its meaning are *euonia* (dedicated devotion) and *pathos* (a feeling of sympathy).

27. See the classic study of love by M. C. D'Arcy, *The Mind and Heart of Love: Lion and Unicorn in a Study of Eros and Agape*, Chapter Four, "Friendship," 104–22.

and breathe without Friendship."[28] It is also true that the cultivation and enjoyment of friends take time, initiative, and effort, commodities in short supply in many of our lives. It may be easier for some who have the time and inclination, but it still requires coming out of our shells and extending ourselves into the stress of interpersonal relationships.

As Plato is more the philosopher of the highest forms of *eros*, Aristotle might be thought of as the one who speaks clearly and profoundly about *philia*. In the *Nicomachean Ethics*, Aristotle gives friendship an integral role in living the good life. He uses three different categories of friendship, describing its quality in ascending order.[29] The lowest form of friendship involves people who know each other, but use one another for personal gain. It is not so much that we should not expect a friend to assist us if we have a need, but that we view the "friend" as one whom we can manipulate for our advantage. Aristotle also includes in this category the common exchange of favors in normal everyday encounters where there is an equal exchange made, and especially when a score is kept and used to manipulate the other. He speaks of this kind of connection between people who come together just to be useful to one another as false friendship. Equally false is the relationship based exclusively on the receiving of pleasure. "Thus the company of witty persons is agreeable, not because of what they are in themselves, but because it is agreeable to us."[30] Such loves die a natural death when there is no longer the need to use an acquaintance or receive pleasure from one.

A true friendship, according to Aristotle is one of "mutual concern and active care."[31] Aristotle says that it "is only between those who are good, and resemble one another in their goodness, that friendship is perfect."[32] This kind of friendship may include the utilitarian kind and that which brings pleasure, but true friendship is built upon the deep and abiding trust that the other person cares about your welfare as you do as well for your friend. Such a friendship makes us better human beings and contributes to the welfare of society.[33]

---

28. Lewis, *The Four Loves*, 56. Lewis speaks of four kinds of love in this volume: Affection, Friendship, Eros, and Charity.

29. *The Ethics of Aristotle*, 227–57.

30. Ibid., 232.

31. Brander, *Love that Works*, 106.

32. *The Ethics of Aristotle*, 233.

33. Aristotle expands these points in the *Ethics*.

## The Understanding of Love: Its Ground, Contours, and Dimensions

The kind of friendship about which Aristotle speaks is further developed in the classical world by Cicero[34] and becomes a cherished value in the Roman world. But the word *philia* is not frequently used in the New Testament. However, some have suggested that friendship should be more widely utilized in describing the human connection with God, especially if friendship is not always viewed as a relationship between equals.[35] The account in the Gospel of John attributes to Jesus the place of friendship for his disciples and he says, "This is my commandment that you love one another as I have loved you. No one has greater love than this, to lay down one's life for one's friends. You are my friends if you do what I command you . . . but I have called you friends, because I have made known to you everything that I have heard from my Father" (John 15:12–16). Liz Carmichael, in her book *Friendship: Interpreting Christian Love* maintains that love may be understood as friendship with God, and carefully traces this theme through classical theology up to the present.[36] For most of us, love is central to friendship, and we value it almost beyond measure.

The third broad category for describing love is expressed in the word, *agape*, one that means unlimited love.[37] It is a form of love that extends beyond the normal limits of human interaction and selflessly reaches out to all of humanity, and indeed to all sentient beings, and goes to the point of need with a caring and healing response.[38] It asks nothing in return and cares only for the well-being of those within the circle of exchange. As we move into an initial discussion of *agape*, it may be helpful to distinguish between appraisal and bestowal. Love that is generated by an *appraisal* sees that the object of love is worthy of love. In this case, the love is evoked by the beauty or the truth or the goodness of the object that is encountered or observed. In other cases, the one who loves may maintain that the person or situation is not attractive and nor inherently lovable, but in need of the response of love. In that case, it is a circumstance of *bestowal* in

---

34. Cicero, *De amicitia*.

35. Thomas Aquinas, for example uses friendship as the fulfillment of the Great Commandments, to love God and neighbor, although his word choice is *caritas*. See Carmichael, *Friendship: Interpreting Christian Love*, Chapter 4, "Thomas Aquinas: '*Caritas is friendship with God*,'" 101–30.

36. Carmichael, *Friendship*. See as well Elizabeth Moltmann-Wendel, in her book *Rediscovering Friendship*. She thoughtfully discusses the male and female image of God and suggests that masculine images of God may have obscured women's experience of Jesus.

37. The Latin word, *caritas*, and the Greek word, *charis*, have a meaning similar to *agape*, but with shades of difference.

38. Post, *Unlimited Love*, 17–20.

## Section II — The Geography of Love

which one gives the love in an unlimited way, but without the motivation of being drawn to the person or situation because of common interests, attractiveness, or charm. Nor is this kind of love given because one finds pleasure or gain in providing care or assistance.[39] The character of *agape* is that it is bestowed regardless of the attractiveness of the person or the pleasure inherent in the situation. It is done for the sake of others in order to heal, care, and increase their well-being.

It is what we have described as the essence of the divine, and it is the word used by John of Patmos in his first letter when he says "God is love." It is also the word chosen by the Apostle Paul as he writes to the Corinthians in order to show them "a still more excellent way" (1 Cor 12:31). This more excellent way is described as follows: "Love is patient; love is kind; love is not envious or boastful or arrogant or rude" (1 Cor 13:4). Jesus is quoted as saying in the Sermon on the Mount, "You have heard it said, 'You shall love your neighbor and hate your enemy.' But I say unto you, Love your enemies and prayer for those who persecute you" (Matt 5:43–44). In the same collection of sayings, Jesus says, "You have heard that it was said, 'An eye for an eye and a tooth for a tooth.' But I say unto you, do not resist an evildoer. But if anyone strikes you on the right cheek, turn the other also; and if anyone wants to sue you and take your coat, give your cloak as well; and if anyone forces you to go one mile, go also the second mile" (Matt 5:38–41). In Pauline theology, it is the *agape* of God that reconciles the human family with God.[40] The Apostle writes, "For I am convinced that neither death, nor life, nor angels, nor rulers, nor things present, nor things to come, nor powers, nor height, nor depth, nor anything else in all creation, will be able to separate us from the love of God in Christ Jesus our Lord" (Rom 8:38–39).

Stephen Post, drawing from the work of Pitirim Sorokin, a leading sociologist of an earlier generation who pioneered the study of love, suggests five essential features of self-giving, altruistic love:

1. Polite behavior is generally expected of all of us, but there may be circumstances in which altruistic, self-giving love (*agape*) is required

---

39. Singer, *The Nature of Love: Plato to Luther*, Vol. 1, 3–22. The three-volume work of Professor Singer is exceptional in its breadth and subtlety as it traces the understanding of love across the centuries.

40. There are several full and profound statements across the history of Christian theology explicating the love of God which is the heart of the gospel, the good news, and how it is received by faith in the heart of the believer. One classic statement about the *agape* of God is the book by the Swedish theologian Anders Nygren, *Agape and Eros*.

and it must take the form of *intensive* caring. Love becomes intensive when it must be strong and concentrated and which requires the one who loves to move beyond self-interest. People such as Martin Luther King, Jr. and Mohandas Gandhi demonstrated this kind of love in settings where casual politeness would have been inadequate.

2. *Agape* is also described as *extensive* by Sorokin and needs to be extended to all those in need, including those who are not lovable and even non-human sentient beings, as was the case with St. Francis of Assisi. Love goes to the suburbs of hell to care for those who suffer.

3. *Agape* has *duration* and does not end when the situation becomes difficult and problems arise. "Love never ends" (1 Cor 13:8). Jesus did not retreat from the crowds, or those who were outcastes, but extended his care to the leper (Mark 1:40–45) and all who came his way.

4. *Agape* is *pure* as well, free from ulterior and hidden motives and unconcerned for the personal needs of the one who loves. It is not ever easy to be free from one's own needs, and indeed the one who loves may find some gratification in selfless love, but it is given without one's own needs as the primary motivation.

5. *Agape* is also described as *adequate* in the sense of providing a wise and appropriate response to the need. Often, and in an effort to be helpful, people reach out to others in a desire to help, but what they provide may not be what is needed. Adequate is a good word, but "appropriate" may be better, as the care we give must be appropriate to the person or the situation.[41]

Daniel Day Williams speaks of *agape* as having five essential qualities.[42] They are:

1. Individuality: Love requires the unique response inherent in an individual; it is not a generic response. The person who views the other as one in need of love cannot view the other as a type, needing a category of love, but needing the special response of a specific individual to a particular need in the person. A mother uniquely gives to her child a selfless gift of love that only she can give to her special child.

---

41. Post, *Unlimited Love*, 133–155, and Sorokin, *The Ways and Powers of Love*, 15–35.

42. *The Spirit and Forms of Love*, 114–122.

## Section II — The Geography of Love

2. Freedom: The gift of love is given in freedom, not driven, for example, by the fate inherent in the phrase "falling in love." Yes, love is given in an historical context, filled with duty, certain conditions, and by a person in transition. But it is freely given nonetheless with an uncertainty about the future, but in hope that it will be appropriate to the need.

3. Action and Suffering: To love is to act, and with the action come feelings, hopes, memory of past actions, and the risk that the act will cause the one who loves discomfort, even pain. When we act in love, we are changed and run the risk of suffering. The parent responds to the needs of her child knowing full well that the response is costly, requiring time, energy, and sacrifice.

4. Causality: Love means that the action taken will change the conditions of the situation. Love is an abstract category without causality, and it will not just be the situation that changes, but the one who loves and the one who receives love. The parent and the child are changed in the giving of love.

5. Impartial Judgment: It is indeed hard, especially in the case of the relationship between parent and child, to be impartial and rationally assess the persons and *situation and provide appropriate love. But impartiality is the high tribute which* loves pays to the other, seeking the true needs of the other and giving the appropriate and adequate response, not the one that is driven by one's own bias.

These categories suggest other words, cognates of love that need some attention as we develop a common language for describing and understanding the gestalt of love. It is possible to suggest dozens of words, and the many languages of the world find words that wrap around the multiple dimensions of love, providing subtlety and nuance that help us say what we feel and want to communicate. I will start with five words, closely related to love, that will help us in our endeavor to journey together across the lovescapes of life.

The first of these is *altruism*, a word used in the social sciences, and which is defined as "a form of helping behavior that provides no anticipated material benefits to the agent and may incur some loss."[43] Excellent research on the evolutionary, neurological, developmental, psychological, social, cultural, and religious aspects of altruism is provided in the volume

---

43. Post, *Unlimited Love*, 59.

entitled *Altruism and Altruistic Love*.⁴⁴ This volume begins with the assumption that altruism is widely considered to be a foundation for the moral life, and that at its core, it is the affirmation of and care for "the other as other."⁴⁵ Altruism, from the Latin root *alter* (meaning "other") is that behavior which is concerned about the welfare of another, especially when that person is in need. The agent of love acts for the well-being of the other as an end in itself rather than a means of internal gratification or public affirmation. It is often a costly intervention and requires self-sacrifice and even loss or suffering to the agent of love. This kind of response to another person or situation is akin to *agape* although *agape* may imply motivation for giving of oneself for the well-being of another person, persons, or unjust situations because there is religious commitment and a deep belief in the value of all human beings created in the image of God. It may involve suffering for the welfare of others because of the linkage with God's love for humanity, which may involve the "suffering" of God. The Hebrew word used in the Bible, *hesed*, speaks of God's steadfast love in being true to the covenant with Israel, even when there is a failure to live faithfully to the promises within the covenant. Those within the covenant cannot be separated from God's mercy (*hesed*).

Another term, closely related to altruistic love, is *care* (*cura*), a form of love that is specifically related to making a response to a person or persons in need; it is "to take care" of them. It is to provide patient and watchful responsibility for the welfare of another, and it often carries with its related meaning, to be weighed down or troubled because the care is so necessary for the well-being of the person in need. Willard Gaylin speaks of care as a fundamental trait of being human, one that develops and matures over time. He views it as a biologically programmed impulse essential for the survival of our species, integral to parenting but essential in all forms of human relationships.⁴⁶ What may distinguish care from other closely related words is the way it is often viewed as integral to our nature to care for our children, a trait that is then transferred to caring for others in need. We provide care for those without food and clothing, those who grieve, and those who are ill.

Closely associated with care is another word, *compassion*, that is also focused on the other, although not necessarily tied to our parental

---

44. Post, et al. Altruism in the study of religious traditions has been discussed in the volume edited by Neusner and Chilton, *Altruism in World Religions*.

45. *Altruism and Altruistic Love*, 3.

46. *Caring*, Chapter 4 "The Nature of Nurture: Food and More," 53–68.

## Section II — The Geography of Love

impulse. Compassion is the form that love takes in response to suffering.[47] Paul Gilbert defines compassion "as behavior that aims to nurture, look after, teach, guide, mentor, soothe, protect, offer feelings of acceptance and belonging—in order to benefit another person."[48] Lynn Underwood points to the subjective quality of compassion, the deep inner feeling that inspires one to respond to the suffering of others, and prefers to use the term "compassionate love" rather than other terms because it represents the inner quality of the one who goes to the point of need in the other.[49] We will give more attention to the rich connotations of compassion as we go along, and give special attention to it when we speak about the centrality of love in the Buddhist tradition in Chapter 4.

Still another concept, akin to the ones we have mentioned and in the family of love is *empathy*. Empathy is the capacity to understand the experiences, feelings, and thoughts of others and to be sensitive to them without having them explain or communicate their situation in a fully explicit manner. It is to be able to identify with another person, sense their struggle and go with them through their suffering. Like compassion, empathy implies having feelings and emotions for the other person or persons. Jeremy Rifkin uses the word "empathic" to describe a fundamental point of view in civilization, a shift in outlook or consciousness that implies understanding the experience, feelings, and suffering of others and caring enough to take action on their behalf. He writes, "Empathy brings together sensations, feelings, emotions, and reasons in a structural way toward the goal of communion with the vast others that stretch beyond our physicality."[50] To have empathy motivates us to respond and care for those in need.

One final word we will introduce here is a more distant cousin, but one in the family of love and important on the journey across life's lovescapes. It is *forgiveness*, which means to cease to feel resentment toward others who have harmed you and (implied) to welcome them back into the circle of communication. To be forgiven is to be pardoned, to not have your offense held against you. It is a word that has deep religious meaning in those traditions that teach their followers that God has revealed the divine expectations for human behavior, ones that are not always followed.

---

47. Two recent books about compassion view it as a way of life, not unlike the Buddhist understanding of compassion. They are: Marc Ian Barasch, *The Compassionate Life: Walking the Path of Kindness* and Paul Gilbert, *The Compassionate Mind*.

48. *The Compassionate Mind*, 193.

49. *Altruism and Altruistic Love*, 72.

50. *The Empathic Civilization*, 172.

## The Understanding of Love: Its Ground, Contours, and Dimensions

God in the Abrahamic religions is said to graciously forgive humans who go against the will and way of God, and religious rituals and practices are taught as a way of dealing with confession and pardon. The Christian faith teaches that we are not only forgiven by the action of Jesus Christ, but called upon to forgive others. The Lord's Prayer invites us to pray for forgiveness and to extend forgiveness (Matt 6:9–13). Forgiveness has the power to shatter the law of the irreversibility of the past, not as a record of all that has happened but in the meaning for us here and now. Forgiveness goes beyond the economy of reciprocity and strict justice and forgives by an act of charity and the gift of love. Those created in the image of God are worthy of loving forgiveness and welcomed back into the family of love.

## CONCLUSION: A GUIDING DEFINITION OF LOVE

We have only just begun in our journey across the lovescapes of life. We have seen that we live in an age of crisis, one filled with vexing problems that seem insoluble. We have suggested that love has a critical role to play in providing insight about these problems and giving motivation and perspective in the effort to solve them and to create a more just and humane world. We have attempted to provide a way of understanding the elusive word *love* and its many cognates. My hope is that we have begun to find a way of talking about love and applying its healing and fulfilling power to our lives and to the world we inhabit. At this point, we review the meaning of love by offering sample definitions from those who have attempted to capture the essence of love.

- Erich Fromm, in his classic study of love, speaks of it as the interpersonal union that has been the ideal virtue in all great humanistic religions and philosophical systems of the last four thousand years of Western and Eastern history. It is a spiritual bonding that preserves one's integrity, a giving of one's true self to the other for their well-being. It involves care, responsibility, respect, and knowledge.[51]

- A more recent definition is given by Stephen G. Post. He writes that, "The essence of love is to affectively affirm and to gratefully delight in the well-being of others; the essence of unlimited love is to extend this form of love to all others in an enduring, intense, effective, and pure manner."[52]

---

51. *The Art of Loving*, 17–31.
52. *Unlimited Love*, 19.

## Section II — The Geography of Love

- M. Scott Peck, in his popular book, *The Road Less Traveled* defines love as "The will to extend one's self for the purpose of nurturing one's own or another's spiritual growth."[53]

- Greg Baer, a medical doctor who specializes in healing relationships defines love: "Real Love is unconditionally caring about the happiness of another person."[54]

- A more recent definition is given by Thomas Jay Oord. His definition of love is: "To love is to act intentionally, in sympathetic response to others (including God), to promote overall well-being."[55]

From these samples, and the others we have alluded to, we have introduced ourselves to the diverse meanings of love. As we continue our discussion of love, we will draw upon the several and diverse nuances of love, but be guided more by those meanings that are agapic in character and stress the generous and gracious spirit and behavior of acceptance, affirmation, and well-being of others, given from a selfless and pure motivation. But we will not ignore love's many-splendored qualities.

So we continue our exploration of the meaning and power of love by turning to the way it has been understood across the centuries. We will then investigate the ways that love provided both a foundation and an ethical framework for many religions of the human family.

---

53. *The Road Less Traveled*, 81.

54. Baer, *Real Love: The Truth about Finding Unconditional Love & Fulfilling Relationships*, 4.

55. Oord, *Defining Love: A Philosophical, Scientific, and Theological Engagement*, 15.

*The Understanding of Love: Its Ground, Contours, and Dimensions*

## STUDY RESOURCES

### Discussion Questions

1. Do you think that love is integral to reality, or is it more simply an ethical value that describes a way of relating to others in fulfilling and helpful ways?
2. Is love primarily a feeling of attraction, an outlook on life, or actions for the benefit of others? Or all of these and more?
3. Which of the Greek words for love (*eros, philia, agape*) do you think best describes what we call "love" in our English usage?
4. In a sentence of two, how would you define love?
5. In what ways would you like love to be a more important part of your life?

### Key Terms and Concepts

- *The metaphysics of love*: the inquiry about whether love is a fundamental part of all of reality.
- *Eros:* the feeling of attraction to that which is filled with goodness, truth, and beauty and which has the capacity to fulfill and complete us.
- *Philia:* friendship that is both fulfilling for us and is also focused on the well-being of the other.
- *Agape:* unlimited love that extends beyond the normal limits of human interaction and selflessly reaches out to all of humanity with a caring and healing response.
- *Altruism*: a form of helping behavior that provides no anticipated material or emotional benefit to the agent and may incur some loss.

### Suggestions for Reference and Reading

1. Brander, Bruce, *Love That Works: The Art and Science of Giving.* Philadelphia: Templeton Foundation Press, 2004.

## Section II — The Geography of Love

2. Nygren, Anders, *Agape and Eros*. Translated by Philip S. Watson. London: S.P.C.K., 1953.

3. Oord, Thomas Jay, *Defining Love: A Philosophical, Scientific, and Theological Engagement*. Grand Rapids: Brazos, 2010.

4. Post, Stephen G., *Unlimited Love: Altruism, Compassion, and Service*. Philadelphia: Templeton Foundation Press, 2003.

5. Williams, Daniel Day, *The Spirit and the Forms of Love*. New York: University Press of America, 1981.

# 3

# The Understanding of Love across History, Tradition, and Culture

## LOVE AS A CONSTANT IN HUMAN EXPERIENCE

WE BEGAN OUR INQUIRY about the meaning of love with a discussion of the way that our immediate circumstances, the region in which we live, and our national and global context are in crisis and in need an infusion of care and compassion. We then turned our attention to finding a way of understanding love in all of its different dimensions and seeking definitions and categories that might guide us in our conversation about love and its application to the challenges we face. As we seek to find ways of applying love to our lives and our world, we will be helped by deepening our understanding of love by exploring the ways that it has been understood across history, and it is to this subject that we now turn.

We suggested that the goal of *Lovescapes, Mapping the Geography of Love* is quite simple, and as we move into a summary of the ways that love has been understood across history, it may be wise to remind ourselves of what we hope to accomplish. We want to understand and describe the meaning of love in all of its rich variety and to explore the ways that love takes expression in human life. As we gain this understanding, we will make the case that love and its many cousins are part of the approach we must take in order to begin to solve the vexing problems of our time. So our goal is to suggest strategies for shaping regional and global policies

# Section II — The Geography of Love

that are loving, compassionate, forgiving, and just, and to provide guidance for becoming more loving persons who will be able to invest our lives in creating a more humane world.

I have spoken with some wise and thoughtful people who, while affirming these goals, have nevertheless cautioned about possible redundancy. I hear, for example, "There is already an abundance of high quality books on the subject of love. Do we really need another one?" The point is well-taken, and I have immersed myself in these books and have been greatly enriched by them. I would answer, with full appreciation of what has gone before, that many of these fine volumes focus on a particular aspect of love and have a slightly different purpose, not always directly related to the place of love and compassion in addressing the particular challenges of our age of crisis. Even those that have been more comprehensive in scope and aimed at incorporating love and compassion into the effort to improve the human condition are inevitably selective and tend to get dated. It would appear, as we review what has gone before, that love is a constant and is so central to the human experience that each generation must re-examine and rediscover the many splendored and life-giving qualities of love. Each generation will do so in a multitude of ways, with reading being only one. But it is one that must be in the mix, drawing upon the rich treasures of former times, and with a clear arrow pointing to contemporary issues. That is our goal.

We turn then to our mapping of love with a brief sketch of the ways that love has been a constant in the human drama across history, traditions, and cultures. We add to our awareness the rich treasures of our heritage. As we do so, we will explore ways that the finest expressions of love may empower us to become better human beings and increase our capacity and commitment to love. So we begin to "count the ways" we might wisely love those closest to us, those in the region in which we live, and indeed the earth and all who dwell in it.

> How do I love thee? Let me count the ways.
> I love thee to the depth and breadth and height
> My soul can reach, when feeling out of sight
> For the ends of Being and ideal Grace.
> I love thee to the level of every day's
> Most quiet need, by sun and candlelight.
> I love thee freely, as men strive for Right;
> I love thee purely, as men turn from Praise.
> I love thee with the passion put to use
> In my old griefs, and with my childhood's faith.

*The Understanding of Love across History, Tradition, and Culture*

> I love thee with a love I seemed to lose
> With my lost saints,—I love thee with the breath,
> Smiles, tears, of all my life!—and, if God choose,
> I shall love thee better after death.[1]

Admittedly, Elizabeth Barrett Browning was speaking to Robert, but I am inspired by the universal character of her words of love and her imaginative metaphors. I think of all the ways it is possible for us to bring love and compassion to a needy world, as difficult as the task may be.

## LOVE IN THE PRELITERATE AND CLASSICAL ERAS

It is not easy to trace the kinds and expressions of love in the early centuries of human existence. There are few if any records of the sorts of connections humans had with one another, although evolutionary patterns may give us some hints.[2] Through the process of natural selection, there were those first humans who were able to adapt to their environment, survive, and reproduce, while others, less able to manage their circumstances, did not stay alive. Over time, there was a survival of the fittest. A certain kind of love may in fact have been one of the essential means of prolonging life.

As evolutionary theory is applied to early human history, three tendencies have been suggested as supporting survival.[3] The first of these conditions is that parents demonstrated care for their infants. Often associated with attachment theory, this care meant that parents would protect the children from predators, both in the natural world and also from other humans. As the children were protected, they began to attach themselves to their parents for security and to the family as a safe haven, an attachment that became imprinted on them and lasting into adulthood. In adulthood, humans would then seek mates who had the capacity to protect and provide security from the range of dangers abundant in this early period of human history.[4]

A second, closely related tendency is that the parents tended to care for and protect each other, thereby preserving the safe environment for the child. There was a commitment to one another. Each parent may have selected a mate that had certain qualities that predicted their ability to provide a safe environment for the family. The man may have been strong

---

1. Browning (1806–1861), *Sonnets from the Portuguese*, 169.
2. Sternberg, *Cupid's Arrow: The Course of Love through Time*, 53–58.
3. Ackerman, *A Natural History of Love*, 131–36.
4. Bowlby, *Attachment and Loss*, Vol. I.

## Section II — The Geography of Love

and healthy, a good hunter, and able to provide sustenance; the woman may have had characteristics that made the home a safe setting and even physical features that evoked the childhood feelings and the attachment imprint of the mate. The third tendency may have been strong sexual feeling for the mate, with some differences in the nature of the attraction between the male and the female. But strong romantic and sexual feelings (passion) for one another ensured offspring and may have contributed to the perseveration of the family unit.

This evolutionary hypothesis would suggest that love, as expressed in care, commitment, and attraction may have been an essential factor in human survival. One author has suggested eight goals rooted in evolutionary theory that point to love as instrumental in survival and reproductive success.[5] They are:

1. Resource display: Reproductive success increases as both male and female find a mate with the most resources to commit to the relationship.
2. Exclusivity: This would include both fidelity and mate guarding.
3. Mutual support and protection.
4. Commitment and marriage.
5. Sexual feelings.
6. Reproduction.
7. Resource sharing.
8. Parental investment in the child's well-being.

Not all scholars would say that evolutionary theory is sufficient to describe the many patterns of survival.[6] Other factors such as the mate's status within the tribe, geography in reference to the availability of food, conditions that limited exposure to disease, and cultural norms and values may have played a central role as well.

There is no question that the understanding of love within cultures has not only influenced survival, but also greatly contributed to the quality of life. It is not possible to describe the way love has been understood and valued in all of the classical cultures, but a few examples will illustrate

---

5. Quoted by Sternberg in *Cupid's Arrow*, 56–57. See Buss, "Sex Differences in Human Mate Preferences: Evolutionary Hypotheses Tested in 87 Cultures," *Behavior and Brain Sciences*.

6. See Grant, *Altruism and Christian Ethics*, 1–33.

## The Understanding of Love across History, Tradition, and Culture

the constancy and priority of love as civilizations developed and ancient societies formed.

We begin our discussion with a brief description of the place of love in the civilization of ancient Egypt. It is all too easy to look at the life of a famous person and to suggest that their life was representative of the kind of experience that all of the people had in the society. In fact, the person's life may have been quite distinct and idiosyncratic, not representative, and this is certainly the case with the person one most easily associates with the love among the Egyptians of the classical era, Cleopatra. What we have with her story, some based in history and some in legend is the influence of erotic love on the great events of her time. She is history's paramour.[7] She was born in Egypt in 69 BCE, the daughter of King Ptolemy XII, who was descended from a Macedonian general. There are no definitive records regarding who her mother may have been, although several theories have been suggested based on the customs of the time.

Many of the accounts of her life have been lost, and there has been some dependence on Plutarch's account written two hundred years later.[8] Plutarch describes her as less than beautiful but very charming and with a strong personality and a musical voice. She was sensitive to international politics, shrewd, and used her glamorous style in her meeting with Mark Antony in Tarsus. She arrived like a goddess, fully aware that she must use her full repertoire in the negotiations with Rome. She knew, for example, that Rome yearned for the mastery of the world and needed Egypt's power, navy, and treasury. What emerged from the conversation in Tarsus is not easy to recreate, but it is clear that Cleopatra and Antony loved one another and established a relationship of respect and a sense of shared mission about the future of the Mediterranean world.[9]

From a review of this story, the hieroglyphic literature of love poems, and the well-researched histories written about ancient Egypt, it is possible to suggest some categories of understanding about love that existed in ancient Egypt. In so doing, care must be exercised not to over-generalize from the one story, but to draw from it and other sources a sense of the

---

7. See Ackerman, *A Natural History of Love*, 3–17.

8. An excellent new account (and Pulitzer Prize winner) of her life has been written by Stacy Schiff, *Cleopatra: A Life*.

9. There are many excellent accounts of the history of Egypt, some giving attention to the influence of the relationship of Cleopatra and Antony. See, for example, the great classic by James Henry Breasted, *A History of Egypt: From the Earliest Ties to the Persian Conquest*. A more recent book on the customs of the ancient Egyptians is Brier and Hobbs, *The Daily Life of the Ancient Egyptians*.

## Section II — The Geography of Love

constancy of love and its influence in the ancient world as well as the modern. Diane Ackerman suggests six categories of understanding:[10]

1. Love's alchemy or power to transform: Egyptians believed in the magic of love, that it could change them and their situation, and Cleopatra had access to this magic.
2. Love as idealizing the beloved in images drawn from nature: A person's features are compared to the stars, flowers, or gems.
3. Love as enslavement: In love, it seems that we are willing to become prisoners of our feelings. "Loves bids me to go, and I follow" even if the destination is dangerous.
4. Love as disabling: Love can be empowering, but a certain kind of love filled with overwhelming emotion has the power to cause us to lose our capability to think clearly and make good decisions.
5. Love as a secret kept from parents: We want to hide our feelings of love from those who would not accept our strong emotions and relationship with one who may not be safe.
6. Love as increasing the power of the senses: Like a drug, our senses are intensified as we are drawn into a love relationship.

Much more could be said about the place of love in ancient Egypt, but perhaps these few characteristics will add to our understanding of the place of love in the ancient world. There may have been many expressions of love as friendship and as selfless compassion in ancient Egypt, but it is erotic and romantic love that gets the headlines. More subtle and influential are the ways that love was understood in ancient Greece. In the case of Plato, the word *eros* is chosen and given a distinctive meaning. As we turn to Plato and then on to Aristotle, we are fully aware that the more common and popular understanding of love in ancient Greece was in reference to the activity of the gods, and that human feelings and expressions of love were thought to be influenced by the gods. It should be observed as well that the homosexual expression of love was accepted within ancient Greece. This observation is important in that many societies and cultures have rejected homosexual union as an acceptable form of human love, and the issue is of great importance in our time and context.

We have already spoken about Platonic love and the place of friendship in the writings of Aristotle, but a brief review might be helpful at this point. All of the various forms of love were present in ancient Greece

10. *A Natural History of Love*, 11–14.

as they probably were in ancient Egypt, but the two ideals found in the writing of Plato and Aristotle have survived across time and continue to influence humankind. By ideal, we mean that there is a certain kind of love that becomes the standard or superior expression of excellence. It epitomizes what love should be and for which we should strive. It is the model from which all other loves are judged. To some extent, it is a love that grows out of appraisal, the experience of being attracted to great beauty, moral character, and intelligence in the object of love. It also has elements of bestowal, taking the ideal of love and applying it to our judgments and behavior about those in our midst.[11] In the case of Plato, this *ideal* or *form* has existence and is not simply a projection of the mind or spirit of the person.

Plato describes love in more than one of his writings, but the full development of love as an ideal for life is in the *Symposium*. Plato was born in Athens in 428 BCE, one year after the death of Pericles and when Socrates was about forty-two years old. Athenian culture was flourishing, and because Plato came from a very distinguished family, his early training must have included all of the richness of Athenian culture. He was exposed to the complexities of politics and governance and the range of philosophies which attempted to describe the best ways of knowing and acting. The question for him and which was central to his philosophy was how it is the humans fit into the overarching scheme of the universe.[12] The *Symposium*, one of more than twenty dialogues, was written in the middle period of Plato's life and represents his most mature, thoughtful, and profound work.

As we described earlier,[13] Plato is very concerned about epistemology, how we are able to know, and ethics, how we should act. He says that true knowledge does not come easily and uses the allegory of the cave to describe this difficult quest for true knowledge. For most humans, understanding is like living in a cave as a prisoner and only being able to see the shadows of reality that are cast by those who walk by a fire. Even if the prisoners were released, they might still be unable to shift their focus. It would require a conversion (*metanoia*), a complete turning around from the world of shadows and appearances to the world of reality. Such a conversion, moving from seeing shadows to seeing reality goes through the

---

11. Singer, *The Nature of Love: From Plato to Luther*, Vol. 1, 23–25. Irving's work is a lucid interpretation of love across the centuries in 3 volumes.

12. Stumpf, *Socrates to Sartre: A History of Philosophy*, 46–79.

13. Chapter 2, 39–41.

## Section II — The Geography of Love

four stages of growth and maturity: imagining, belief, thinking, and on to knowledge. True knowledge comes when one is released from preoccupation with sensible objects and begins to understand the world of *ideals* or *forms*. These ideals or forms are eternal patterns of which the objects are only copies.

It is into this frame of reference that Plato speaks about love (*eros*). It is *eros* or desire that motivates and inspires humans to move out of the cave, from the mundane observation to the beautiful object, and then on to the beautiful thought and finally to the essence of Beauty itself. The phrase, Platonic love, which has come into our language, refers to a life of love which seeks to know the ultimately real—goodness, truth, and beauty. It is not a life rooted in the senses, but a life of the mind, motivated by love that empowers one to move toward maturity and to be able to live the virtuous life of thoughtful contemplation. Much of the rest of Plato's philosophy regarding the moral life, politics led by the philosopher-king, and the understanding of the cosmos flow from the foundation the love-centered life.[14]

Aristotle, a student of Plato's, but differing with him on some issues, also leaves a profound legacy in his writing about love. For Aristotle, love has more to do with *philia* or friendship than with *eros*. Once again, Aristotle, like Plato, has a comprehensive philosophy covering all aspects of the cosmos and human life. His understanding of love fits within this larger framework, the foundation of which is rationalism, the use of reason to understand, and the habits of right thinking which lead to right choice and right behavior. It is in his work the *Nicomachean Ethics* that Aristotle speaks about love, one aspect of his treatment of ethics.

Aristotle moves partially away from Plato in regard to the separate existence of *ideals/forms* and says that these ideals of love are present in actual human relationships. As we described earlier,[15] Aristotle speaks about three different kinds of friendship, beginning with the one that is least noble and moving to the one that is most virtuous. The first kind of friendship is a relationship in which one person exploits the other for personal gain, a relationship that is essentially false in character. The second is similar, a friendship that is based exclusively on receiving pleasure from another. A true friendship, however, is based upon a genuine concern for the other, trust, fidelity, and active care. It is only this kind of friendship

---

14. For a good summary of Plato's view of love, see Morgan's *Love: Plato, the Bible, and Freud*, 5–46. Singer's Vol. 1 in *The Nature of Love*, 47–87 offers a profound interpretation of Plato's view of love as well.

15. Chapter 2, 42–43.

that is true and that will lead to the good and happy life. "But it is only between those who are good, and resemble one another in their goodness, that friendship is perfect. Such friends are both good in themselves, and, so far as they are good, desire the good of one another."[16]

The Romans, too, found ways of thinking about love and expressed all forms of love. There were noble values that were present in the culture, but as in all periods of history, these noble values were not always consistently followed. As one might expect, ancient Rome had its rules and laws about human behavior; it was a culture that was structured and that took law seriously.[17] For example, marriage was essentially a family contract with more emphasis placed on the way life was managed than on the deep feelings of attraction between the marriage partners. As in most cultures, so in Rome there were different classes, and behavioral patterns and expectations differed between the classes. For example, slaves were not allowed to marry. In the upper classes, monogamy and restraint were written into the culture and praised, in part because of the need for efficiency and order, but sexual freedom and intemperance were the order of the day. Children were valued and respected, and the marriage contract served to provide a safe and nurturing environment for children. Within the marriage, one in which the wife was seen as inferior, sex was for "making babies" more than an expression of fondness and commitment. Infidelity was common, and not infrequently it was engaged in for raw pleasure and occasionally because of romantic attraction, although these trysts were not necessarily based on friendship and mutual respect. Many remained single and divorce was common.

Lucretius, the first-century BCE Epicurean poet-philosopher, extolled married life and wished that it could be a central feature of the life of the empire, lived out with fidelity and trust. He warned against passionate love based solely on sexual attraction and romantic feelings and called it destructive madness, recognizing the natural tendencies of human beings.[18] Relationships of pure passion were common in ancient Rome, as he observed and expected, but regretted.

Ovid, the last great poet of the Augustan age (47 BCE–17 CE), has moved well beyond the idealism of Plato and Aristotle and even the

16. *The Ethics of Aristotle*, 233.

17. Of the many books on the history of Rome, De Burgh's *The Legacy of the Ancient World*, 298–303 provides and succinct description of the place of law ancient Rome.

18. Oates, *The Stoic and Epicurean Philosophers*. See section on Lucretius, *On the Nature of Things*, Book IV, 137–162. Observed by Brander in *Love That Works*, 27.

## Section II — The Geography of Love

lingering hope of Lucretius. He is quite direct in speaking about love as sexual attraction. His book, *The Art of Love*, essentially assumes that any woman his readers might want to woo is married. The challenge is part of the fun in that the real pleasure comes from seducing a married woman whose husband is both protective of his wife and jealous of those who may show an interest.[19] To gain permission would spoil the fun in that the challenge would be gone. In Ovid, we find a champion of transgression, perhaps cynical but also realistic in his description.

Rome also had its defenders of the noble and virtuous life. No less a person than the Emperor Marcus Aurelius (121–180 CE) spoke profoundly about the good life in his *Meditations*, as did a freed slave, Epictetus (60–110 CE) in his *Discourses*. Both were part of the Stoic school of thought, founded by Zeno in the year 308 BCE in Athens. Stoic philosophy taught that virtue is the only good, and that the virtuous person is one who has obtained happiness through knowledge. The virtuous person finds happiness within and lives independently of the influences of the world. Happiness comes from self-mastery, not yielding to passions and emotions. The wise person then seeks to regulate life in harmony with universal reason (logos), which is the highest duty. An essential part of this duty is to care for (love) one another. People "exist for the sake of one another. Teach them then or bear with them."[20]

Epictetus, in the section on Friendship in his *Discourses*, argues that those who have the power to love are those who reason well and are not deceived by appearances and driven by passion. He writes, "Whoever then has knowledge of good things, would know how to love them; but how could one who cannot distinguish good things from evil and things indifferent from both have power to love? Therefore the wise man alone has the power to love."[21] True friendship and love depend upon wisdom and discernment.

The view of love in ancient Rome was rooted in both the ideals of reason and then written into law in order to shape the cultural values of the early Republic and later the Empire. In ancient Rome as in most cultures, there was not consistency in adhering to these values. The following norms were taught and incorporated into laws and social expectations:

19. Ovid, *The Art of Love*, translated by Rolfe Humphries, 65. See also Nehring, *A Vindication of Love*, 86.

20. Marcus Aurelius, *Meditations*, Book VIII, in *The Stoic and Epic Philosophers*, 552.

21. Epictetus, *Discourses of Epictetus*, Chapter XXII, "On Friendship" in *The Stoic and Epic Philosophers*, 330–331.

1. Society must be guided by laws based on justice and which protect and respect the citizens. Justice becomes the tangible and corporate expression of love and compassion. Slaves and aliens were not always protected by the laws.
2. Marriage was as much a way of managing the details of family life as it was a relationship of attraction and commitment. Many Romans found ways to express freely the passionate and sensual dimensions of love with others beside their spouses. A few of its philosophers and poets not only acknowledged that this was the way of human behavior, but even noted that pleasure gained from this behavior was to be celebrated.
3. Other Roman poets and philosophers extolled the norms of the more reasoned and disciplined life. They argued for a life based upon the rational understanding of the order and reason built into the universe (logos). When discerned by reason, this pattern suggested a life of self-mastery and respect and care for others.

## LOVE IN THE MIDDLE AGES

As the Roman Empire declined, there was a vacuum in government structures and order, especially in Europe, and people found ways to organize their corporate lives more regionally.[22] This period of time, the Middle Ages, is generally dated from about 500–1500 CE, with the early part of this period seen as a decline. The period from the ninth to the sixteenth century is often viewed as resurgence in the region. It was organized in a feudal system which had as its basis the relation of lord to vassal. In this system, all land was parceled out for a fee by the lords to the vassals. It was characterized by homage with the expectation of service by tenants, even to the point of taking up arms in the case of threat by a neighboring lord. There were regional courts that adjudicated grievances and conflicts. The primary overarching structure in this latter part of the Middle Ages was the Holy Roman Empire, consisting primarily of a loose confederation of German and Italian territories under the suzerainty of an emperor, an alliance lasting into the early 1800s.

---

22. In this subsection, I will focus more on Europe and Christianity in the discussion about love, and I will devote the next chapter to other regions of the world and the religions and ethical norms of these regions.

## Section II — The Geography of Love

Part of the power vacuum in the Middle Ages was filled by the Christian church. One of the church's leading theologians, Augustine (354–430 CE), reflected on the decline of the Roman Empire and the role of the church in the uses of power and the ordering of human society.[23] His views about society and many other aspects of faith and life in a prophetic way anticipated the period of the Middle Ages and were to influence the way society was organized in this period of history. He was born in Thagaste in the African province of Numidia. His father was not religious, but his mother, Monica, was a devout Christian. At the age of sixteen, Augustine began the study of rhetoric in Carthage, a port city filled with temptations for a young man. Though his mother's influence was present, he nevertheless discarded his faith and values and took a mistress with whom he had a son. At the same time, he was a brilliant student and he applied his extraordinary mind to the study of rhetoric.

Coupled with the study of his discipline, Augustine read *Hortensius* by Cicero, which was an exhortation to search for philosophical wisdom. He pursued this quest with diligence, hoping to find intellectual certainty. His nominal understanding of Christianity was not satisfactory, and he remained perplexed by the problem of evil. Why would a good and all-powerful God allow it? In search of an answer to this perplexing problem, he turned to Manichaeism, a philosophical system that taught a dualistic understanding of the universe, with the principle of light or goodness and the principle of darkness or evil existing side by side. He began to see his own tendency to yield to the tug of his senses as connected to the power of darkness.

In time, he was to move away from this position, accepting full responsibility for his moral failure and not blaming it on an external force. He then became somewhat attracted to a point of view whose followers were called the Academics (Skeptics), but also sensed in this point of view both arrogance and cynicism. He felt it was too easy to simply criticize the views of others without offering an alternative. His career in rhetoric took him to Milan, where he was introduced to Neo-Platonism and read the *Enneads* by Plotinus. He was also influenced in Milan by Ambrose, the Bishop of Milan, and was drawn back to his Christian roots.[24] He applied and integrated his understanding of Neo-Platonism to Christianity and found a credible place to stand. In time, he became an integral part of the

---

23. See *The City of God*.

24. For an autobiographical account of the early life of Augustine, see his classic work, *St. Augustine's Confessions*. See Book VIII, 171 for an account of his conversion.

church, becoming the Bishop of Hippo and providing profound reflections on the confluence of faith and reason.[25]

His writing was prolific, and his influence of theology on the Christian church would be hard to overstate.[26] It was in this systematic theological understanding that Augustine's treatment of love emerged. It is rooted in his moral philosophy and in particular his view of the nature of the human moral constitution. Augustine tends to agree with the ancient Greek philosophers that happiness is goal of human life, and it comes by living the good life. Aristotle, for example, argues that happiness is achieved when a person fulfills the inherent natural functions through a well-balanced life. Augustine moves beyond Aristotle at this point and maintains that true happiness in not found in the natural order; it is only achieved in the supernatural realm. It is achieved when there is relationship established with the divine. Augustine writes in the *Confessions*: "Oh God Thou has created us for Thyself so that our hearts are restless until they find their rest in Thee."[27] It is in harmonious union with God that humans find true peace and happiness.

But this union is elusive, given the human tendency to love inappropriately. Humans will inevitably love, moving beyond themselves to give their affection to an object of love. A person may love (1) physical objects; (2) other persons; or even (3) oneself. From these loves, a person can derive a measure of satisfaction, and the objects of love are good in themselves. But the one who gives a full and complete love to these objects mistakes the manner of love and expectations to be received by this love and will remain discontented and restless. Each object of love needs a certain kind of love with an appropriate expectation, such as the love of food for meeting the need of hunger. One should not expect the object of love to meet more than the particular need that corresponds to the object. The most basic human need for true inner contentment and serenity can only be met by spiritual union with God. To give one's love to God is to find ultimate satisfaction or true happiness.[28]

The objects of love are not interchangeable, and it is the human tendency to substitute a thing or a person for the infinite. There are legitimate

---

25. See Cochrane, *Christianity and Classical Culture* for a comprehensive treatment of Augustine's life and the context of his time. There is a good selection of the writings of Augustine in Clark, *Augustine of Hippo: Selected Writings*, translation and introduction, a volume in *The Classics of Western Spirituality*.

26. See Singer, Vol. 1 *The Nature of Love: From Plato to Luther*, 163–70.

27. *The Confessions of St. Augustine*, Book I, 1.

28. I follow the interpretation of Augustine's view of love in Stumpf, *Socrates to Sartre*, 144–47.

## Section II — The Geography of Love

forms of attraction to the natural world with all of its beauty and complexity. There is appropriate love for others, those closest to us and to those in need. But when the natural world, material possessions, or other persons are given primary loyalty and viewed as the way to fulfillment, then the expectations are misplaced and disillusionment occurs. Love becomes disordered when we give our truest and deepest love an object of love other than God; it cannot give us ultimate happiness. Disordered love produces all forms of pathology in human life, and we lose our way, as do our associations and corporate structures as they too become filled with disordered love. We (as individuals and the society we inhabit), if driven by disordered love can only be reconstructed when we are converted to the reordering of love. We are to love God first and foremost, and then others, ourselves, and the objects in the natural world properly. We must rid ourselves of all self-pride and misplaced love and give ourselves in love to God. Only then will we find our way to inner peace and equanimity.

Augustine maintains that the heart of the problem is our free will and our tendency to abuse it as we place our affections on objects, power, and praise, believing that they will ultimately satisfy us. It is not easy to emancipate ourselves from these temptations; they have great power. We can only be free of this tyranny by putting our faith in God and being empowered by God's grace. Grace comes to us as we put our faith in Jesus Christ, the Mediator between God and humankind, who himself became mortal that we might be made eternal. God gives what God asks, and Augustine prays, "God, ask what you will, and give what you ask."

Augustine maintains that these same principles prevail in society as well. It occurs when we try to apply justice, the corporate expression of love and the natural expression of the eternal law to the ordering of society. He develops this theme in *The City of God*, in which he speaks about those who love God on the one hand, and those who love themselves on the other (the City of the World). Augustine argues that much of the disorder in society, even the collapse of the Empire around him, is the result of misplaced love and misguided values. Space does not allow the full explanation of his views of history and government, but these views were to be influential for centuries. They are read, understood, and given new life in the writings of Thomas Aquinas (1225–1274).

As we fast-forward to the thirteenth century CE, we note that Augustine lived at the time of the decline of the Roman Empire, signaling the beginning of the Middle Ages, and Aquinas lived in the full flowering of this thousand-year period in Western history. The fast-forward to

## The Understanding of Love across History, Tradition, and Culture

Aquinas does jump over other important historical expressions of love, and perhaps most importantly the concept of romantic and courtly love, and we will return to it. But for now, the move to Aquinas enables us to continue to develop the themes of love which are present in the Christian tradition.[29]

The great achievement of Aquinas was that he was able to bring together and synthesize so much of what had gone before in Greek philosophy and Christian theology. He was especially indebted to Aristotle, whose philosophical system was recast in Christian form and evolved into a comprehensive worldview called scholasticism. The essential method of scholasticism was dialectical, relying chiefly on logical deduction. Various viewpoints were placed next to each other, and then through reasoned disputation, a scholarly and preferred point of view was chosen, one that integrated faith and reason. A good example of this methodology and one of the best known arguments that came from this method and developed by Aquinas was the so-called proofs for the existence of God.[30] His theological system was comprehensive in scope, and it was within this system that Aquinas developed his understanding of love for God and for neighbor.

Aquinas developed his theological system in the context of the influence of Peter Lombard (c. 1100–1159), whose *Four Books of Opinions* or *Sentences* were the primary source for theological refection in this period of time. Lombard's writing contained a collection of the theological problems of faith with their solutions selected from the best patristic sources. The *Sentences* address the issue of love, and Lombard drawing upon Aristotle (love as friendship) and the church fathers maintained that love was akin to friendship best exemplified in the way that Jesus laid down his life for his friends and enemies. *Caritas*, a Latin translation of 1 Corinthians 13:13 (Greek, *agape*), became the key word, and there was some debate on how best to define the word as it appears in 1 Corinthians 13:13: "And now faith, hope, and *caritas* abide, but the greatest of these is *caritas*." The father of Thomas, Albert the Great, a fine theologian, explored six meanings of the term in good scholastic fashion, and then settled on the following definition of *caritas*: "love is a connection or bond by which all things are joined in unspeakable friendship and indissoluble union."[31] He did not

---

29. Carmichael in *Friendship: Interpreting Christian Love* traces the development of the different views of love through the Middle Ages, and then speaks of Aquinas as "the greatest theoretician" of these views. I will follow her interpretation of the views of Aquinas, 101–28.

30. See Stumpf, *Socrates to Sartre*, 181–84.

31. Carmichael in *Friendship*, 103.

## Section II — The Geography of Love

fully endorse the idea that *caritas* was equivalent to *amicitia* (friendship), but Thomas did, and he identified love as friendship (*caritas* is *amicitia*) consistently across his career of teaching and writing.

His argument for this interpretation is that *caritas* and *amicitia* are the same because both demonstrate the full qualities of love. He goes on, utilizing the scholastic method, to counter several views, but argues poignantly against the point of view that friendship is not the full expression of love because it depends too heavily upon mutuality, a view of Aristotle. Aquinas maintained that friendship extends beyond those from whom we receive satisfaction in the relationship. He argues that God extends friendship to all of the human family, needing nothing in return, but offering through the Holy Spirit a transforming relationship filled with *caritas*. His argument proposes the following objects of love or friendship, as we are infused with love by the Spirit of God:[32]

1. The first and primary form is our loving friendship with God. We are to love God "with our whole heart" (Deut 6:5). This kind of love goes beyond just the enjoyment of God, although it is a blessing, to the deeper dimension of awesome wonder and heartfelt praise. This love for God is expressed in a life devoted to the will and way of God and nurtured through prayer and the sacraments.

2. The second form of friendship love is for our self and our own body. He quotes Leviticus 19:18, that we are to "love our neighbor (friend) as yourself" and argues that to love ourselves is the acknowledgement and expression of the full union of God within us. It is not a self-love that gratifies our lower nature, but a love that leads to the perfection of our rational nature.

3. Finally, Aquinas maintains that friendship love is for the benefit of our neighbor. We are to love all people, even our enemies, not just those from whom we receive love and fulfillment.

With great care and wisdom, Thomas takes on every possible objection and counter argument, making the case that the best understanding of love is friendship.

Toward the end of the Middle Ages, and pointing to a new historical era, Martin Luther (1483-1546) enters the Christian scene and articulates an interpretation of love that differs from that of Thomas Aquinas. Luther had read the works of his predecessors, Augustine and Aquinas, but it

---

32. For a full development of the ways that Aquinas' understanding of love prevails and is interpreted in the Catholic tradition, see Vacek, *Love, Human and Divine: The Heart of Christian Ethics*.

was another medieval scholar who had an even greater influence on him, William of Ockham (1280–1349). Ockham, called by Luther "my beloved William," had resisted the rational system of Aquinas based on natural theology and the rational arguments for the existence of God such as causality. Natural reason, Thomas maintained, can lead us to God by way of the proofs of the existence of God, arguing for example that all that moves and happens have a cause, but what is needed to explain this pattern is a First Cause, namely, God. Ockham argued that we must depend more on an empirical methodology and our experience. We cannot argue back through causes and find God. Knowledge of God is rather a gift of grace and is assured by an act of faith. Luther found support for this view in Augustine, and it was this foundation that caused Luther to emphasize that the initiative of God rather than human reason was the way we know God. Our problem, Luther maintained, was not so much inadequate reasoning, but the bondage of the will that must be emancipated by the love of God, and when liberated, enables us to know by an act of faith. This kind of knowledge of God is personal and relational.

It was into this frame of reference that Luther spoke about love, referring to *agape* as the free gift of God, love that liberates and connects us to God. It is bestowed on us, and we grasp it and make it our own by an act of faith. Agape precedes human love and is superior to it in every way. Luther would turn to the Apostle Paul, "But God proves his love for us in that while we were sinners, Christ died for us" (Rom 5:8). Further, "God's love has been poured into our hearts through Holy Spirit that has been given to us" (Rom 5:5). It is not that we deserve this love, but that it is given to us by the free expression of God who is love and loves us unconditionally.[33]

A follower of the Lutheran way, twentieth-century Swedish theologian Anders Nygren, grasped fully what Luther was teaching and developed it in his classic work, *Agape and Eros*. Nygren's exposition of agape is based on four foundational points:[34]

1. God's love, *agape*, is spontaneous and freely given, not motivated by need or external influence. It is not driven by the quality of the object of love, and it arises solely out of the nature of God.

2. It is therefore not motivated by the search for goodness. It does not discriminate on the basis of the value of what it chooses to love. Even the sinful, those who resist the will and way of God as readily as those

---

33. See Singer, *The Nature of Love*, Vol. 1, 265–341 for an interpretation of Luther's understanding of love.

34. Singer in *The Nature of Love*, Vol. 1, refers to Nygren's views, 275–78.

## Section II — The Geography of Love

who are committed to the will and way of God, are fully loved. God's mercy and loving-kindness are there for all.

3. It is also creative, appropriate, adequate, and discerning, giving the kind of love that is necessary to heal and make whole. A common metaphor for the loving-kindness of God's love is that it is like the love of a parent who would make any sacrifice for the well-being of their child.

4. In addition, it is the initiator of a relationship that is transforming. *Agape* brings salvation or healing, and with the transforming healing comes the empowerment and motivation to love our neighbor—and indeed all of humankind.

Luther argued that God's love for us, and the command to love others, are truly *agape* rather than *eros* or *philia*. He maintained that it is not our effort to obey a law or our reason that grasps ultimate truth that motivates our love, but the Spirit of God who is love and is present in our lives.

> "Since these promises of God are holy, true, righteous, free, and peaceful words, full of goodness, the soul which clings to them with a firm faith will be so closely united with them and altogether absorbed by them that it not only will share in all their power but will be saturated and intoxicated by them. If a touch of Christ healed, how much more will this most tender spiritual touch, this absorbing of the Word, communicate to the soul all things that belong to the Word."[35]

He would go on to teach that being transformed by God's love, we should then love our neighbor with the same sort of love.

Running concurrently with these Christian affirmations of love through the medieval era was another understanding of love that was to blossom in this period. It is best described as courtly love and later romantic love, and it was a view that has had great influence and energy across the centuries into our time.[36] It is not all that easy to define in a simple sentence in that this understanding of love developed over several centuries and in different countries and cultures. It is, however, essentially a Western understanding, though similar understandings were present in other cultures as well. It is most closely related to *eros*, and it is often a love that is bestowed but also one that has appraisal in that the object of love is attractive. Singer maintains that courtly love, the clear predecessor

---

35. Luther, *Three Treatises: The Freedom of the Christian*, 283–84.
36. The title of Vol. 2 of Singer's book, *The Nature of Love, Courtly and Romantic*.

of romantic love "affirms that love between human beings is in itself authentic and magnificent. It is love based on natural inclinations, such as sexual desire, and yet directed toward highly moral and aesthetic values."[37] Sometimes abused, this sort of love was not fundamentally exploitive, but respectful and desiring the joy and well-being of the beloved.

The idealistic love of Plato sought to transcend the world of the senses, and Christian love was often focused more on the love between God and humankind. This new love was clearly about love between humans. It was a fundamental shift from unilateral love to mutual love.[38] Singer underlines five essential qualities of courtly love:[39]

1. The first is the affirmation that sexual love between men and women is an experience of value, a pleasure worth striving for. We take this observation for granted in our time, but in the eleventh century, it was not an accepted value.

2. Courtly and romantic love enriches and fulfills both the lover and the beloved. It is not degrading, but uplifting and ennobling.

3. Because it has these qualities, sexual love cannot be reduced to mere sexual attraction or instinct. It has the capacity to bring two people together creating a bond that adds joy and fulfillment in life.

4. What made this love awkward and uncomfortable for the church community was that it was not necessarily associated with marriage. It was, on occasion even between a married woman and an unmarried knight or troubadour. Neither was it an intrusion on another's privacy or the course of their life, but a polite and respectful attraction and artful courting; it was a *courtly* initiative.

5. This kind of love was often intense and passionate as it brought two people together and joined them in an experience that was pleasurable and enriching. In many cases it allowed people to rise above the mundane routine of their day-to-day experiences and duties.

This love flourished from the eleventh century to the end of the thirteenth century chiefly in the south of France and the north of Italy. It emerged in part as a reaction to the teaching by the church that love should be understood almost exclusively as God's love for human beings. But people were lonely, especially as they returned from the Crusades. They saw relationships of attraction between women and men on their travels

---

37. Ibid., 35.
38. Ackerman, *The Natural History of Love*, 51.
39. Vol. 2, 23–32.

## Section II — The Geography of Love

and learned about other understandings and expressions of human love. Women, bound to clearly defined roles and absent husbands, often longed for more human contact. For example, William IX, Duke of Aquitaine (1071–1127), upon returning from the Crusades began to compose songs of love and yearning, now recognized as the first troubadour love songs. He had seen passionate love expressed in other parts of the world, and he began to write songs with words that spoke about "the union of souls," a genuinely ideal form of love.

While not always in opposition to the church, the movement for the legitimate expression of passionate love did begin in Europe as a reaction to Christianity. The church's doctrine of marriage was challenged by those who in spirit longed for a more free expression of human love.[40] The love stories of Tristan and Isolde, Abelard and Heloise, and Dante and Beatrice are compelling, often sad, and full of the human emotion we call love.[41] Its full expression is present is Shakespeare's *Romeo and Juliet*, a story that is important in the transition from courtly love to romantic love.

## LOVE IN MODERN TIMES

As life changed from the medieval patterns of feudal life with what is often viewed in the stereotype of "the handsome knights courting beautiful maidens," courtly love became closer to what we now understand as romantic love. There were comparable experiences and feelings, but different circumstances and ways of understanding love as the Middle Ages merged into the Renaissance, the Enlightenment, the industrial age, and into the modern era.[42] Romantic feeling, akin to those in courtly love, became more rooted in a philosophical movement known as Romanticism and the shift from the one to the other is gradual.

Essentially romantic love goes beyond courting with the goal of union with another, to an idealistic appreciation of nature, a value that gives meaning to the spiritual longings rooted in human nature.[43] This movement known as Romanticism begins to emerge as the eighteenth

---

40. De Rougemont, *Love in the Western World*, 74.

41. See Nehring, *The Vindication of Love*, 111–24.

42. One of the best expositions of these changes is the book by De Rougemont, *Love in the Western World*. De Rougemont explores the psychology of love from the legend of Tristan and Isolde straight through to Hollywood, focusing on the inescapable tension between marriage and passion.

43. Singer, Vol. 2, *Courtly and Romantic*, 285.

century flows into the nineteenth century. Goethe and Rousseau were precursors of the movement known as Romanticism, and it was Byron, Shelley, and Keats and many others who were to speak directly about human love as Romantics. As Keats says in one of his letters, "Love is my religion—I could die for that." They would affirm the essential conditions of courtly love and apply them to their own context:

- Sexual love between men and women as an ideal that ennobles both the lover and beloved;
- Sexual expression as a spiritual goal that cannot be reduced to physical passion;
- The value and joy of courtship;
- A deep and abiding union with the other.

The difference between courtly love and romanticism reflects the intellectual changes and development from medieval times to modern times. These changes included making courtly love more suitable to a changing world, no longer supporting older forms of Christianity or the feudal institution of matrimony.[44]

In the late nineteenth and early twentieth centuries, there were those who were critical of philosophical Romanticism and questioned the value of romantic love as a guide in human relationships. But romantic love lives on, is experienced by most of us at some point in our lives, and will most likely endure, but the accuracy of the feelings as accounts of reality will continue to be fundamentally challenged, as delightful as these feelings may be.[45] People such as Kierkegaard, Tolstoy, and Nietzsche were to speak about romantic feelings as false allusion and projection of wishful fantasies, pointing to what Freud would develop more fully. However with Kierkegaard and Tolstoy, we observe noble attempts at preserving a more virtuous form of love rooted in the Christian ideal of *agape*.[46]

It was Sigmund Freud (1856–1939), probing beneath the surface into the depths of the human psyche, who would quite dramatically call into question the validity of romantic feelings. Prior to Freud's bold inquiry into the nature of the human psyche, the traditional view of the feelings of sexual and romantic love blossoming in puberty and early adulthood was

---

44. Ibid, 300–301.

45. No less a rigorous philosopher than Bertrand Russell speaks about the feelings of romantic love as intense delight, but acknowledges that they do not necessarily provide a true picture of reality.

46. Kierkegaard, *Works of Love*, and Tolstoy, *Where Love is, God is Also*.

## Section II — The Geography of Love

commonly accepted. Freud's bold probe however would challenge this traditional view and spark a lively discussion. For example, Freud explored the uncharted territory of early childhood and postulated that children had sexual feelings in the erogenous zones of their bodies. He went on to develop the theory of the Oedipus complex, a somewhat shocking view that a baby longs for one of the parents and even wishes to kill the other, who is seen as a rival. In a swirl of ambivalence, the baby may love and hate both parents, and its heterosexual and homosexual instincts clash. Fortunately for the baby, amnesia sets in during later childhood and the child represses its sexual feelings. But as the child reaches adolescence and begins looking for an acceptable (non-incestuous) love partner, the young person will unconsciously choose a partner that reminds him or her of the parent who was the object of the infant's love. He also expressed that view that traditional foreplay, kisses, caresses, and oral sex were the attempt to return to the pleasure of nursing at one's mother's breast. Inevitably, this development of human sexuality leads to difficulties in later life, as the free expression of one's sexual impulses often leads to perversion and repressed sexuality leads to neurosis. As one falls in love and a mate is chosen, the decision is made not on the basis of wisdom, but more on the basis of the repressed feeling of the idealized parent loved in childhood. The lover transfers these feelings to the chosen mate who may not be able to live up to the need of the person who is bestowing the love. Hours on the couch![47]

By mid-twentieth century, love had become an important subject of scholarly inquiry and artistic expression. Psychologists and social critics such as Theodore Reik, Pitirim Sorokin, and Erich Fromm, philosophers as different as George Santayana, Jean-Paul Sartre, and Herbert Marcuse, and literary critics and novelists such as D. H. Lawrence and Marcel Proust write about the wonder and magic of love that fills human life.[48] The story is too long to tell here, and we will touch on it in later chapters. Suffice to say, it is a fascinating one which has the capacity to deepen our self-understanding and enrich our lives.

---

47. See Ackerman, *A Natural History of Love*, 123–30, and Freud, *Sexuality and the Psychology of Love*. Freud's views are also treated in Morgan's *Love: Plato, the Bible and Freud*.

48. Bloom in *Love and Friendship* and Nehring, *A Vindication of Love*, in different ways trace the theme of love in literature.

*The Understanding of Love across History, Tradition, and Culture*

## LOVE IN CONTEMPORARY TIMES

It would be remiss if we did not introduce one other approach to love, that of scientific inquiry, an exploration of both the social sciences and the natural sciences. The exploration of love in these past few decades has gone in numerous directions, with no one view prevailing. But what Pitirim Sorokin attempted in his scientific inquiry about love in mid-twentieth century has in fact been repeated in recent decades.[49]

Sorokin's approach was rooted in the social sciences, using methodologies from both psychology and sociology. His exploration has been continued across the social sciences, and we offer here a brief summary of the work that is currently being done.[50]

One illustration growing out of the social sciences might be called the interview and analysis approach or more technically, the phenomenology of love. It utilizes a carefully designed research questionnaire, does extensive interviews with several populations, and then seeks to find common elements, styles, or expressions of love.[51] The approach has uncovered a broad range of behavior called love, but which is quite different in expression. For example, Abraham Maslow discovered what he call B-love and D-love, the first being love for the other and the second being a "love" driven by needs and deficiencies.[52] Other social scientists have attempted to discern a typology of love and have listed several love-styles, including *eros* (physical attraction), *ludus* (playful), and *storge* (affectionate).[53] Robert J. Sternberg speaks about "a Duplex Theory of Love," in which he argues that love is both a structure (a triangular subtheory) and a development (a sub-theory as a story). It is a complex and helpful analysis in which he describes one possible triangular love with the points of the triangle being intimacy, passion, and decision/commitment.[54]

---

49. Sorokin, *The Ways and Powers of Love: Types, Factors, and Techniques of Moral Transformation*.

50. See the volume edited by Sternberg and Weis, *The New Psychology of Love* for an excellent summary of current research about love being done in the social sciences. The volume edited by Post, et al., *Altruism and Altruistic Love* has excellent essays pointed more directly at love as altruism.

51. Oord, *Defining Love: A Philosophical, Scientific, and Theological Engagement*, 66–67.

52. Noted by Oord in *Defining Love*, 67 with a full description in Maslow's book, *The Further Reaches of Human Nature*.

53. Also noted by Oord. One example given is that of John Alan Lee, "Love-Styles," in Sternberg and Barnes, *The Psychology of Love*, 38–67.

54. Sternberg and Weis, eds., *The New Psychology of Love*, 184–99. Note that there

## Section II — The Geography of Love

A second description of love growing out of the social sciences might be called positive psychology, which shifts the emphasis in social science research from the study of pathology and mental illness, an earlier focus, to the study of positive life experiences.[55] One emphasis in this movement is on the life-changing character of positive outlooks such as optimism and hope. Another stresses the life-giving outcomes of forgiveness, gratitude, and positive emotions.[56] One major theme in the category of positive psychology is attachment theory, the view that the relationship that an infant has with its mother (or other significant caregiver) greatly influences the child's development and inclines it in life to close and loving relationships. In adult life, the one with a close relationship with one's mother or caregiver is more likely to show compassion to others.[57] It is this point and its broad implications that we will expand in Chapter Five.

One other example of the study of love growing out of the social sciences is the way that different cultures define and experience love. Some forms of love appear to be cross cultural and nearly universal whereas other forms of love tend to be expressed differently from culture to culture. Debra Lieberman and Elaine Hatfield in their article, "Passionate Love: Cross-Cultural and Evolutionary Perspectives," suggest that passionate love is a cultural universal, but certain culture values influence the way it is understood and called love. They argue, for example, that romantic love fits well within the individualistic culture of the United States whereas in the more collectivistic culture of China other values are given a higher priority and romantic feeling must give way to honor the wishes and guidance of parents.[58]

What is significant about the abundance of research in social and cultural sciences is that love and altruistic behavior are now more accepted as a respectable area of research, and that self-giving love, as

---

are two different books on the psychology of love, one published in 1988 and then a new version published in 2006.

55. Oord, *Defining Love*, 69. See Snyder and Lopez, eds., *Handbook of Positive Psychology of Love*.

56. See Post, et al., eds. *Altruism and Altruistic Love* for several essays that reflect the trend toward positive psychology and the place of love in human interaction. A companion volume edited by Post, et al., *Research on Altruism & Love* has a helpful annotated bibliography. The classic work of Sorokin, *The Ways and Power of Love: Types, Factors, and Techniques of Moral Transformation* remains a guide and inspiration.

57. Oord in *Defining Love* references the article by Mikulincer, et al., "Attachment, Caregiving, And Altruism: Boosting Attachment Security Increases Compassion and Helping."

58. In Sternberg and Weis, eds., *The New Psychology of Love*, 274–297.

## The Understanding of Love across History, Tradition, and Culture

opposed to need-based attachment, is common in human interaction. There is an increasing interest in the general topic of love in the natural sciences as well, and once again, we will look only briefly at these developments.[59]

As one might expect, there has been serious research on love in the biological sciences. Thomas Oord in *Defining Love* provides an excellent summary of the ways that Charles Darwin opened the door to scientific inquiry on the theme of love and guides the reader through recent research as well, raising the interesting question of whether other species may express a form of love.[60] Sternberg and Weis offer six essays in *The New Psychology of Love* on the biological understanding of love.[61] There is a broad range of approaches that might be classified in the two categories of evolutionary theories and behavior theories. For example, Douglas T. Kenrick in "A Dynamical Evolutionary View of Love" argues that love is based in certain decision biases that evolved to serve genetic interests and to facilitate reproduction.[62] These biases influence people's attention, memory, and decision-making in reference to mate selection, causing them to be more altruistic toward a stranger than with one's relatives with whom one shares genes. He does suggest that there are different kinds of love appropriate in different relationships and that the expression of love may differ across cultures. It is important to note that he understands love to be an instinctive part of human nature.

Phillip Shaver and Mario Mikulincer, in their essay "A Behavioral Systems Approach to Romantic Love Relationships: Attachment, Caregiving, and Sex," argue that there are three dominant behavioral systems: attachment, caregiving, and sex. The purpose of these systems is to ensure a person's security by making her or him stay close to others who can provide necessary support and security.[63] The attachment system is engaged when the person providing the security is not present and a threat is encountered.

---

59. Richard Dawkins in *The Selfish Gene* and *The God Delusion* has raised the ante in the debate with his view that even *agape* love has evolutionary and survival motives. Others have argued this position, such as Edward O. Wilson in several books on sociobiology such as *On Human Nature*. Grant in *Altruism and Christian Ethics* argues persuasively with Dawkins on this point.

60. *Defining Love*, 97–136.

61. *The New Psychology of Love*, 16–145.

62. Ibid., 15–34.

63. Ibid., 35–64.

## Section II — The Geography of Love

The literature about love has also developed in heart and brain research as well, although not as specifically targeted toward love, but focused on human well-being, which has the component of love present. Again, let me provide just a few brief examples. Three medical doctors, Thomas Lewis, Fari Amini, and Richard Lannon focus on linkage between love and brain research in their volume, *A General Theory of Love*.[64] These authors, drawing upon new brain research, describe the human need for intimacy, proposing that our nervous systems are not self-contained and actually connect with those people who are close to us. There is a silent rhythm that makes up the life force of the body and is intrinsic to it. These wordless links determine our mood, improve our health, and change the structure of our brains. In one sense, they argue, who we are and who we are becoming depends on whom we love.[65] Love is at the core of our physical make-up and our behavior.

Another medical doctor, Daniel G. Amen, in a slightly more popular vein, suggests that our brain is determinative of our psychic health, and that there are ways to improve our mental and emotional health by medicines and meditative practices. While the capacity to love and be loved is not singled out in his several books, there is the clear implication that his brain prescriptions would increase our capacity to give and receive love.[66] Another book, widely circulated and well-received at a more popular level, entitled *The HeartMath Solution,* argues a similar case for the role of the heart in human flourishing.[67] The research undergirding the book is intended to demonstrate the way that the heart is intimately connected to human well-being. Once again, love is not singled out as the only human experience that increases human well-being, but it is certainly one of them. Again, with the aid of meditative practices (the intuitive intelligence of our own hearts), one's life can be substantially improved, and there is the likelihood of the increased capacity to love and be loved.

The meaning and place of love is developing into a major area of study in the social and natural sciences, a topic we will address in succeeding chapters. It always has been present in the broad sense of the arts, in philosophy, history, literature, visual arts, and religious studies. We will

---

64. Published in 2000.

65. See Chapter Three, "Archimedes' Principle: How We Sense the Inner World of Other Hearts," 35–65.

66. See, for example, *Healing the Hardware of the Soul: Change Your Brain Change Your Life*.

67. Childre and Martin with Beech, *The HeartMath Solution*.

sample these inquiries as a way illustrating the geography of love, turning next to the ways that love has been understood in religious traditions of the human family.

# Section II — The Geography of Love

## STUDY RESOURCES

## Discussion Questions

1. Are human beings, as they mature, ever able to be sufficiently free from self-interest and express selfless love in the sense of *agape* love?
2. There are many different kinds of love. Do you think these different understandings of love are related and have characteristics in common?
3. Is it possible for love, as first expressed in sincere and caring ways, to become "disordered?" If so, how and why does this happen?
4. Do you think that romantic love is a healthy emotion, improving human relationships, or it is simply infatuation based on personal need and a false ideal of the beloved?
5. In what ways might love and compassion influence regional, national, and international programs and policies? Or are the ideas of love and compassion too sentimental and idealistic and have little value in the real world of politics and diplomacy?

## Key Terms and Concepts

- *Attachment theory:* an infant's attachment to its primary caregiver which is imprinted on the child's psyche and inclines it to close and intimate relationships in adult life. If the infant/child is separated from the caregiver, the child can become depressed, desperate, and emotionally disturbed, also characteristics that might occur in adulthood.
- *Courtly love:* the affirmation that feelings of attraction and the passionate expression of love between human beings are in themselves both authentic and magnificent.
- *Disordered love:* the view of Augustine that love can easily be misplaced. In particular it is when a person gives total love to anything in the created world rather than to God. When this happens, then the person will be discontented in life.
- *Ideals or forms:* Plato's view that there is an ideal or form for objects and ideas that has an existence apart from the objects and ideas, such

as perfect justice, which our laws can only approximate or perfect love, which we will strive for but never quite reach.

- *Platonic love:* a love that is not rooted in the senses, but which is focused on the ideals of goodness, truth, and beauty.
- *Romanticism:* the view, finding its finest expression in the nineteenth century, that affirms an idealistic appreciation of nature, a value that gives meaning to the spiritual longings of the human soul.

## Suggestions for Reference and Reading

1. Ackerman, Diane, *A Natural History of Love.* New York: Random House, 1994.
2. De Rougemont, Denis, *Love in the Western World.* Princeton: Princeton University Press, 1983.
3. Nehring, Cristina, *A Vindication of Love: Reclaiming Romance for the Twenty-First Century.* New York: HarperCollins Publishers, 2009.
4. Singer, Irving, *The Nature of Love,* in 3 volumes. Chicago: The University of Chicago Press, 1984.
5. Sternberg, Robert J., *Cupid's Arrow: The Course of Love through Time.* Cambridge: Cambridge University Press, 1988.
6. Sternberg, Robert J. and Karin Weis, *The New Psychology of Love.* New Haven: Yale University Press, 2006.
7. Stumpf, Samuel Enoch, *Socrates to Sartre: A History of Philosophy.* New York: McGraw Hill, 1988, Fourth Edition.

# 4

# The Understanding of Love within the World Religions

## LOVE AS INTEGRAL TO THE WORLD RELIGIONS

OUR DISCUSSION BEGAN WITH a brief description of the world being in a state of crisis, noting that nearly every age might be called an age of crisis, depending upon where one lives and the circumstances in one's environment. Our argument is that the challenges we currently face are especially vexing because they are truly global, require a new consciousness and awareness, and demand creative and sophisticated solutions. The argument went on to suggest that love and compassion, while not the technical solutions to many of the problems we face, nevertheless contribute to the attitude and perspective required for finding humane and just solutions.

The word *love* and its many cognates are used in a variety of ways across history, languages, and cultures. In particular, love has a multitude of meanings in contemporary English. Some definitions and a proposed common universe of discourse were introduced so that our discussion about love might be grounded and stay on track. We borrowed from an earlier age and used three Greek words as a place to start, ones commonly used to distinguish the various forms of love. The first was *agape*, which has been defined as pure and unlimited love.[1] The second word

---

1. See the small book by Templeton, *Agape Love*, 1. See as well the volume by Post, *Unlimited Love: Altruism, Compassion, and Service*, 11–39.

## The Understanding of Love within the World Religions

was *philia* (*phileo*, v.) and the most common understanding of this word is friendship. It was the word chosen by Aristotle for human friendship, and Thomas Aquinas, influenced by Aristotle, used it for describing the human relationship with God. The discussion went on to speak about *eros* and defined it as attraction, including physical attraction in the sense of sexual feelings, love, and appreciation for the marvelous world in which we live, and also a life goal that goes beyond the senses to the love and appreciation of the good, the true, and the beautiful, as in Plato's thought.

Our next endeavor was to provide a very brief description (glimpses only) of the understanding of love in historical eras, intellectual, literary, and artistic traditions, and a range of cultures. It was underlined that love seems to be a constant in human experience, and it is described in a variety of ways, from the classical era through the Middle Ages and on to the modern period. We then observed that the contemporary period in which we live values the way love has been expressed and described in the past, but has added a distinctly scientific approach, drawing upon both the natural and the social sciences in the quest to fully understand love. With this introduction to lovescapes, my hope is that we have begun to gain a better understanding of the diverse geography of love.

There is another important part of the topography of love, one that has already been introduced, but needs more careful description and analysis. It is the way that love and compassion, and their many cousins, have been central to the great religious traditions of the human family, both in terms of belief and especially in terms of practice. Again, this topic is more suited to a book than a chapter, so our descriptions will be limited, but perhaps they will give an initial understanding that can lead to further inquiry. As we look at the understanding and suggested practice of love within the religions of the world, we will divide these religious traditions into four broad categories: (1) love in representative religious and philosophical outlooks in the classical period; (2) love within the indigenous wisdom traditions; (3) love within the religious outlooks in transcendent monism found, for example, in Hinduism and Buddhism; and (4) love in the Abrahamic monotheistic traditions.

## LOVE WITHIN THE RELIGIOUS AND PHILOSOPHICAL OUTLOOK OF CLASSICAL CULTURE

Our goal in this section will be to review briefly how love was understood and practiced in the philosophical traditions and religious life of

## Section II — The Geography of Love

the Greco-Roman world.[2] We will look at these outlooks in the classical era, ancient Greece and Rome, as representative of the classical culture that was to exercise great influence on the western world.[3] It is also very important to note that these most influential points of view were in many ways more philosophical than religious and that the records describing the place of love in religious practices are somewhat limited.[4] However, these more philosophical and ethical ideas of self-giving love and friendship were to take a religious form, especially in Christianity and Islam.

As we have mentioned, Plato used the word *eros* to speak about love. His viewpoint does contain the notion of attraction, but it goes far beyond what we ordinarily associate with the English word *erotic*, derived from *eros*. In fact, his theories, profound and insightful, are important and influential in any description of love not only in the Greco-Roman world, but in our time as well. We attempted to describe them in Chapter 3 as we emphasized one aspect of Plato's view, namely that *eros*, fundamental to human development, goes though stages of maturity. With his well-known allegory of the cave, Plato taught that humans begin by loving only shadows and appearances, move on to the attractions of the senses, and as we mature we advance to contemplating (loving) ultimate reality as our mind grasps the ideals of goodness, truth, and beauty.

Aristotle, in contrast to Plato, maintained that love was not so much contemplation of the *ideals* or *forms* as it was an understanding of the way in which the ideals and forms take expression in tangible ways. It is from this frame of reference that he used the word *philia*, defined most basically as friendship, and while accurate, friendship is not sufficiently inclusive of the full meaning of the term. The word also describes nearly every form of attachment, ranging from kinship to participation in the political system (*polis*). It also implied, especially in the early period of Greek thought the notion of virtue (*arête*). What is meant by virtue is courage, and that the one with courage is a person who can be trusted and counted on in difficult circumstances. *Philia* is often associated with kinship and references family members as a model of those who can be counted on to help. Implied in this understanding is that there are others, aliens, to whom one

---

2. See Chapter 3, 58–63. There is always risk in brief summaries, appearing to make simple what is really very complex. I take the risk, keenly and humbly aware of the dangers of distortion.

3. We will look at other traditions indigenous to Indian subcontinent, Asia, and Africa as well.

4. Berchman, Chapter 1 "Altruism in Greco-Roman Philosophy" in Neusner and Chilton, eds., *Altruism in World Religions*, 1.

may be polite, but reliance upon them is risky. There is a clear connection between friendship, kinship, courage (virtue) and fidelity.[5]

It is Aristotle who refines the concept of *philia* and develops a full theory of friendship that includes caring about the welfare of others, an understanding which we could easily call love.[6] To some extent Aristotle agrees with his teacher, Plato, and acknowledges that friendship does have components of self-interest, but Aristotle asserts that care for oneself requires the concern for the welfare of others. To review, Aristotle's view has the following components:

1. He maintains that human beings are naturally social, that to be with others is the pathway to happiness, and to be happy is the goal of life.
2. This pathway is a virtuous endeavor because in true friendship we care for the welfare of the other person. We may expect that our friend will care for our welfare, but we do not offer friendship for our own interests and pleasures (false friendship), even though we know that friendship often includes reciprocity.
3. To be truly interested in the concerns of the other is not to open ourselves to the intrusion of the concerns of others, but is a way of expanding our interests that leads to an informed and wise expression of friendship.
4. This kind of friendship includes both our kinship and household (*oikos*) and the city (*polis*). Friendship as it is expressed within the *polis* becomes the basis for justice, which is nothing less than our care for the well-being of others.
5. Being virtuous is to practice justice and to share with others a commitment to the common good. Unanimity is a form of political friendship, as friends seek the common good.
6. Those who are "friends" with themselves or who have self-love are free to love because they are rational and able to use reason to understand the needs of others and the ways to show concern for them.

Epicurus, the practical philosopher, born when Aristotle was in his forties, rejected basic elements in Aristotle's argument. He argued that the greatest good is pleasure, understood as the absence of pain and anxiety. He maintained that friendship is only good as it nurtures the state of

---

5. Ibid., 4.
6. Aristotle develops his views in both the *Nicomachean Ethics* and the *Politics*.

## Section II — The Geography of Love

*ataxaria* (tranquility).[7] Friendship has value as it contributes to happiness and peace of mind, but Epicurus focused almost exclusively on personal friendship, not association in the political realm in which one seeks the common good. Politics for Epicurus is like being in a prison, an occupation that the wise person will avoid leading because it creates stress and anxiety. The real value of friendship, for Epicurus, is not so much in seeking the good of others, but in cultivating a commitment or contract not to harm others or be harmed by them. Friendship has instrumental value as it increases the pleasures of happiness. Justice for Epicurus is not the obligation to seek the welfare of others but to pledge not to harm others and to ask them not to harm us. Friendship then, in the teaching of Epicurus, while exceedingly important, is self-centered, instrumental, and utilitarian in character, offering pleasure rather than leading to altruism.

Glancing quickly at the Roman side of the Greco-Roman world, we note that Cicero (106–43 BCE), the Roman philosopher, following Stoic thought[8] stressed the need for rationality and maintained that true friendship can only exist among the wise and virtuous. Only those who agree on their views of life and appreciate each other's virtue can be true friends. Seneca (4–65 CE), also a Roman philosopher, and incidentally a teacher of Nero, followed the Stoic tradition of rationality and argued that it is only the wise person who knows how to love properly, and therefore true friendship exists solely among sages. A fundamental question arises as to whether these kinds of friendships and expressions of love, articulated by Cicero and Seneca, have any altruistic motives or whether they are driven almost exclusively by self-interest. Does one make friends in order to improve one's own life and cultivate one's mind, or is there a genuine interest in the well-being of others? Does one really need the company of others, or is it possible to become self-sufficient, having friends as they are convenient but not necessary in order to achieve happiness or one's aim in life?

In summary, it is safe to say that while there were differences in the understanding of love and friendship among the various philosophers and schools of thought in the Greco-Roman period, these viewpoints had the common thread of maintaining that friendship was a complex mixture of self-love, self-interest, and altruistic behavior. There was also agreement

---

7. Berchman, *Altruism in World Religions*, 14.

8. Stoicism, founded by Zeno (340–265 BCE), maintains that reality is a rational order in which nature is controlled by laws of reason, interpreted in the pattern of pantheism. Human lives are guided by Providence against which it is futile to resist and to which wise people willingly submit. See Smith, ed., *Philosophers Speak for Themselves: From Thales to Plato*, 17–21.

*The Understanding of Love within the World Religions*

that love (both *eros* and *philia*) is an extremely important dimension of human experience and, in some cases, even the goal of life.

As the Common Era dawned, new concerns emerged, in part as a result of the deep and profound changes in the Roman Empire. The search for truth and meaning, once detached and purely rational, became personal and religious. People became more preoccupied with personal salvation and saw that interaction with the gods or God was a way of finding one's purpose in life and securing one's eternal destiny. Divine grace was introduced, and love for God and others, based on will more than reason, became a central concern.

## LOVE WITHIN THE INDIGENOUS WISDOM TRADITIONS

The phrase indigenous wisdom traditions refers to the religious outlook of populations often called first peoples because they were the first inhabitants of certain parts of the world. For the most part, the areas in which they lived were later colonized by foreigners. These people accumulated great wisdom across the centuries as they learned how to live with nature, with each other, and with the foreigners who arrived on their shores. We have chosen the word indigenous in preference over fourth world peoples in that the terms First World (highly industrialized), Second World (Socialist bloc), and Third World (developing) are terms in transition, as would be Fourth World because of the enormous changes occurring globally.[9]

These indigenous people differed as they faced a variety of challenges inherent in the regions where they lived.[10] But what they had in common was a holistic vision of reality, a deep belief that the world was a complex and patterned mixture of living spirits, nature, and people with common needs and concerns. The religious outlook of these peoples is not a separate piece of life that can be studied in isolation from the rest of life, but it is the worldview itself. Most of them believed that their true home, nature, was permeated with spirits which animated it, hence the term *animist*. These peoples generally had myths that explained the origins and forces of nature and historical roots of their existence. Many of these cultures have attempted to preserve the languages, beliefs, and values which gave

---

9. See Burger, *The Gaia Atlas of First Peoples*, 16–18.

10. See Ferguson, *Exploring the Spirituality of the World Religions*, Chapter 2 "Indigenous Wisdom Traditions," 23–40.

## Section II — The Geography of Love

cohesion to their cultures and way of life, but the preservation has been difficult as these peoples entered into the modern world.

The attempt to preserve the values of their worldviews has attracted the attention of people around the world because these values speak poignantly to many critical challenges facing all who call earth their home. All of the people of the earth must face issues such as global warming and tribal conflict. It may be easy to idealize these cultures, failing to recognize that these indigenous peoples were not necessarily noble in all their activities. But their sense of interdependency with Mother Earth and their belief in the order and sanctity of community life can be informative, and it points to their view of love. Let us listen to their words:[11]

- "Every part of the earth is sacred to my people. Every shining pine needle, every sandy shore, every mist in the dark woods, every clearing and humming insect is holy in the memory and experience of my people." A Duwamish Chief.

- "One has only to develop a relationship with a certain place, where the land knows you, and experience that the trees, the Earth, and Nature are extending their love and light to you to know there is so much we can receive from the Earth to fill our hearts and souls." Inti Melasquez, Inca.

- "We Indian people are not supposed to say, 'This land in mine.' We only use it. It is the white man who buys land and puts a fence around it. Indians are not supposed to do that, because the land belongs to all Indians, it belongs to God, as you call it. The land is part of our body, and we are part of the land." Buffalo Tiger, Miccosukee.

- "An Innu hunter's prestige comes not from the wealth he accumulates but from what he gives away. When a hunter kills caribou or other games he shares with everyone else in the camp." Daniel Ashini, Innu.

One well-known author and teacher, Don Miguel Ruiz, has attempted to preserve the values of his indigenous culture, the Toltec of Southern Mexico.[12] We will use his writing as representative of the indigenous tradi-

---

11. Quoted by Beversluis, ed., *Sourcebook of the World's Religions*, 43–44.

12. His books include *The Four Agreements*; *The Voice of Knowledge*; *Prayers: A Communion with Our Creator,*; and *The Mastery of Love* from which we learn about this indigenous tradition's view of love, interpreted and made contemporary by Don Miguel Ruiz. It is important to note that the widely circulated writings of Carlos Castaneda, such as *The Teachings of Don Juan: A Yaqui Way of Knowledge* also represent an indigenous tradition of Mexico. A good account of the Toltec tradition is in

## The Understanding of Love within the World Religions

tion of wisdom, fully aware that it is distinctive and does not express the views of all the wisdom traditions. But we chose it because the writings of Don Miguel Ruiz have been well-received, widely read, and because of the wisdom it contains for our time.

The teachings and culture of the Toltec people were somewhat hidden for hundreds of years, lost in the mist and maze of history. There is now good historical evidence suggesting that the Toltec people had an advanced culture that lasted for over a thousand years. In the 1920s, there were many archeological discoveries suggesting that such a culture did thrive, built pyramids, and went through several phases of development. It began to fade as a forceful tribe in approximately 750 CE with the burning of the major city, Teotihuacan, located twenty-five miles northeast of Mexico City. A new city, Tula, was founded and appeared to thrive, but it too disappeared in 1170 CE, most likely overrun by another group of people. It is likely that those who were left became the victims of the invasion of Hernando Cortes.

The descendants of the Toltecs believe that the original people possessed sacred knowledge, and that this knowledge can be recovered and shared with the modern world. In the 1960s, the anthropologist Carlos Castaneda did research in the region, and the Toltec heritage began to be studied and appreciated. A Mexican medical doctor, Don Miguel Ruiz, has understood that his calling is to tell others about the Toltec Way of Life. His book, *The Four Freedoms* began to be studied, and new way of life built on the Toltec teaching became attractive to many people. At the heart of the Toltec teaching is the belief that most human beings live in a kind of prison of fear; we have wounded minds. We grow up in a way that inculcates fear in our consciousness, and we lose our natural innocence and capacity to love. Much in our lives is controlled by fear; for example this fear shapes the view we have of ourselves, our view of others, and certainly the choices we make in life.

It is possible to be set free from the prison of fear, to find our true nature, and to live a life of happiness, freedom, and love. But it is not easy and will require the effort of a great warrior. It will mean gaining mastery of several components of one's life. The first is the Mastery of Awareness, to learn who we really are. This is the first step to freedom as we face ourselves with courage and learn the truth about our identity. It is all too easy, in large measure because of fear, to be bound to our conditioning, to rationalize our behavior, to justify our perceptions, and to end up going

---

Rosenthal's *Toltec Wisdom*.

## Section II — The Geography of Love

through life controlled by fear rather than reality. The mastery of awareness teaches us to focus our attention on who we really are and why we think, feel, and act the way we do. As we discover our true identity, we are emancipated from the fear that has controlled us for so long.

The second mastery is the Mastery of Transformation. This process and the resulting awareness teach us how to become spiritual warriors. It empowers us to overcome our false perceptions and change the life-shaping dream of our life. We develop a new vision about who we are and can become. We get rid of the resentments, the anger, the internal turmoil, the tangle of fearful emotions, and emerge on the other side with a true understanding of ourselves. As Jesus said, "The truth will set you free."

There is then the Mastery of Intent, which is not the same as intention.[13] Intent is more akin to opening one's life to the power of the Infinite, a concept not unlike the Tao in Taoist thought. We learn how to align our lives with the *logos* of the universe, and this can only be done by surrendering ourselves to the Infinite and then living lives in harmony with the Infinite or Intent. It is not rational intention or the attempt to achieve what we want in life. It is rather yielding to what is ultimately real, and as we do, we find ourselves and become the channels of the Infinite.

As we gain these masteries, we become those who learn how to love; we reach the Mastery of Love. We get off the track of fear and start on the track of love.[14] It is important to note that the love we gain is self-love, and with this self-love we realize that we are no longer driven by all that we think we need. In fact we can relax and do not have to seek anything that comes from another. The tyranny of always wanting, what Buddhists describe as the source of human suffering, disappears, and we can become those who truly love others. We no longer view the world through the lens of our needs, but become free to show love to others. The love that we give to others has several characteristics, described in the following way by Miguel Ruiz:

1. Love has no obligations. Fear is full of obligations. In the track of fear, whatever we do is because we *have* to do it, and we expect other people to do something because they *have* to do it.

2. Love has no expectations. Fear is full of expectations. With fear we do things because we expect that others are going to do the same. This is why fear hurts and love doesn't hurt.

---

13. Rosenthal, *Toltec Wisdom*, 25–26.
14. *The Mastery of Love*, 55–71.

3. Love is based on respect. Fear doesn't respect anything, including itself. If I feel sorry for you, it means I don't respect you.

4. Love is ruthless; it doesn't feel sorry for anyone, but it does have compassion. Fear is full of pity; it feels sorry for everyone. You feel sorry for me when you don't respect me, when you don't think I am strong enough to make it.

5. Love is completely responsible. Fear avoids responsibility, but this doesn't mean that it's not responsible. Trying to avoid responsibility is one of the biggest mistakes we make because every action has a consequence.

6. Love is always kind. Fear is always unkind. With fear we are full of obligations, full of expectations, with no respect, avoiding responsibility, and feeling sorry.

7. Love is unconditional. Fear is full of conditions. In the track of fear, I love you *if* you fit into the image I make of you.

8. In the track of love, there is justice. If you make a mistake, you pay only once for that mistake, and if you truly love yourself, you learn from that mistake. In the track of fear, there is no justice.

The goal then of the follower of Toltec wisdom is to yield to the Spirit or God (Nagual), be transformed, and become a channel of the Infinite. In so doing, one achieves inner peace and true happiness and becomes a loving person.

## LOVE WITHIN THE TRADITIONS OF TRANSCENDENTAL MONISM

There is a great religious heritage that grows out of the ancient cultures of the Indian subcontinent and South and East Asia. From this region came the religions of Hinduism, Buddhism, and Confucianism, and several other religious traditions.[15] What nearly all of these great religions have in common is the belief that all of reality is essentially one. It differs from the view that there is a personal God who may be understood as one subject among many. The spiritual quest in these religious traditions is to gain a viewpoint from beyond (enlightenment), and to find harmony with the One, however it may be understood.

---

15. In addition to those mentioned, there are others including Jainism, Taoism, Shinto, Zoroastrianism, and Sikhism.

## Section II — The Geography of Love

We will focus on the three religious traditions mentioned above and begin with Hinduism.[16] It is an ancient religion and had its beginnings with the migration of Aryan people from the North into India. The migration lasted from approximately 1900–1600 BCE, and these Aryan people brought with them the literature known as the Vedas. The Indus civilization was already present as Aryans arrived, but it had fallen into disarray, and the culture that emerged was in part a fusion of Indus and Aryan beliefs and practices. At the heart of the early forms of Hinduism, a term that essentially means the belief of the people of India, was the quest for inner peace and harmony that comes from union and harmony with the One. This quest was viewed as the responsibility of each individual. There was guidance, but no external intervention, as each person sought to resolve the inner tensions that accompany life and find the way to tranquility and contentment. Hinduism is a religion that defines tranquility as the blessed condition that humanity can know as one achieves enlightenment and lives in harmony with the One, a tranquility of being for which all else should be sacrificed.

The sacred pathway was initially taught in an oral form, but in time a literature emerged called the Vedas, a term meaning sacred wisdom. By 800 BCE there were three collections including the best-known Rigveda as well as the Samaveda and the Ayurveda. There was another independent collection that was accepted later, and it was called the Atharvaveda, a collection of poetry that guided the priests. The literature is vast, varied, and wise; it requires careful reading, especially if one has not grown up in the tradition, and it offers a worldview and a way of life in which love plays a vital role. The worldview and its intrinsic pattern of life had several components:[17]

1. The first was an understanding of human nature which included the daily rounds of life with all of their challenges. But it also included the notion of *atman*, one's inner being or soul, which lived beyond the life of the body and the daily rounds of life.

2. A second foundational belief was that the universe had structure and order, a point of view that invited each person to find their way and achieve harmony with rhythm of the universe.

---

16. For a good discussion of ethics within Hinduism, and the role of love and compassion in particular, see Morgan and Lawton, eds., *Ethical Issues in Six Religious Traditions*, 1–60. See as well Runzo and Martin, eds., *Ethics in the World Religions*, 177–96.

17. Nielsen, et al., *Religions of the World*, 103–5.

3. Part of the structure included three distinct realms, the earthly, the atmosphere, and the sky that was beyond human sight and which was the realm of mystery and eternal light.

4. All of the actions, patterns, and rhythms of this three-storied universe were controlled by an impersonal principle called *rta*, a term that was later replaced with the word *dharma*. These terms do not refer to a personal transcendent God, as in the Abrahamic monotheistic religions, but to the structure of the universe based on truth and justice. When *rta* or *dharma* is followed, then there is peace and order. The religious rituals and the practices of yoga empower that practitioner to inculcate these values.

Many other features of the complex religion of Hinduism might be mentioned including the belief in many gods; the pattern of karma, samsara, and rebirth; the caste system; and the four stages of life. These additional beliefs are germane to a full understanding of Hinduism, but we will focus more on those beliefs that directly shape the ethical values of Hinduism. The moral character of the religion is intimately connected with the four affirmations mentioned above. These affirmations should be viewed as inherent in the order of the universe, based on truth and justice. They are foundational for ethical guidance and lead to the ethic of love and compassion.

A commitment to living an ethical life in keeping with the order of the universe grows out of this worldview. A code of conduct, developed over the centuries, has prescriptions of living the ethical life, not unlike the role exercised by the Ten Commandments in the biblical-based religions. It is called the "Ten Vedic Restraints" or the *Yama*.[18] Basic to each one is a concern for the other.

- Yama 1 is noninjury or *ahimsa*, the practice of not harming others by thought, word, or deed, and living a kindly life, revering all beings as an expression of the One Divine energy. This often implies a vegetarian diet as respect for and the prevention of injury to other beings.

- Yama 2 is truthfulness or *satya*, the practice of speaking only that which is true, kind, and helpful and refraining from lying or betraying promises.

- Yama 3 is non-stealing or *asteya*, the practice of controlling one's desires and respecting the lives and property of others.

---

18. Published by the Himalayan Academy, Kapa'a, Hawaii, 2004.

## Section II — The Geography of Love

- Yama 4 is godly conduct or *brahmacharya*, the practice of living faithfully within marriage, seeking the company of ethical people, and dressing and speaking modestly.
- Yama 5 is patience or *kshama*, the practice of coping with trying circumstances, living in harmony with others, caring for children, and remaining poised and under self-control in good times as well as challenging times.
- Yama 6 is steadfastness or *dhriti*, the practice of being steady with a clear purpose and goal, firm in decisions, overcoming obstacles and fear of failure, and sustained by prayer.
- Yama 7 is compassion or *daya*, the practice seeing the divine everywhere, being kind to people, animals, plants and the earth itself, and extending sympathy for the needs and suffering of others.
- Yama 8 is honesty or *arjava*, the act of being honorable at all times, renouncing any deception, obeying the law, never cheating, and facing oneself honestly.
- Yama 9 is moderation or *mitahara*, the practice of being moderate in appetite, eating a vegetarian diet, drinking wisely, and avoiding ostentation.
- Yama 10 is purity or *saucha*, having integrity in all thought, speech, and behavior, and by daily meditation, overcoming temptations of self-destructive behavior.

One of the best known Indian Hindus of the modern era was Mohandas Gandhi (1869–1948). He was not a Brahmin, but born into the merchant class and became a lawyer. He was not a religious scholar, but a practitioner, and it was his religious practices as a faithful Hindu that guided him in his leadership of independence for India. He was greatly influenced by the *Bhagavad Gita* and its simple, yet profound truth. He practiced the Yamas and put a special emphasis on *ahimsa*, the commitment to not taking life and respecting all of life; and *satyagraha*, the practice of "speaking truth to power" and practicing nonviolent and civil disobedience. His influence, rooted in the practice of these forms of love and compassion, lives on in India and many parts of the world.

Buddhism, both in its classical form and its contemporary expression, places love and compassion at the center of its ethical understanding.[19] The

---

19. See both Runzo and Martin, eds., *Ethics in the World Religions*, 219–33 and Morgan and Lawton, eds., *Ethical Issues in Six Religious Traditions*, 61–117 for good

ethical teaching of Buddhism, as it does with Hinduism, grows out of the larger understanding of what is ultimately real, its cosmology, although Buddhism generally does not linger on cosmology and moves directly to practice. The foundation for the Buddhist understanding of the reality is the Four Noble Truths, although in different ages and traditions, the interpretation of these is somewhat varied.[20] The Four Noble Truths are:

1. Life is filled with suffering (*dukkha*), and human unrest is universal. Life is not what we expect or want it to be. This understanding includes not only aging, pain, and disease, but also mental and emotional sorrow.
2. Pain and suffering are caused by attachment and craving (*tanha*), our desire to have and possess. There is the desire for sensual pleasures, for possessions and wealth, reputation, and power believing that having all of this will bring satisfaction. But ironically, in gaining these, we feel empty.
3. There can be an end to suffering. Buddha taught that we must let go of our craving and root out the need for attachments. When we do, our suffering will cease. But the path of gaining release from craving is not easy.
4. There is a way called the Noble Eight-fold Path, which joined with the Four Noble Truths constitutes the *dharma* or foundational teaching of Buddhism.

The Noble Eight-fold Path has the following components, interwoven in an intersecting circle:

1. The right view, or having understanding and seeing things as they are.
2. The right intention or thinking wholesome thoughts and practicing loving-kindness, empathy, and compassion toward all of creation.
3. The right speech, being truthful and kind in what we say.
4. The right action, the art of living in a positive and constructive way.
5. The right livelihood, earning a living in a way that reflects our values.
6. The right effort, nurturing our spiritual life.
7. The right mindfulness, paying close attention to our present circumstances and being aware of our surroundings.

---

introductions to the ethical teachings of Buddhism.

20. See Ferguson, *Exploring the Spirituality of the World Religions*, 105–6.

## Section II — The Geography of Love

8. The right concentration, focusing our minds and channeling them toward the goals of wisdom and enlightenment.

From this foundation comes the compassionate life.[21] The Dalai Lama, perhaps the leading spokesperson for Buddhism in the world today, maintains that a good heart, cultivated by the practice of following the eight steps in the noble path, and a range of practices including meditation (method) and the cultivation of the mind (wisdom), can transform us and make us into loving and compassionate people. It becomes the *bodhisattva's* (or Buddhist pilgrim's) way of life, overcoming negative emotions such as anger and hatred and maintaining a balanced and happy state of mind. There are a range of practices (*bodhichitta*) to sustain a balanced and happy state of mind which empower one to be compassionate. In one book, the Dalai Lama suggests seven steps in a quest to expand our capacity to love.[22] There is the foundation of acknowledging the suffering of all people, whether friend of foe, and knowing that the one who loves and has compassion cannot bear the suffering of others. The seven steps are:

1. Recognizing that all people are your friends.
2. Appreciating the kindness that has been shown to you.
3. Offering this same kindness to others.
4. Learning to love.
5. Understanding the difference between love and attachment.
6. Understanding love as the basis of human rights.
7. Consciously widening the circle of love.

Another well-known leader of Buddhism, a Vietnamese Zen Buddhist Monk, Thich Nhat Hanh, also teaches the centrality of love and compassion in human behavior.[23] He underscores that loving-kindness (*maître*) has four elements: the capacity to bring happiness to the other; showing compassion (*karuna*) to and easing the pain of the one who suffers; having joy inside and sharing it with others; and having internal freedom and bringing freedom, both internal and external, to others. In all of his teaching, Thich Nhat Hanh is clear that love and compassion flow from the transformed person, the one who is mindful and on the path toward enlightenment.

21. The Dalai Lama, *The Compassionate Life*.
22. *How to Expand Love: Widening the Circle of Loving Relationships*, 41–182.
23. See his books, *True Love: A Practice for Awakening the Heart*; and *Teachings on Love*.

## The Understanding of Love within the World Religions

The American Buddhist nun Pema Chodron underscores the Buddhist teaching that love and compassion are not always present in us and easily demonstrated to others. She emphasizes that showing love and compassion require the practice of bodhichitta, the basic human wisdom that can help drive away the sorrows of the world.[24] She teaches that we must be free or awakened from the confused mind and illusions and cultivate the unbiased mind and good heart. Only then, after careful cultivation, will we be true to our calling to be loving and compassionate people, able to ease the suffering of others and bring them peace and purpose.

The Chinese sages and the teachers of Confucianism in particular focused almost exclusively on the practice of love and compassion and its application to social and political situations.[25] It must be noted, however, that there is a continual theme in Confucian thought that human behavior becomes ethical as it lines up with the guidance of *T'ien* or heaven in the sense of ultimate reality or the dwelling of ancestral spirits. So it too, and its Chinese cousin, Taoism with its teaching on the eternal Tao, is legitimately viewed as within the family of transcendental monism, and calls on human beings to live in harmony with *T'ien* or the Tao, though with different assumptions and in different ways.

Confucius and Confucian thought in general have often been characterized by a focus on external ritual and a sense of propriety (*li*), perhaps without a full appreciation of the subtle meaning of *li* that goes well beyond the rules that should govern family life. Confucius did address the concerns of respect, and wanted the fundamental value of being respectful of others to become more central to an environment that cast restraint to the wind in the pursuit of self-aggrandizement, the desire for wealth, and the abuse of power. To Confucius, this behavior appeared to be harmful to Chinese society. What was needed was a return to the traditional values that once were foundational to a just and stable social order in China. A new order, overcoming the selfish plunge toward self-destruction, should be based on appropriate customs, the consideration of others, and respecting the dignity of all. There must be a return to appropriate consideration of others (*shu*), respecting the rights of others, and yielding to the concerns of others in empathy (*ren* or *jen*). What was needed was the cultivation of the spiritual values that treat people with reverence and as having sacred worth.

---

24. *No Time to Lose: A Timely Guide to the Way of the Bodhisattva*, 1.

25. Karen Armstrong, *Twelve Steps to a Compassionate Life*, 40ff. I will follow her description of the situation in China in the time of Confucius.

## Section II — The Geography of Love

Not only should these fundamental values of respect for others be applied in the family, but also in the larger society and state. Confucius was quite specific in their application. He identifies five relationships in the family (broadly understood) and prescribes appropriate behavior for each. They include father-son, elder and younger brother, friend with friend, husband and wife, and ruler to ministers and subjects. Each of these relationships, including the ruler to minister and subjects, and friend with friend, has characteristics of the family, and therefore society may be understood as an extended family. Each one is mutual, reciprocal, and respectful of age and seniority:[26]

1. There is kindness in the father, filial piety (*hsiao*) in the son.
2. There is gentility in the elder brother, humility and respect in the younger brother.
3. There is humane consideration in elders, deference in juniors.
4. There is righteous behavior in the husband, obedience in the wife.
5. There is benevolence in rulers, loyalty in ministers and subjects.

Ideally, in each of these relationships, there is the presence of internal motivation that produces behavior that is truly humane (*ren* or *jen*) and the application of external practices that are appropriate and circumspect in regard to rites and ceremonies (*li*). An ideal relationship has both; it has the inner resources of goodness, benevolence, and love; and the external form of respect and appropriate behavior that demonstrates respect. The qualities of family relationships provide the basis and model for social relationships and the structures of society.

Confucius was very aware that not all people will be motivated to show love and respect, and he strongly urges teaching in the schools and religious gatherings that have these values as a fundamental part of the curriculum. Education should lead to a third ideal, in addition to *ren* and *li*, and that is the ideal of *chun tzu* which might be translated as the superior or mature person. Confucius points out that there are different kinds of people in society, but it is the sage who embodies and teaches wisdom, one who is the model of *chun tzu* who has a very important responsibility in shaping the values of society. In fact, the sage should become the ruler, or the ruler the sage, and exercise *te*, which is the virtuous power to order society. If the people sense that the ruler respects them and has their

---

26. There is patriarchy and inequitable distribution of power in these patterns, but Confucius was concerned about traditional values that would encourage and sustain order.

interests at heart, there will be respect and adherence to the principles and practices that make for a stable and peaceful society. Indeed, the ruler needs to learn the "arts of peace" much like the other arts of music, poetry, and great learning; all are essential to the well-being of society.

As a final dimension of the place of love and compassion within Confucianism, there is the sense of the Heavenly Mandate. When the fundamental values of *ren, li, chun tzu,* and *te* are present, there is the likelihood of the regularity of the seasons, a good harvest, the correct balance of *yin* and *yang,* and peace. The ruler will lead with the approval of heaven and there will be harmony in society. In many ways, while Chinese rulers did not always pay attention to Confucius, and have not since his time, his teaching nevertheless has lasting value in that he applies the principles of being truly humane in governance. He taught respect for all, not just respect in individual modes of behavior, but respect built into the political systems which lead to a more just and peaceful society and world.[27]

## LOVE WITHIN THE ABRAHAMIC MONOTHEISTIC RELIGIONS

We begin with Judaism, the first and foundational religion of the Abrahamic traditions. While it may not be accurate to call the religion of the early Hebrews, going back to the travels of Abraham, Judaism, descendants of these Hebrew beginnings (c. 2000–1000 BCE) drew upon the experiences and beliefs of these people to form what has become the religion of Judaism. At the heart of Judaism is the belief in *one God* who is personal and relational, an affirmation that also became the cornerstone of Christianity and Islam. The Hebrew people believed that they had a *covenant with God*, the Creator of all, who is active in history and shaping their destiny. It was not so much nature in which the divine presence was discerned, but in history, and God had called them to live faithfully within their historical circumstances, following the guidance of *Torah*. If these Hebrew people lived in fidelity to the covenant, they believed they would be blessed with a land, called *Canaan, Israel,* or *Palestine,* and they would flourish as a people.

The story of the Hebrew Bible, following the early accounts of creation and other pre-historical "events," traces this complex pattern of belief that their history was a sacred story that invests life with transcendent meaning. From Abraham, to the Patriarchs, on to Moses and Joshua, then to the monarchy under David and Solomon, through the great prophets, the

27. See Ferguson, *Exploring the Spirituality of the World Religions*, 125–26.

## Section II — The Geography of Love

exile and return, and the presence of alien governments, the history unfolds. In it is the pattern of faithfulness and unfaithfulness to the covenant, and obedience and disobedience to Torah and *mitzvah* (commandment). Out of this experience came the growth of their scriptures and in these sacred writings one finds ethical guidance and the double commandment to love God with one's whole being and to love one's neighbor as oneself. The sage Hillel, an older contemporary of Jesus, was challenged to recite the entire Torah while he stood on one leg. Hillel replied: "What is hateful to yourself, do not to your fellow man. That is the whole of the Torah and the remainder is but commentary. Go study it."[28] Jesus would later express this teaching in the positive in the Golden Rule.

In time the rabbis, reflecting on the suffering caused by war, would ground the teachings of love and compassion in the universal value of *shalom* and several of their other foundational theological affirmations. They would speak about peace (*shalom*) as both a longing and ethical commandment. It came to mean not just the absence of conflict, but the reconciliation of enemies and a fundamental change of heart that would result in love and compassion. In addition, the rabbis taught that human beings are created in the image of God, and to express enmity to another human being should be regarded as a denial of God; murder became not simply a crime against humanity, but a sacrilege and a desecration of God's image.[29]

Current teaching in the ethics of Judaism is often framed in three major categories which have implications for the practice of love and compassion.[30] The first is *tzedakah* or righteousness, and it is often applied to charitable giving in the pursuit of justice. It is based on the biblical imperative that all needy humans deserve help, especially if they have been oppressed by injustice.[31] The most important commentary on the meaning of *tzedakah* is written by Rabbi Moses Maimonides in the twelfth century, and it has become known as "Maimonides' Ladder of *Tzedakah*." Carefully and thoughtfully, Maimonides lists eight ways of giving to others (charity) in order of importance with the lowest form of charity being to give grudgingly to those in need and the highest level being to give to help a person before they become impoverished or victims of injustice.

---

28. Quoted by Armstrong, *Twelve Steps to a Compassionate Life*, 50–51.

29. Ibid., 53. Heschel in *God in Search of Man: A Philosophy of Judaism*, 412, postulates that in Judaism, the issue of being human can never be treated in isolation, but only in relation to God.

30. Sometimes summarized with the title of "good deeds."

31. See Diamant and Cooper, *Living a Jewish Life*, 68–78; Robinson, *Essential Judaism*, 234–39; and Neusner and Chilton, editors, *Altruism in World Religions*, 31–51.

## The Understanding of Love within the World Religions

A second category of good deeds is *gemilut hassadim* or charity, but it is more fundamental and demanding than merely writing checks for charitable causes. It emphasizes acts of loving kindness that call for person's involvement in the lives of others and face-to-face encounters with real need. These acts of loving kindness are not exclusively for the poor, but can be given to anyone. They include, for example, feeding the hungry, helping people find jobs, visiting the elderly and sick, teaching people to read, providing shelter for the homeless, saving animals from suffering, caring for orphans, and honoring those who have died.[32]

The third category is *tikkum olam*, often called "repair the world." The traditional teaching of *tikkun olam* focused on performing the *mitzvot*, such as keeping kosher and lighting the *Shabbat* candles, but it has developed into taking on the most challenging macroscopic problems of the world such as working for social justice, world peace, and the restoration of the environment.

Love and compassion are foundational to Jewish ethical life. The commandments to love God and one's neighbor are made tangible and specific in Jewish teaching, ever revised so that all who are faithful to their religious heritage have guidance. They are reminded again and again that the foundation of Torah is "I and Thou," that the righteous life is based on a personal and loving relationship with God and neighbor.[33]

The Christian faith in its origins was informed by the Hebrew Bible, often called the Old Testament within the Christian church. To a large degree, it is the narratives and the teaching of the Hebrew Scriptures that guided the early Christian church and helped to shape its ethical codes. The Bible of the first generations of Christians was the Hebrew Bible, and in this Scripture they sought guidance for their beliefs and practices. Of course there are other factors that explain the variance from Judaism and the distinctive beliefs and practices within Christianity, not the least of which are the life and teachings of Jesus and the ministry and writings of his disciples such as Luke, John, and Paul. But the Hebrew Bible is foundational, especially for the early Jewish converts to Christianity.

Love and compassion in the Hebrew Bible are expressed primarily through the stories. They are not abstract concepts, but the themes and plots of the actions which are described. One story, the story of Moses, is prototypical and captures the essence of this teaching. The primary elements of love and compassion are in his story:

32. Diamant and Cooper, 75.
33. See Buber, *I and Thou*.

## Section II — The Geography of Love

- There is the deep belief in one God who is personal and relational and guides Moses.
- There is the covenant, one that is renewed in the time of Moses (Exod 19:3–8).
- There is the Exodus, the event/idea of emancipation and redemption, being set free from bondage.
- There is Torah, the deep belief that human societies function best under the rule of law, especially in the law that is inspired and given by God that insures justice (Exod 20).

These "gifts" from the life of Moses help us to understand the way love is understood in the Hebrew Bible. In summary, let me mention three dimensions.

The first dimension of love is seen in the way that the divine love is manifested in the lives of the Hebrew people. God's love for humankind is *patient and unconditional*. These features of love are rooted in the covenant and are especially evident when the Hebrew people are unfaithful and fail to keep the expectations of the covenant; God still loves these people. It is seen in many stories of the Hebrew Bible, and paradigmatically in the story of Abraham and Sarah and in the classic account of David's reign and failures.

A second aspect of divine love is God's *activity on behalf of the people*; God takes the initiative, pursues an unfaithful people, and acts on their behalf. He gives insight and courage to Moses and gives strength and comfort to Esther. The author of Second Isaiah reflects: "In his love and pity, he redeemed them" (Isa 63:9).

A third dimension of the Hebrew Bible's understanding of love has to do with the place of *Torah (law), which serves the public good*. Love and compassion are more than personal emotions; they are also they endeavor to create social structures which insure that justice prevails. This theme is expressed across the teaching of the prophets and is present in the Ten Commandments (Deut 5), which have both personal and social guidance in regard to the moral life and the place of justice in society.

Jesus drew upon these concepts in his teaching, and he refers directly to the *shema* as foundational: "Hear, O, Israel: The Lord is one Lord; and you shall love the Lord your God with all your heart, and with all your soul, and with all your might" (Deut 6:5). He adds the passage from Lev 19:18, "that we are to love our neighbor as we love ourselves," and then speaks of these passages as the essence of "the law and the prophets."

## The Understanding of Love within the World Religions

It is this understanding of love that becomes a central part of Christian teaching and which finds its way into the New Testament. It is supplemented with other stories and concepts, but not fundamentally altered. At the foundation of the New Testament teaching about love, and hence the Christian view of love is the foundational statement that "God is love" (1 John 4:8). This statement is one of the very few direct statements about God, (with "God is light," 1 John 1:5, and "God is Spirit," John 4:24).The majority of the other references that define God are metaphorical and in the negative (God is not limited, etc.). The statement may have been more intended for pastoral care and nurture, but it does have ontological implications as well. God has expressed this love toward the human family, and indeed the whole earth and the universe in many ways (John 1:1, 1:14; Heb 1:1), and the ultimate expression of God's love toward humanity is the coming of Jesus (John 3:16; Rom 5:8; 1 John 4:9–10).[34]

God's love for us transforms us and reconciles us to God, to others, and to ourselves (Rom 8:1–2; 1 John 4:16–21). In the thought of Paul in particular, we see a strong emphasis on transformation by the Spirit of God and the new law of love being written on our hearts. It is called a fruit of God's Spirit in our lives (Gal 5:22). So the mark of the Christian life is love, with a special emphasis on *agape* love. Jesus is direct with his immediate followers and says that they are to have the double commandment of love (to love God and one's neighbor) at the center of their lives. Even a critical reading of the New Testament accounts would suggest Jesus is the epitome and model of love.[35] For example:

- He has compassion on the five thousand, heals the sick, and then feeds them (Matt 14:13–21).
- He heals and meets the needs of all who come to him (Matt 8:1–17; 15:21; Luke 6:26–37).
- He teaches the Golden Rule: "Do to others as you would have them do to you" (Luke 6:31).
- Even in death, the actions of Jesus are exemplary, as he faces death with courage and asks God to forgive those responsible for his crucifixion (Luke 22:34).

---

34. See the work of Vacek, *Love, Human and Divine: The Heart of Christian Ethics*.

35. The Jesus scholarship regarding access to the authentic sayings of Jesus is complex, but I am taking the position that the main events of the life of Jesus and his central teaching can be accessed and understood.

## Section II — The Geography of Love

Here again, love has both a personal expression as in caring for individuals, and it has a social implication as in creating just and human social structures.[36]

The Apostle Paul continues to teach that *agape* is at the foundation of the Christian faith, affirming that it was out of love that God came to the human family in Jesus, reconciling humankind to God and calling the human family to a life of love.[37] In guiding the new Christians at Corinth, he says, "And I will show you a still more excellent way" (1 Cor 12:31). Paul is guiding this new Christian community, and he writes about the preeminence of love. His logic is clear, that if I do a range of noble acts, but do not have love as the motivation, then they are empty gestures. Love is also very tangible and practical: "Love is patient; love is kind; love is not envious or boastful or arrogant or rude. It does not insist on its own way; it is not irritable or resentful" (1 Cor 13:4–6). Love is permanent and never ending. Other gifts and noble acts will pass away, but "faith, hope, and love abide, these three; and the greatest of these is love" (1 Cor 13:13). Love is the very heartbeat of the Christian faith, both in belief and practice.

Islam, influenced in its formation by both Jewish and Christian teaching, also maintains that love and compassion are rooted in the character of God and makes these values fundamental to its ethical teaching.[38] The clear authority for Muslims about their beliefs and practices is the Quran, a profound and complex volume that is the foundation of Islam. The Quran gives love and compassion a central place in Islamic thought.

The first and foundational affirmation about love in Islam comes in one of the names of God (Allah) which is *al-Wadud* (Love). In the Quran there are many references to God's love for humankind.[39] There is the as-

---

36. See the book by Jackson, *Christian Charity and Social Justice*.

37. Nygren, in his classical work on love, *Agape and Eros*, argues that *agape* overshadows all other forms of love in Christian understanding. Other forms of love are mentioned in the Bible and are carefully described by Morris in *Testaments of Love: A Study of Love in the Bible*.

38. The affirmation of love as central to Islamic thought and practice was underlined in the publication of "A Common Word Between Us and You." It is a document prepared by Muslim scholars and sent in October, 2007 to Christian leaders around the world, inviting them to join with Muslim communities in the affirmation and practice the two love commandments: to love God with our whole being and our neighbor as ourselves.

39. There are good and reliable translations of the Quran, although Muslims contend that reading the Quran in Arabic is the best way to fully understand the meaning. See Wagner, *Opening the Qur'an: Introducing Islam's Holy Book* for an excellent introduction to the Quran for a non-Muslim.

surance that God is all-loving, that he is all-compassionate, and that he is all-merciful.[40] The opening words of the Quran are: "In the name of Allah, Most Gracious, Most Merciful. Praise be to Allah, the Cherisher and Sustainer of the Worlds."

A second affirmation of the centrality of love and compassion in Islam comes from viewing Muhammad as the model of compassionate and fair treatment of his contemporaries. The Quran (33:21) describes him as *uswa hasana*, a "beautiful model" who was sent "as a mercy to the worlds" (21:107).[41] Islam teaches that the love of God necessitates the love of the Prophet, and the love of the Prophet necessitates the love of God; they are interwoven. The teaching about love, modeled by Muhammad, often speaks about the many kinds of love as evident in the life of Muhammad, but makes clear that only the love of God is real love and all other love is metaphorical love, although this kind of second level love is legitimate and a gift of God.[42] Muhammad's early years were filled with his own grief with the loss of his parents and the resulting poverty he experience without their support. These early years gave him genuine empathy for the needy and the marginalized. His first marriage taught him a great deal about the role and place of women, and while he shared the patriarchal values of his time, in a quite remarkable way he respected and honored women.[43]

A third dimension of the Islamic understanding of love and compassion is evident in its teachings and traditions. One of its holidays, for

40. An excellent account of love within Islam is given to us by Seyyed Hossien Nasr in *The Heart of Islam: Enduring Values for Humanity*, 209-15. The distinguished scholar of Islam, John L. Esposito, in his superb study, *Islam: The Straight Path*, 68-114, stresses the place of love and compassion in the beliefs and practices of Islam.

41. Asma Afsarudin, Professor of Arabic and Islamic Studies at the University of Notre Dame, writes: "For believing Muslims, the Prophet is the moral exemplar for all time and the best of humankind" (*The First Muslims: History and Memory*, 16). The biographical account of the life of Muhammad by Tariq Ramadan, *In the Footsteps of the Prophet: Lessons from the Life of Muhammad*, speaks again and again of the loving qualities of Muhammad.

42. Nasr, *The Heart of Islam*, 212.

43. There are recent books written by Muslim women who speak about the discrimination they have felt in Islam. See Asra Q. Nomani, *Standing Alone: An American Woman's Struggle for the Soul of Islam*, Irshad Maji, *The Trouble with Islam Today: A Muslim's Call for Reform in Her Faith*, and the books by Ayaan Hirsi Ali such as *Nomad, From Islam to America: A Personal Journey Through the Clash of Civilizations; Infidel;* and *The Caged Virgin: An Emancipation Proclamation for Women and Islam*. It is not always easy to interpret the discrimination against women as the official teaching of a religion or whether the discrimination grows more out of the culture, but it is clear that the defense of the treatment is often religious in tone. This observation is not exclusively about Islam and could also be made about Judaism or Christianity.

## Section II — The Geography of Love

example, celebrates *Ishq* or the divine love of God. But perhaps the most obvious demonstration of the centrality of love and compassion in Islam is one of the Five Pillars, the *Zakat* or annual charity. It is expected that adult Muslims pay 2.5 percent of their annual income to charity with the money going to the poor, the needy, destitute new Muslims, people drowning in debt, travelers with few financial resources, refugee relief foundations, widows, orphans, poor relatives, and causes for freeing slaves. In more general terms, Islam emphasizes being kind to family members, honoring parents, feeding the poor, fighting against injustice, freeing slaves, and even being kind to animals.

One of Islam's more mystical branches, the Sufi tradition, is especially focused on love and it views the universe as a projection of God whose essence is love. For example, a great Sufi philosopher, Ibn al-Arabi, saw God as the "Beloved" everywhere, and reflected on how God loves through the creation. The Sufi tradition, in its philosophical teaching, but more through its poetry and practice, has found comfort and guidance in understanding God as infinite love. The poetry of Mawlana Jala al-Din Rumi has been widely read and circulated, bringing insight to many.[44]

Many other religious traditions might have been selected to illustrate the special place of love in the religious experience of humankind, and reference will be made to some of these as we speak about the topography of love in other domains. But perhaps these central religious traditions will be illustrative and informative. We turn now to an exploration of how it is that human beings develop or lack the capacity for having love and compassion as a central component of their lives.

---

44. Ernst, *The Teachings of Sufism*, 172–78.

## STUDY RESOURCES

## Discussion Questions

1. Are the views of love in the classical period of history (ancient Greece and Rome) altruistic in character or more oriented to self-fulfillment?

2. In what ways does the Toltec view of the human capacity to love depend upon self-awareness and personal maturity? How does one reach higher levels of self-awareness and personal maturity?

3. In what sense do the religions of Transcendent Monism (Hinduism, Buddhism, Confucianism, etc.) rely on inner transformation and empowerment in order to increase the human capacity to love?

4. Are there ways for the three Abrahamic monotheistic religions to find common ground in their shared ethic of love? Or is the perpetual tension between them inevitable because of diverse beliefs and cultures?

5. Why have these three Abrahamic monotheistic religions, which teach that love and compassion are the center of their ethical code, been violent and why do they continue to have elements of violence in their corporate behavior?

## Key Terms and Concepts

- *Stoicism:* An influential philosophical movement founded by Zeno (340–265 BCE) that maintained that reality, including nature is fundamentally rational in character. Human lives are governed by this rational "Providence" which guides them and against which it is futile to resist and to which wise people willingly submit.

- *Toltec Wisdom:* A view of life of the indigenous people in Southern Mexico in the middle of the first millennium of the Common Era that maintained that the capacity to be free, fulfilled, and to love was based upon the mastery of self-awareness.

- *Yama:* The Ten Vedic restraints or guidelines for life that give ethical guidance to Hindus.

- *Bodhisattva:* A person within Buddhism who aspires to attain enlightenment in order to relieve the suffering of others.

**Section II** — The Geography of Love

- *Li*: A central Confucian value that instructs Confucians in living with propriety (appropriate behavior) that treats others with respect.
- *Torah*: The law or instruction of God, contained in the first five books of the Hebrew Bible, that guides Jewish people and others in ways that lead to justice and the common good.
- *Zakat*: The Muslim annual charity expected to be given by mature Muslims to assist people in need: one of the Five Pillars of Islam.

## Suggestions for Reference and Reading

1. Aristotle, translated by J. A. K. Thomson, *The Ethics of Aristotle*. New York: Penguin Books, 1958.
2. His Holiness the Dalai Lama, translated by Jeffrey Hopkins, *How to Expand Love*. New York: Atria Books, 2005.
3. Diamant, Anita and Howard Cooper, *Living a Jewish Life: Jewish Traditions, Customs, and Values for Today's Families*. New York: HarperResource, 1991.
4. Nasr, Seyyed Hossein, *The Heart of Islam: Enduring Values for Humanity*. New York: HarperSanFrancisco: 2004.
5. Neusner, Jacob and Bruce Chilton, eds., *Altruism in World Religions*. Washington, D.C.: Georgetown University Press, 2005.
6. Ruiz, Don Miguel, *The Mastery of Love*. San Rafael, CA: Amber-Allen Publishing, 1999.
7. Runzo, Joseph and Nancy M. Martin, eds., *Ethics in the World Religions*. Oxford: Oneworld, Vol. III, 2001.
8. Vacek, Edward Collins, *Love, Human and Divine: The Heart of Christian Ethics* Washington, D.C.: Georgetown University Press, 1994.

**SECTION III**

# The Development of Love

In Section II, The Geography of Love, we began with the ways that love is understood in the human family, suggested definitions of love and its cognates, and offered a partial universe of discourse that would enable at least the beginnings of a clear and logical conversation. We went on to explore the complex and diverse terrain of love by providing "sightings" of love across history, traditions, and cultures. We then offered a walk across the hills and valleys of the religious landscape of human family, noting that love is integral to the ethical codes of most religions.

We turn now to an exploration of the development of love, the ways that human beings develop or do not develop the capacity to be those who love. We will look first at the environmental factors that shape humans and either increase or dictate against gaining the capacity to be loving people. In the following chapter, "Endowed for Love," we will probe theories about how we are made and "wired" for love, examining the nature side of the nature-nurture discussion. In Chapter Seven, we turn to the ways that love can be cultivated in order to produce the fruitful crops and beautiful flowers of loving people and just and peaceful societies.

> What's the earth with all its art, verse music worth
> Compared with love, found, gained and kept?
>
> —Robert Browning

# 5

# The Nurturing Environment

## MOVING TOWARD THE LIFE OF LOVE

WE HAVE MAINTAINED THAT our world is in a state of crisis, knowing full well that people in other times may have also thought they lived in a time of trouble.[1] There is a risk in using crisis language in that speaking about the world being in so much difficulty can easily become an empty cliché. But I want to stay with the phrase, asking readers to find their way into the reality of our times. We have also implied that there are signs of hope, and that the very presence of hope is a motivating factor in finding solutions to the overwhelming problems we face. As Gordon Brown of the United Kingdom writes regarding one of our current challenges: "Globalization may have unleashed change of a scale, scope, and speed unprecedented in human history—but it has also given our species an unprecedented opportunity to act in concert in order to master the forces that buffet us."[2] Our thesis is that those who bring the spirit of hope and an attitude of love and compassion to this troubled world offer a perspective that will not necessarily solve many of more technical problems that have to do global infrastructure and environment concerns, but it will contribute to the conviction that our challenging problems can be solved and that there

---

1. See for example the book by Sorokin, *The Crisis of Our Age*.
2. Gordon Brown, "Take Back the Future," *Newsweek*, May 5, 2011, 7. Gordon Brown is the former British prime minister and is the author of *Beyond the Crash: Overcoming the First Crisis of Globalization*.

## Section III — The Development of Love

are just and humane solutions to them. Love motivates us to find these solutions for the well-being of people everywhere, for ecological issues, for corporate structures, for international conflict, for global infrastructure, and for improving the prevailing norms and values that profoundly influence strategies for change. We need a culture of empathy, compassion, and earth community.[3]

The strategy we are suggesting is to find ways to increase the human capacity to live lives that are constantly moving toward being centered in love and compassion. In Section III, we are examining another aspect of lovescapes, the ways that we might cultivate love and compassion in our lives. We move first to the nurture side of the nature-nurture conversation, and explore how it is that the environment we inhabit influences our capacity to love.[4] In Chapter 6, we will explore the ways that our nature shapes our ability to love, and then in Chapter 7, we will suggest ways that we can take the initiative and use a variety of means to increase our ability to be loving and compassionate people.

Across the twentieth century, there were a wide variety of theories about human development, many of them persuasive and standing the test of time. They are a treasure for those of us who struggle to understand how it is that we move through life, the changes that occur, and how we reach levels of maturity. In our new century, we receive guidance from several approaches of the human movement toward maturity which expand our understanding. Many of these approaches are rigorously scientific in character and we will explore them in Chapter 6. Not all of these studies of human development include the development of the capacity to love, but many of them speak about other characteristics that have affinity with "love development."[5] We will briefly review these many views about human development and suggest the possible overlaps with the development of the capacity to love and be compassionate.

---

3. See Rifkin's *The Empathic Civilization: The Race to Global Consciousness in a World in Crisis*. See as well David C. Korten, *The Great Turning: From Empire to Earth Community*.

4. See the new book by Evelyn Fox Keller, *The Mirage of Space between Nature and Nurture* for a thoughtful account of the connections between nature and nurture in human development.

5. One, for example, that might provide some guidance for a theory of love development is James Fowler's *Stages of Faith: The Psychology of Human Development and the Quest for Meaning*. The classic work of Sorokin, *The Ways and Power of Love: Types, Factors, and Techniques of Moral Transformation*, first published in 1954, suggests a wide range of factors that cultivate love.

## AN ECOLOGICAL PERSPECTIVE

We begin our review of these several understandings of human development with a commitment to synthesis and inclusivity, drawing the most helpful insights from them in order to understand better how to cultivate more loving ways. My conviction is that each of these views explains important dimensions of our growth toward maturity, and that drawing upon the point of view of each of them will suggest a more holistic understanding of human development. There are very real differences between them, and the literature describing the differences and the dialogue between the spokespersons for these views not only point out these differences but suggest ways for synthesis and a more comprehensive understanding. Few of them, in fact, are intended to describe all aspects of human growth and development; most focus on one aspect such as a particular behavior, as for example cognitive and language development or social or moral development. Others focus on pathology, articulating ways that the growth process has been blocked and derailed.[6]

Another point of view, and one that I find persuasive, especially on the nurture side of the continuum, is the ecological approach of Urie Bronfenbrenner.[7] He argues that human growth and development are shaped by all aspects of the interaction between human beings and their surroundings. He also maintains that the best way to change human behavior, making it more healthy and responsible, is to change the environment. This point of view may not give sufficient attention to the nature side of the continuum, but it certainly underlines how we are fundamentally shaped by our environment. What makes Bronfenbrenner's work so credible is that he refuses to suggest that only one aspect of our given circumstances, such as our relationship to our parents, is the exclusive cause of our behavior or our mental and emotional distress. His view is inclusive, or as he prefers to call it, ecological. It has the following "building blocks":[8]

---

6. The work of Anita Woolfolk, *Educational Psychology* (Eleventh Edition) provides an excellent summary of the those developmental theories that are helpful in education, although less is said about the earlier theorists such as Freud and Jung and those views that focus more on mental illness and healing. Her views, and the views of those whose work she clearly describes, do tend to intimately connect the nature-nurture division as illustrated by Keller in *The Mirage of Space between Nature and Nurture*.

7. *The Ecology of Human Development: Experiments by Nature and Design.*

8. Ibid., 3-15.

## Section III — The Development of Love

1. Human development is formed by the way a person perceives and deals with his or her environment. Bronfenbrenner writes, "Thus development is defined in this work as a lasting change in the way in which a person perceives and deals with his environment."

2. The environments are several, with the more immediate and primary ones nested in the larger frames of reference. As Bronfenbrenner puts it, "The ecological environment is conceived as a set of nested structures, each inside the next, like a set of Russian dolls."

3. To explain behavior, one must look beyond single settings and pay attention to the relations between the several settings of a person's life. As Bronfenbrenner writes, "The next step, however, already leads off the beaten track for it requires looking beyond single settings to the relationship between them."

4. A person's behavior is often shaped by events occurring in the person's absence. As Bronfenbrenner puts it, this factor "evokes a hypothesis that the person's development is profoundly affected by the events occurring in settings in which a person is not even present."

5. These several environments are in flux and may influence a person's behavior in different ways as the patterns change across space and time. Bronfenbrenner writes, "Finally, there is the striking phenomenon pertaining to settings at all three levels of the ecological environment outlined above: with any culture or subculture, settings of a given kind—such as homes, streets, or offices—tend to be very much alike, whereas between cultures they are distinctly different."

An analysis of the shaping environment requires theoretical models that address these complexities; they need to be substantive and use methods that factor in the many-sided influences.

Bronfenbrenner does provide a description of these several shaping influences. He speaks, for example about *dyads* or two-person systems such as mother-child or caregiver and child. He goes on to describe the "dyads plus" systems such as the expansion in the environment of parent-child to the larger family. He then describes the several settings in which these groupings function, such as pre-school care, school, and parents' work, all within a complex subculture and the larger culture of a society and a changing historical setting. The model goes way beyond the analysis of the behavior of individuals in terms of single shaping influences and includes systems both within and between settings, and ones that can be modified and expanded.[9] His view argues for the transformative power of the following systems:

- There is the immediate setting which includes people such as parents who shape an individual's development first hand or the *microsystem*.
- There is the linkage between the settings, the primary one and those in which the developing person either participates or does not participate but which shapes the immediate setting. It is called *mesosystems* in those settings in which the child participates and *exosystems* in those in which the child does not participate.
- He then expands his "nested" theory and describes "the overarching patterns of ideology and organizations of the social institutions common to a particular culture or subculture."[10] He calls this pattern the *macrosystem*.

What he suggests in his ecological model is not totally new; most of these building blocks are present and discussed in the social sciences. What is especially helpful, however, is the way that he integrates them and links them to the course of human development. He argues that the use of this ecological model should shape public policy in that it suggests a way of creating environments that are life-giving and enable humans to flourish. He does value the more narrowly conceived views of human development, such as the decontextualized system of Piaget, and draws upon them for the framing of an integrative view; he often integrates them into his more comprehensive system. In our discussion of the ways that humans develop into more loving and compassionate people who help to address regional, national, and global problems, we will attempt to learn from several models, but will lean toward an application of Dr. Bronfenbrenner's ecology of human development.

## THE MODELS OF HUMAN DEVELOPMENT

We must be selective in describing these models; they are numerous and profound and have been written in nearly every era of history. Our criteria for selection are: (1) those which are more recent and are based upon

---

9. Anthropologists, sociologists, economists, and historians often speak about the shaping influences of culture, economic systems, and of historical change, and their influence on the ways we frame the world around us. For example, Joseph E. Stiglitz, winner of the Nobel Prize in Economics, writes about the power of economic systems in *Globalization and Its Discontents*. My library is full of comparable books.

10. Bronfenbrenner, 8.

## Section III — The Development of Love

research;[11] and (2) those which are rooted primarily in the social sciences and speak at least indirectly to the development of our capacity to be loving and compassionate people.

We begin with the view of one of the founders of human psychology, Sigmund Freud (1856–1939). Freud, a Copernican figure in the field of psychology, has been uniquely influential in understanding human development even though his views have been challenged and substantially modified within the practice of psychoanalysis.[12] But in a profound way, he invited all those seeking to understand human development to look deeper and beyond the obvious shaping influences. He is especially remembered as the founder of the psychoanalysis school of therapy, an approach to therapy that is known for looking beneath the surface for the causes of pathological behavior.

He studied medicine at the University of Vienna and became interested in the treatment of neurosis, went on to study in Paris, and then, back in Vienna, began to treat patients with a methodology that used hypnosis, free association, and dream interpretation. He not only developed a therapeutic technique for the treatment of hysteria and neurosis but advanced an elaborate theory that included observations about human culture and religion.[13] The following is a brief and selective summary of his views.

Freud maintains that human beings, like other organisms, want to preserve a *state of equilibrium*. They are equipped to do this by their nervous system which functions to reduce and control stimuli. Our mental life is intimately related to this system and especially helps us manage the pleasure and pain associated with the stimuli. These stimuli are both external and internal (instinctual) with the internal stimuli functioning as our signal for danger and awareness of needs. These instincts have the following characteristics:

- An impetus or intrusion that demands energy.

---

11. There are many views, profound and persuasive, which have grown out of philosophical and religious reflection, ones that go back to Buddha, Plato, and Jesus, etc. and move across the span history into the rise of developmental psychology. We will draw upon these earlier insights as well, especially in Chapter Seven.

12. One interesting challenge comes from Armand M. Nicholi, a professor at Harvard in his book, *The Question of God: C. S. Lewis and Sigmund Freud Debate God, Love, Sex and the Meaning of Life*.

13. See for example his books, *Totem and Taboo, Moses and Monotheism*, and *the Future of an Illusion*. His book, *A General Introduction to Psychoanalysis*, provides an introduction to his basic theories, and there are excellent summaries of his views such as J. Stanley, ed., *The Standard Edition of the Complete Psychological Works of Sigmund Freud*, 1959.

- An aim to reach satisfaction by abolishing the source of the stimulation.
- An object that enables us to achieve our aim.
- A source or the somatic process from which the stimulus originates.

Instincts then manifest themselves in our mental and emotional life, which is filled with ideas or wishes for objects and behavior that we think will protect us and meet our needs.

These wishes may be *conscious, preconscious, or unconscious*. If unconscious, they are prevented from surfacing to the conscious level by repression, and we have a tendency to resist attempts to bring them into consciousness because of fear and possible discomfort. An essential component of therapy is to help clients surface these hidden needs and wishes. It is done in a variety of ways that increase awareness of how we function which leads to greater health and freedom (equilibrium). In its simplest form, Freud maintains that we have an *ego* as our guide to reality which mediates between the unconscious *id* that seeks pleasure and the challenges of the external world that might create pain. We also have a *superego* which functions as a societal-imposed conscience in reference to our behavior. Many have thought that this description of our inner life, the way that the reality principle (ego) controls the pleasure principle, is one of Freud's most important contributions to human understanding.

He goes on to develop these theories in some detail, and he suggests the several mechanisms we use to preserve our equilibrium. How is it that the ego holds life together in light of the challenges of both the internal and external stimuli? It is the feeling of anxiety that makes us aware of our needs and possible danger, and we then resort to a range of mental and emotional responses to ease our anxiety. They are:

- Identification: the process of orienting the self to something such as an object, a person, or a group with the resulting feeling of close emotional association; as for example, the infant putting objects in its mouth as a defense against hunger; or when anxiety occurs and the challenges appear, the child identifies with mother or father as a source of comfort and security.[14]

---

14. Sherry Turkle, a professor of psychology at the Massachusetts Institute of Technology and with a background in psychoanalysis, writes about this identification occurring with computers and robots in children in her book, *Alone Together: Why We Expect More from Technology and Less from Each Other*.

## Section III — The Development of Love

- Projection: the process of warding off threats and attributing the danger to another person or situation instead of seeing it as a threat to oneself ("the storm will pass over us"), or projecting an ideal situation that will bring pleasure or comfort as in a fantasy.
- Sublimation: the process of changing an instinct without blocking it, which allows, for example, a sexual striving to be satisfied in a non-sexual and more acceptable way.
- Repression: the process that pushes the threat out of our consciousness, although as Freud notes, the threat does not go away and will reappear in unexpected forms.
- Reaction-Formation: the process of exaggerating the opposition or threat and overcompensating, as in the case of one who compulsively worries about germs or must have perfect order in the house in order to feel equilibrium.
- Rationalization: the process of dealing with objectionable instinctual demands by satisfying them under the cloak of socially acceptable reasons.
- Regression: the process of dealing with frustration by returning to an earlier period of life in which satisfaction was obtained.

Freud mentions other means of maintaining equilibrium, but these at least are suggestive of his approach, and they have become an important part of our self-understanding and language.

He further develops his view of human development and behavior with his theory about sexual instincts or the *libido*, that force by which the sexual instinct is represented in the mind as a need or a threat to our equilibrium. There are stages through which we attempt to maintain equilibrium and get our needs met. The first stage of this tendency, and one that was a bit of a shock to Freud's generation, has to do with the sexuality of infants. He describes the baby's pattern of auto-erotic touch aimed at pleasure, a practice called *narcissism* by Freud, and a pattern of behavior that may continue into adult life. What we later call love is the attraction to objects connected with feelings that satisfy us, such as feeding, care, protection, and cuddling. But this process is complex, and as we develop, we have feelings of *ambivalence,* or stated dramatically by Freud, feelings of attraction when our needs are met or feelings of hatred when others deprive us of our need for love. The negative feeling may manifests itself in aggression, sadism, or may be directed at ourselves (*masochism*).

## The Nurturing Environment

All of these inner complexities carry over into adult life and shape our way of relating to others, the means we use to solve conflicts, and more profoundly, how we develop as persons with identity and character. As implied, Freud was bold enough to project his theories on to culture and history. For example, he postulates that universal prohibitions like those on incest are controlled by the illusions within religious beliefs and practices. But for our purposes, we can use those parts of his theories that have withstood the test of time and criticism as a way of reflecting on our capacity to become people motivated by love and compassion.

In short, Freud is not optimistic about the possibility of becoming loving and compassionate people. In fact, Freud is persuaded that the possibility of harmonizing human sexuality and socially accepted mores makes him fundamentally opposed to all idealistic thinking about the nature of love.[15] He consistently maintains that the goal of communal unity, mutual support, and personal happiness is not achievable. However he does argue for an effort that meets the needs of and sustains a more peaceful civilization, but it will come at the expense individual fulfillment. He speaks about the two types of attraction or love, one that is egoistic which is self-oriented and one that is altruistic which seeks social unity even at the expense of happiness for the individual. When addressing *agape* love, as for example in the life of St. Francis, he argues that such behavior does not do justice to the giver of such love, and that not all people are worthy of it.[16]

What then might we take from Sigmund Freud, his school of psychoanalysis, and his many followers who further developed his views? The lessons are many for our study of love. The first is that we do have undercurrents that shape our behavior, and these patterns within us, often unconscious and repressed, are difficult to access. They do have an influence on our capacity to be loving and compassionate people, and in many cases block our ability to have genuine empathy for others.

It follows that we need to be keenly aware that we are complex, and this complexity does not always make it easy to be a caring person or to give ourselves to building a more just and humane society and world. Freud invites us to be realistic about our ability to practice altruism.

Freud does offer a pattern for becoming more self-aware through psychoanalysis and its many offshoots. By becoming more self-aware, we

---

15. Singer, *The Nature of Love*: Vol. 3, *The Modern World*, 150. Singer's treatment of Freud's understanding of love is perceptive.

16. These themes are developed in *Civilization and its Discontents*.

## Section III — The Development of Love

gain both some freedom from the unconscious forces that shape our behavior, and we become better able to manage the negative messages that urge us to be egoistic and harmful to ourselves and others in our self-seeking. While we may not choose the path of psychoanalysis, we can nevertheless learn that we need to be quite intentional about improving our psychic health and finding ways of achieving levels of maturity that encourage more empathy and compassionate behavior.

We turn now to other views of human development based in rigorous research that temper a simple and occasionally pious idealism about the human capacity for love and compassion. These views tend to be less ideological and pessimistic than Freud about progress toward the formation of a more empathic culture. A person, less well known than Freud, but in many ways as influential is Jean Piaget (1896–1980) who, along with Freud, tended to view human development in terms of stages. Freud focused on the stages of psychosexual development whereas Piaget described cognitive development using the pattern of stages. He argued that in these stages of progress, the thinking of a child involves more than the simple addition of knowledge and skills. According to his stage theory, the child matures through four stages, and his or her cognitive development moves from sensorimotor to preoperational to concrete operational to formal.[17]

Piaget operates from the fundamental assumption that human beings move through these stages of development toward maturity because of the unfolding of the biological changes that are genetically programmed.[18] Parents and teachers have less influence on this biological aspect of our growth, although they insure that children have the nourishment and care they need to be healthy. However, both nature and nurture are clearly present in the child's development. There are several facts that nudge the biological changes forward. For example, the range of activities of the children cultivates growth; it is their interaction with the environment from which they learn. As they observe, experiment, and organize information, their thinking process changes and matures. As they engage in these activities, children interact with others and there is learning from others.

---

17. Piaget's theories are developed in his many books written over several decades. They include *The Construction of Reality in the Child*, 1954, *Origins of Intelligence in Children*, 1963, *The Science of Education and the Psychology of the Child*, 1970, and *The Equilibrium of Cognitive Structures: The Central Problem of Intellectual Development*, 1985.

18. I am guided in my comments by Woolfolk in *Educational Psychology*, 32–42.

## The Nurturing Environment

This learning might be describes as the social transmission of knowledge and understanding.

Piaget goes on to describe how the thinking of a child processes these new discoveries. There is a tendency to organize the information into patterns; psychological structures or systems emerge for understanding and interacting with the world. As the child matures, these structures become more complex. Children will also adapt to their environment by assimilating new information, putting it into the categories already in place, and then accommodating one's thinking and behavior to new situations and information. As with Freud, Piaget says that the child organizes this new information in a way that provides inner equilibrium or balance. Children make sense of it all in ways that bring balance and order.

Piaget divides this process of change, learning, and equilibrium in the four stages of cognitive development. They are:

1. In infancy (0–2), the child is in the sensorimotor stage because the child's thinking involves seeing, hearing, moving, touching, taste, etc. The child begins to make use of imitation and memory, begins to recognize that objects exist even if they are not observed, and moves from reaction to goal-centered activity.

2. In early childhood (2–7), the child is in the preoperational stage. The child gradually develops the use of language and to think operations through in logical order, but still has difficulty seeing another person's point of view.

3. From later elementary school to middle school (ages 7–11), the child becomes able to solve concrete problems in a logical way, understands how to classify and change, understands that a person or an object remains the same over time, and to think back in a reverse fashion about an event.

4. From the early teenage years to adult (ages 11–adult), the person begins to solve abstract problems in logical ways, becomes more scientific in thinking, and develops concerns about identity and social issues.

Some have criticized Piaget's classifications and argued that not all people reach stage four or only use this level of thinking in limited areas, and some move beyond stage 4 to levels of profound abstraction and integration. More recently, there is an increasing tendency to move away from the structure of stages because there is so much individuality and difference in each person's development. In addition, there is the view that these

## Section III — The Development of Love

processes of change are more continuous than they seem, not abrupt, and that many people use modes of thinking of more than one stage simultaneously. Still others, and Urie Bronfenbrenner is one of them in his ecology of human development, introduce a social-cultural perspective, suggesting that movement through stages of development is profoundly influenced by external circumstances and is not primarily the product of a biological programming.[19] But all human development theorists must read Piaget carefully; his work is thorough and profound. In many ways, he does point the way to the current emphasis on human development being rooted in biological factors. For our purposes in regard to understanding the human capacity to be loving and compassionate, he speaks directly to the issues of physical development as being interwoven with our mental, emotional, and social development. It is a complex mosaic. His views on cognitive and language development contribute to our thesis that the fully developed person has greater potential to become a person for others. The expression and application of love and compassion require empathic understanding and the subtle and nuanced use of language.

There are many development theorists who focus on the social and moral development in addition to the psychosexual development (Freud) and cognitive and language development (Piaget). One of them, influenced by Freud and whose influence has been significant, is Erik Erikson (1902–1994). He used stages as a frame of reference and in particular provided a way of understanding the needs of young people in relation to society. He maintains that each of the stages has its particular goals, concerns, accomplishments, and dangers, and that they are interdependent. The successes within a later stage may depend on the accomplishments that are achieved and the conflicts resolved in an earlier stage. At each stage, the individual faces a developmental crisis, often an internal conflict between two alternatives, one positive and life-giving and another harmful and blocking growth. The way the individual resolves the developmental crisis will have a lasting impact on the individual's self-image and view of the world. For example, the adolescent will face a crisis of a developing a healthy identity but will be challenged in this time of life by role confusion. The choices made about work, values, and commitments to others

---

19. A Russian scholar, Lev Semenovich Vygotsky, less well known in the West, did extensive research on the social sources of individual thinking. He argues that cognitive and language development are shaped more by environment and less by an internal, biological processes as the child moves through stages.

## The Nurturing Environment

such as a life partner will shape and clarify one's identity and form the contours of the person's life.[20]

Erikson lays out eight stages as follows:[21]

1. There is the infant, from birth to 12–18 months who has the needs of nourishment and security and will learn in this stage either *trust or basic mistrust*. The infant needs a loving and trusting relationship with a caregiver who meets these needs or the infant will develop a sense of mistrust.

2. There is the small child, ages 18 months to 3 years, who needs to learn about the body's needs and physical skills such as walking, grasping, and controlling the sphincter. The child who learns these tasks will develop *autonomy or develop shame and doubt* if they are not learned.

3. There is the stage of 3 to 6 years in which the child becomes more independent and self-sufficient and will face the challenge of *initiative versus guilt*, the latter coming if the initiative toward independence is too forceful and overly controlled by the caregiver.

4. From 6 to 12 years, the challenge is between the feelings of *industry versus inferiority*, as the child learns new skills, but risks in this challenge of learning the feelings of failure and incompetence.

5. In adolescence, there is the increased importance of peer relationships and the developmental crisis of *identity versus role confusion*. The young person must begin to achieve a sense of identity in occupation, gender roles, politics, and religion, or remain confused about essential identity.

6. In young adulthood, the challenge is successfully developing love relationships, with the development crisis being *intimacy versus isolation*.

7. In middle adulthood, each adult must find good ways to make a contribution to society and support the next generation. The development crisis is between *generativity and stagnation*.

8. In late adulthood, there must be culmination of a sense of acceptance of oneself and a sense of fulfillment, so the challenge is between *ego integrity and despair*.

---

20. Erikson, *Identity: Youth and Crisis*. Erikson's book, *Young Man Luther*, applies his theory to a person in history.
21. Woolfolk, *Educational Psychology*, Table 3–4, 83.

## Section III — The Development of Love

Each of our pathways and manner of addressing these identity crises may differ, but they are suggestive of the characteristics of the healthy and mature person. These pioneers of developmental psychology, Freud, Piaget, and Erikson, all contribute to our inquiry about the nature of love development. Freud is somewhat pessimistic about the human capacity to love in unlimited and self-giving ways. Piaget focuses more on cognitive and language development than on interpersonal relationships. Freud's contribution is to counsel caution about adopting an overly idealistic view of love and compassion. Piaget does not address the issues of love and compassion directly, but suggests the path of the child from dependency to adult competency, and adult competency is a necessary component to being able to express wise and appropriate caring of others. The challenge of giving thoughtful and sensitive love to others requires a reasoned approach and the sensitive use of language. Addressing the pressing issues of a region, country, or the global context in compassionate ways will need extraordinary sophistication, as Freud suggests, and it may mean personal sacrifice on the part of individuals to build a more humane civilization.

In the work of Erikson, the structure of the "development crisis" of the various stages of life suggests the way to maturity, and how it is that human beings find a sense of personal acceptance and the steps of development that lead to personal fulfillment. This pattern suggests three guiding principles for the formation of a loving and compassionate person, one who is able to care for others as individuals and provide energy and guidance for the development of a society that empowers people to flourish. They are:

1. Supportive caregivers and an affirming context enable people to mature and have the potential to be free from a view of the world shaped exclusively by their own pronounced and unmet needs.

2. Clear choices must be made along the way, some in the early stages of life made with the encouragement of supporting parents or others. But later, more independent, intentional choices are made by the individual that lead to self-fulfillment and responsible living. If these choices are not made, it may mean the failure to establish a clear identity, life-giving relationships, and meaningful work with the possible result of self-destructive patterns of living.

3. Maturity encourages the capacity to be a loving and compassionate person while immaturity blocks love and compassion. It is this thesis that we will continue to develop.

## The Nurturing Environment

I want to include in this brief survey two other people who have dealt with the issues of human development, Lawrence Kohlberg in moral development and James Fowler in faith development. I select these two, from among many others, in that their work points to ways which human beings develop the capacity to be loving and compassionate.[22] I begin with Lawrence Kohlberg, whose views of moral development are based in part upon Piaget's ideas.[23] Kohlberg also employs the structure of levels and stages, and he argues that human beings mature in their moral development through three levels and six stages, with stage five and six not always being clearly separate. The levels are:

- Preconventional, the period in which moral judgments are based solely on a person's needs and perceptions.

- Conventional, the period in which moral judgments are based upon the expectations of society and law.

- Post-conventional, the period in which the moral judgments are based on thoughtful and carefully chosen personal principles of love and justice, not necessarily determined by the conventional views in society.

Each of these levels has two stages as follows:

Level One: Preconventional moral reasoning in which judgment is based on personal needs and the rules of others.

The first stage is controlled by a punishment-obedience orientation, one in which the developing person obeys rules to avoid punishment, and a good or bad action is determined by physical consequences.

Stage 2 functions in terms of personal reward, with the personal needs of the developing person determining what is right and wrong.

Level Two: Conventional moral reasoning in which judgment is based on the approval others, family expectations, traditional values, and the laws of society.

---

22. I have been influenced by several other authors who have written about the various dimensions of human development. Among them are the work of Carol Gilligan, *In a Different Voice: Psychological Theory and Women's Development*; Robert Kegan, *The Evolving Self: Problem and Process in Human Development*; Abraham Maslow, *Toward a Psychology of Being*; Carl Rogers, *On Becoming a Person*; and B. F. Skinner, *Beyond Freedom & Dignity*. I have also read with interest those books focused more on seasons and passages in adult life such as Gail Sheehy, *Passages: Predictable Crises of Adult Life* and Daniel J. Levinson, *The Seasons of a Man's Life*.

23. Kohlberg's views are in several publications, but his definitive work is found in *The Philosophy of Moral Development*. See the summary of Kohlberg's view by Woolfolk in *Educational Psychology*, 98–99.

## Section III — The Development of Love

Stage 3 has the orientation of the good boy/good girl, an orientation that often means "nice" and one in which the developing person makes moral judgments in reference to what pleases and is approved by others.

Stage 4 has the structure of "law and order," one in which the developing person understands the laws to be absolute and enforced by authority that must be respected.

Level Three: Post-conventional reasoning in which judgment is based self-determined principles.

Stage 5 has the design of a social contract, and good is understood by the developing person as living by socially arranged agreements and covenants.

Stage 6 has the orientation of universally understood ethical principles, one in which the individual makes moral judgments in terms of conscience and in reference to concepts such as justice, human dignity, and equality.

Kohlberg has developed this frame of reference by studying the behavior of both children and adults and by placing them in a case study frame of reference. He has invited individuals to make moral judgments in reference to hypothetical situations out of which the patterns of moral reasoning emerged. His views have been criticized by those who suggest that moral development is not a logically sequenced pattern, but one in which people have more than one frame of reference in making ethical judgments. Critics also point out that from time to time people regress in their moral behavior or move back and forth between stages. He has been challenged as well by those who maintain that moral choices are not as dependent on reasoning as Kohlberg suggests, but often shaped by the circumstances of one's life, one's emotional state, and personal relationships.

His pattern of moral development does speak directly to our desire to understand how one becomes a more loving and compassionate person. If one clearly places altruism and self-giving unlimited love as the highest standard of human behavior, it is clear that those who have reached stages 5 and 6 in Kohlberg's theory of moral reasoning are better able to express altruistic love and compassion. They have become relatively free from the controlling influence of their own personal needs and the approval of others and can move toward the choice of demonstrating empathy and caring in personal relationships and responsible actions that improve the welfare of others.

James W. Fowler served as a professor at Harvard University and was for many years a Professor of Theology and Human Development at

Emory University and Director of the Center for Faith Development there. His particular interest has been faith development, the way that human beings develop meaning in their lives. The term *faith development* has often been exclusively associated with religious meaning, but his theories are not solely about a religious orientation but a dynamic system of images, values, and commitments that guide one across the lifespan. Fowler, influenced by those developmental psychologists that have been mentioned such as Piaget, Erikson, and Kohlberg, shaped his understanding of the human meaning in the structure of stages.[24] He maintains that there are 6 stages of faith, or the quest for meaning, but is clear that these should not necessarily be understood as an inevitable progression through life. He says that there may be progression, but that each stage has its own integrity and may be appropriate for a particular age or the circumstances of one's life. Those who have read his work have occasionally spoken of later stages of development as more mature and life-giving for an individual, and perhaps a case can be made for this point of view. Fowler, however, gave some resistance to this point of view and argued that meaning can be found at the various stages. He notes that the early stages are especially appropriate for younger children in that these stages are connected to their development. He also pointed out that it is possible to remain in one of the later stages (3–5) and find meaning in life that provides health, stability, and fulfillment. His research also suggests that many conventional churches teach and practice a faith that has many characteristics of Stage 3.

He begins with *infancy*, not calling it so much a stage as a foundational beginning point in life. In infancy, there is *undifferentiated faith* in which the infant learns about mutuality and trust and grows in reference to the quality of care offered by parents and the immediate community, such as the religious community in which pre-images of God and meaning may be present. Here, the Erikson thesis of the development crisis in infancy, that of learning trust or mistrust is foundational.

Stage 1 in Fowler's view emerges in *early childhood* and is called *intuitive-projective*. In this stage the young child's thought patterns are pre-operational, with fact and fantasy mingled together and episodic. As faith is introduced in story and play, there is the rise of imagination and the formation of images that point beyond the immediacy of the surroundings

---

24. His definitive work is entitled *Stages of Faith: The Psychology of Human Development and the Quest for Meaning*. He has written several articles and books, one of which is especially important in our effort to understand "love development," *Becoming Adult, Becoming Christian: Adult Development and Christian Faith*.

to the numinous and the ground of being. The child senses that there is something "beyond" which holds it all together and gives it meaning.

In stage 2, *childhood*, as the child reaches school age, the primal images develop and meaning takes the form of *mythic-literal faith*. There is the increase of narrative and an introduction to stories of faith that suggest to the child that there is a spiritual world and a transcendent, ultimate environment. There is some sorting out of fact and fantasy and the narrative suggests meaning. If the religious community of the child is Christian, then the child may learn that God created the world; that there was judgment and floods occurred; and that Jesus, who is the Son of God, loved the children who came to him.

Stage 3, which is that of the *adolescent*, is called by Fowler the *synthetic-conventional*. There is the rise of formal operations in thinking and the onset of emotionally charged puberty. Third person or conventional views are assumed, both in terms of belief and expected behavior, although the beliefs may not always be fully accepted internally, and externally the expected behavior may not always be practiced. Adolescents challenge the prescribed views in order to gain independence. At this point in life, the young person begins to explore issues of identity and meaning, begins to form relationships, assumes roles, and cares deeply about peer acceptance. The adolescent hears new stories in the context of a community of faith and begins to make commitments of belief and moral behavior. There are new stories and the story line becomes applicable to life. Meaning is "out there" and can be grasped and internalized, often understood in the monotheistic traditions in terms of a personal relationship with God.

In *young adulthood*, Stage 4, the mode of faith is called by Fowler *individuative-reflective*. In this stage, the young adult begins to express the new and developing identity in reference to values, images of power, and a mega-story that helps the young person to make connections that are upheld by transcendent meaning. The young adult is now using full formal operations, and thought patterns have a systematic character. There is the challenging task of clarifying boundaries of self and one's worldview, and often commitments are made with the internal statement: "This makes sense and works for me." There are commitments to ideologies and outlooks about the world from the standpoint of a reflective, self-aware identity.

In Stage 5, *adulthood*, there is a more *conjunctive faith* or connected and inclusive frame of reference. A new sense of calling or vocation may emerge, complemented by a new theological outlook. The boundaries of

Stage 4 become more porous and open to fundamental questions, often brought on by new experiences. It is possible that a "second naiveté" will develop, with more openness and peace about the disruptive invasions of spirit, shafts of light from "the cloud of unknowing," touching one's deepest self. We see new perspectives not as threats to our way of framing meaning and faith, but opportunities for deeper understanding of the Mystery. There is recognition of particularity, that all faith formations are contextual and relative rather than absolute, and that we must face the reality of finitude. We become more open to other faith formations, learning from faith and meaning constructions that are different from our own and which might enrich and complete us.

In Stage 6, *universalizing faith*, not altogether different from Erik Erikson's stage 6, Fowler says that it may be possible for us to form a partnership and be more integrated with Being or the transcendent dimension of reality. In this integration, we begin to live easily in the world with a sense of integrity and with a sense of partnership with Love, however it may be understood. We move beyond the paradoxes of Stage 5 and reaffirm our fundamental trust in the process of becoming a person and forming a life of caring. We may move to what Thomas Berry calls the Great Work, the goal of replacing the distorted dream of an industrial technological paradise with the dream of partnership with the Earth and all of its creatures, a partnership based on respecting our home, planet earth, and our interdependency with all who share this home.[25]

As there was with Lawrence Kohlberg in his views of moral development, so there is much to learn from James Fowler in his exploration of stages of faith regarding our capacity to love and express compassion. In the concluding section of the book, I will try to provide tangible applications of lessons about love, but at this point, I want to underline three primary lessons from the work of James Fowler:

1. The first is that he adds the *dimension of meaning and faith* to the intricate web of linkages and connections in the human pattern of growth and development. While he asserts that it is possible to find a stage of faith appropriate for the needs of a person at a particular point in life, he does imply that there is a movement toward a more mature understanding of life's meaning and experience of the transcendent.

25. See Berry's book edited by Mary Evelyn Tucker, *The Sacred Universe: Earth, Spirituality, and Religion in the Twenty-First Century*, Chapter 10 "A Ecologically Sensitive Spirituality," 129–38. See as well his book, *The Dream of the Earth*, Chapter 15 "The Dream of the Earth: Our Way into the Future," 194–215.

**Section III** — The Development of Love

2. The movement beyond stages 3 and 4 leads to a great capacity to see beyond the confines of one's own needs and cultural frame of reference. We develop the capacity to *have an empathic understanding* of those who have a different culture and understanding of transcendence and ultimate meaning.

3. As this new understanding develops, it begins to *shape one's sense of vocation*, and invites responsible participation in the building of a world in which we work for reconciliation and a social order based on a just peace.

## THE SETTINGS FOR GROWTH

In our review of theories of human development, we have learned that human beings are formed by the way they perceive and deal with their environment. To illustrate, let me quote William Johnston in his introduction to a well-known medieval book on spirituality about the environment of the Middle Ages. Medieval people inherited and assumed a way of understanding the world. He writes: "It is an age when, in spite of troubles and rumbling presages of a coming storm, Europe was deeply religious: faith penetrated to the very hearts of the people and influenced not only their art, music, and literature, but every aspect of their lives..." The people "took for granted a Church, a faith, and a sacramental life that are no longer accepted without question by many readers today."[26]

As then, so there is now a sort of gestalt, a configuration, structure, and pattern of physical, biological, personal, cultural, historical, and global influences that function as a unit to shape us. It is called by Urie Bronfenbrenner an ecology of human development and one that is not easily broken into separate parts. One theory of human development is called Gestalt psychology, which resists the tendency to isolate only a few shaping influences in our development.[27] Yet it is helpful to see the various components of our environment and how they combine to contribute to (or block) our growth. To review, we have seen the following pattern:

---

26. Johnston, ed., in the Introduction to *The Cloud of Unknowing*, 29.

27. Gestalt psychology, a movement that began in the early part of the twentieth century attempted to study human behavior in a holistic manner. Frederick Perls, among others developed gestalt therapy. See, for example, the book by Perls, et al., *Gestalt Therapy: Excitement and Growth in the Human Personality*.

*The Nurturing Environment*

1. The process of human growth and development involves an individual self, moving through the stages of life with increasing capabilities and a measure of freedom and choice as life progresses.

2. The individual, as life progresses beyond childhood, attempts to navigate a complex array of shaping influences in order to create a life of meaning and contentment.

3. The environment which must be navigated is layered, vast, complex, and changing.

4. Individuals often directly participate in these shaping influences such as participation in a family or school. But sometimes we do not participate in more indirect influences, and we may not be fully aware of them. For example, Freud speaks of the human tendency of repression and the presence of the unconscious in the human psyche. Others speak of social and historical influences that we unconsciously assume as "the way things are."

5. Bronfenbrenner speaks of these shaping influences as microsystems (dyads such as child and parent); mesosystems (dyads plus, that is, the expansion of the dyad to include other influences in the primary environment); exosystems (dyads plus, that is, ones in which the individual does not participate); and macrosystems (overarching patterns of cultures and subcultures).

6. We have noted as well that these shaping influences may be understood on a spectrum ranging from positive and life-giving to negative and life-denying.

7. There are influences that are life-giving enable and empower us to exercise more freedom. We are emancipated from controlling needs and able to make choices that lead to inner contentment, satisfying relationships, and lives with meaning and responsibility.

8. There are influences that are life-denying and block our growth; we remain in stages of development that are driven by our immediate needs. We have little freedom and do not thrive and flourish.

Our thesis, briefly expressed in points 7 and 8 above is that those environments with their many shaping influences impact our capacity to express love and show compassion. It is also important to explore the characteristics of those environments that maximize our capacity to be caring and empathic people, and in successive chapters, there will be an expansion of the study of these characteristics. But initially, we will limit our remarks

## Section III — The Development of Love

to illustrations and examples from the human development theories we have mentioned. These views suggest some conditions that should exist in the several stages and settings of our lives if we are to mature and increase our capacity to express love and compassion. Attention will be paid to the relationship of stages, settings, and their continual change.

The first setting, the *primary context* (or microsystem) into which one is born and spends the early years of life, usually understood as a family with parents, should have at the very least four basic conditions:

1. There should be food to meet the hunger needs of the infant.

2. There should be protective shelter, a safe home in which to explore, play, and experiment.

3. There should be an accepting and nurturing presence of parents or caregivers.

4. There should be a good balance of freedom that leads to independence and boundaries that guide in the formation of moral and religious commitments.

In such a setting, the infant will learn about loving and trusting relationships rather than move into later stages of life with mistrust and the inability to connect with others in caring and understanding ways. As the child develops there will be the development of cognitive and language skills and as there is movement toward adolescence, issues of autonomy, identity, moral development, and religious commitments are explored and commitments made. The microsystem continues through life and will be either a safe haven for intimate relationships and a common life shared with those most dear, or a setting that is filled with conflict and stress, exacerbating one's needs for security and intimacy.

The second setting, one I choose to call *regional* (both mesosytsem and exosystem) include the extended family, nursery care, schools, clubs and teams, religious communities, settings for work and career, places to have a family, settings in which to exercise our political views, and ultimately places to retire. Often these regions have a distinctive subculture and a way of seeing the world. Not infrequently these subcultures and cultures take the form of an exosystem with forces of influence in which we do not participate and that impact us in ways that are beyond our awareness. In the mobile American culture, we frequently change these settings as we move through life, but often look back to them as home. These settings are life-giving when they have the following conditions:

1. These settings should provide the growing child with an appropriate balance of freedom and structure, room to develop autonomy and independence, and boundaries to prevent harmful and self-destructive behavior.
2. The settings should provide a way to develop relationships and begin to explore one's sexuality. It is in these settings that one begins intimate relationships that may lead to life partnerships.
3. These settings should provide opportunities to learn about the culture in which one lives, the larger world in all of its many dimensions, and to develop skills that will lead to meaningful work. In fact, it is regional settings that often become the place in which one selects a career path and moves through the stages of a career, although careers may be lived out nationally and internationally.
4. It is often in these settings that an individual moves through the stages of moral development and makes choices regarding life's meaning and religious beliefs and practices. Ideally, resources such as social groups and religious communities are available to assist an individual in these critical areas of development.

It is in our regional settings where most of us grow up and move into adulthood with all the challenges and rewards of life partnerships, careers, and the expression of our sense of vocation, meaning, and deepest values.

Still another setting, the *national*, has characteristics of a macrosystem with overarching patterns of structure and energy that shape our development and the ways we live our lives. We are keenly aware of the national context in which we live, and we know it has a powerful shaping influence on us. We are reminded daily of the challenges inherent in this setting and wish for a nation that has the following characteristics:

1. We want a nation that is just, that gives us the security to know that we have access to adequate food, high quality health care, opportunities for good schooling, and protection and equal rights under the law.
2. We want a nation at peace and to know that we are safe from external threat.
3. We want a nation that has an economy in which we are assured of good employment and a high quality of life.
4. We want a nation that has a promising future, one that will be a healthy context for our children.

**Section III** — The Development of Love

As national elections occur, these issues become central in our voting decisions and our desires for national setting in which there is potential for the good life.

A final setting that has a profound shaping influence on our development is *global in character* and it too has the overarching patterns of the macrosystem. At a minimum, we hope for a world that has the following characteristics:

1. It should be a world in which all of the people are relatively free from the threat of violent conflict and war.
2. It should be a world with adequate global infrastructure to address natural disasters and bring immediate relief for the victims.
3. It should be a world in which there is a more equitable distribution of wealth, one that is in the process of eliminating poverty and all of its harmful consequences.
4. It should be a world in which the basic needs of all, needs for good nutrition and safe water, a quality education, adequate health care, and fair treatment under law are present.

Without these conditions, our world will remain conflicted and filled with many who suffer daily. The majority of the world's population will not easily become people who will experience the joys and challenges of love and compassion nor will they be able to participate in giving love and compassion to others.

## CONCLUSION: DESIRED OUTCOMES

In speaking about love and compassion, one runs the risk of uttering empty and hackneyed platitudes, a risk about which I am keenly aware. I am also conscious of the need to take the generalizations that may appear to be clichés to the level of practice. Our goal in Section IV will be to speak directly to the practice of love in the several contexts of our lives, by speaking about love and compassion in the primary settings of life, their presence in regional and national settings, and then addressing the very complex issue of the place of love and compassion on the global scale. Our present goal in this section is to examine the ways that we can become more loving and compassionate people by looking at shaping influences in our lives (nurture). We will also explore our natural endowment and how it determines that our basic needs and physical characteristics may contribute to our capacity to care (nature). We will then identify some ways that we can take the initiative to become more loving and compassionate people, the desired outcome of our endeavor.

Before we move to the question of nature in the nature-nurture continuum, I want to suggest a simple design for moving toward our desired outcome. What I say is partly personal and has shaped my writing and living. It is present as well in the vast literature on love, and it is certainly encouraged by those who engage in the healing and transformative professions. I will come back to the formula from time to time and want it to be up front as we develop our theme. It has three steps or levels, not necessarily in successive order and often intertwined. They are essential to our progress toward our desired outcomes and might be summarized as *head, heart,* and *hand.*

The first is that we move toward becoming caring people as we gain knowledge and become informed about the needs of individuals, societies, nations, and the world. We need to understand the intensity and complexity of these needs if we are to make a loving response to them. Our minds (*head*) must be engaged for us to comprehend both the universality of the needs and ways that we might assume responsibility for them in a tangible way. Without this knowledge, our tendencies will likely be to stay focused on meeting our own needs. It may take the form of a selfish quest for wealth, reputation, and power, goals that are constantly placed before us as the way to happiness. But happiness does not consist in the abundance of things possessed or power and prestige. It consists rather in the quality of our lives and the character of our behavior.

A second level of response is that of our *heart*; the way the needs of those near us, those in our larger circle, and indeed the needs of people across the world get inside of us and to our emotions. My own movement toward an endeavor to become a more compassionate person picked up speed when I went beyond a basic knowledge of the suffering in the world, started to see it first hand, and then began to care about it. I developed feelings of love, compassion, caring, and empathy for those within my circle, and as I traveled the world, I was put in touch with the devastating character of poverty, the tragic circumstances of people who experienced natural disaster, and those who were victims of injustice and war. My heart was changed and must continue to be changed daily.

I then began to act in the ways that were possible and appropriate for me, and ways that were not always easy and convenient. I was motivated. I found that I could use my *hands*, and that I could live with the fact that they might occasionally get "dirty" if I engaged in caring behavior. I made mistakes, had inappropriate assumptions, and occasionally made poor judgments, but I ventured out into the world. My primary way became teaching and providing pastoral care and using whatever financial resources to which I had access. I participated on boards and committees of organizations that engaged in helping people improve the quality of their lives. I offered what I could.[28] Head, heart, hand; learning, feeling, doing, integrated; the way forward.

## STUDY RESOURCES

### Discussion Questions

1. In your judgment, are we more shaped in our development by our environment or by the way we are made?
2. Are you optimistic about our capacity to reach levels of maturity that enable us to act freely and responsibly and to become loving and compassionate people?
3. Which one of the various representatives of theories of human development do you find most persuasive? Least persuasive?
4. How much are we influenced by macrosystems, the overarching patterns of ideology and social institutions common to a particular culture or subculture?
5. How might we begin to engage our head, heart, and hand in becoming more caring and compassionate people?

### Key Terms and Concepts

- *Ecological Perspective:* the view that human growth and development are shaped by all aspects of the interaction between humans and their environment.
- *Exosystem:* the view in human development theory that humans are often shaped by influences in which they do not actively participate.

---

28. Mark 12:42, "two small copper coins."

- *Unconscious:* a term used by Sigmund Freud that describes repressed wishes and needs that are prevented from surfacing because of fear and possible discomfort.
- *Developmental Crisis:* a term used by Erik Erikson to describe the challenge in stages of development to decide to move in a healthy way toward maturity or to resort to a more negative state of being.
- *Post-Conventional:* a term used by Lawrence Kohlberg to describe when a person makes a moral judgment based on self-determined principles.
- *Synthetic-Conventional:* a stage of faith described by James Fowler when the adolescent accepts third person or conventional views about meaning and religious faith.

## Suggestions for Reference and Reading

1. Bronfenbrenner, Urie, *The Ecology of Human Development: Experiments by Nature and Design.* Cambridge, MA: Harvard University Press, 1979.
2. Erikson, Erik H., *Identity: Youth and Crisis.* New York: W. W. Norton & Company, 1968.
3. Fowler, James W., *Stages of Faith: The Psychology of Human Development and the Quest for Meaning.* San Francisco: Harper & Row Publishers, 1981.
4. Freud, Sigmund, *A General Introduction to Psychoanalysis.* New York: Permabooks, 1958, first published in 1924.
5. Kohlberg, Lawrence, *The Philosophy of Moral Development.* New York: Harper & Row, 1981.
6. Piaget, Jean, *Science of Education and the Psychology of the Child.* New York: Viking, 1969.
7. Woolfolk, Anita, *Educational Psychology,* 11th edition. Upper Saddle River, NJ: Merrill, 2010.

# 6

# Endowed for Love

## NATURE'S SIDE OF THE NATURE-NURTURE CONTINUUM

IN CHAPTER FIVE, THERE was an exploration of the ways that our capacity to love, be compassionate, and express empathy are shaped by the nurture we receive through the early years of our lives and then enhanced in our adult years as our relationships and circumstances are supportive and life-giving. Wise and caring nurture has a profoundly positive influence on our maturity and well-being, and these qualities in turn enable us to be compassionate people. My thesis is that our capacity to love is significantly increased as we grow and develop into mature persons. The capacity to express all forms of love depends to a large extent on one's sense of integrity, the ability to wisely manage stress and anxiety, one's inner contentment and sense of well-being, and the freedom from the controlling influence of our needs for affirmation and security. In fact, just a few decades ago, many social scientists and advocates for the life of love would have placed the primary emphasis on the way we interact with and are formed by our environment as the source of our ability to love and to become a person for others.

While few would discount environmental factors in forming us, there has been a turn toward giving more attention to nature in the nature-nurture continuum. Both have been present in understanding human development, but new scholarship and theories on the natural science side of the ledger have generated a renewed appreciation for the way humans are formed and why they behave as they do. I have been especially conscious of the extraordinary forming influence of nature as I have observed the growth and development of our adopted grandson, a boy with special needs who struggles with being developmentally delayed, with Attention-Deficit-Hyperactivity-Disorder, and with being on the autism continuum. The best nurture will help but not remove the need for medical intervention to manage his behavior.

The national and international discussion of the increase in the number of children who are autistic is but one example of the attention being given to how we develop in reference to our natural inheritance. The devastating disease, Alzheimer's, dramatically affecting human behavior, has also brought the reality of natural conditioning and brain health to the forefront of our attention. Over the past decade, both the technical journals and the more popular news magazines have pointed to our genetic structure, and words such as genomes and bi-polar, and expressions such as "the way we are wired" or "the way we are programmed," and initials such as ADHD and DNA have become a part of our conversations. *Time* magazine has had a series of articles on topics that in previous generations might have been discussed in reference to the influence of our environment. Among them are: October 25, 2004, "The God Gene"; January 17, 2005, "The Science of Happiness"; and June 6, 2011, "The Science of Optimism." Few have questioned that romantic love has a physical component, but it was emphasized in *National Geographic*, February, 2006 in the article entitled, "Love: The Chemical Reaction."

A more technical and scientific study by three medical doctors begins a discussion about love with a chapter entitled "The Hearts Castle: Science Joins the Search for Love."[1] In a newly revised book *The New Psychology of Love*, the lead articles are about biological theories of love with special attention to evolution.[2] Michael Dowd, a clergy person turned scientist, writes in his book on evolution about evolutionary spirituality.[3] Doc Childre and Howard Martin write in *The HeartMath Solution* that appropriate care for our hearts can help us "maintain emotional clarity in the midst of chaos" and assist us to "achieve peak mental and intuitive performance."[4]

While on leave in Princeton during the fall of 2010, I audited a course on brain science and became more keenly aware of the ways our brain

---

1. Lewis, et al., *A General Theory of Love*, 3–15.
2. Sternberg and Weis, eds., *The New Psychology of Love*.
3. *Thank God for Evolution*, 209–48.
4. Cover page.

# Section III — The Development of Love

grants or blocks our capacity to love and show compassion. Daniel Amen, a medical doctor has made brain research more accessible to lay readers and speaks about how it is possible to "enhance your brain to improve your work, love, and spiritual life."[5] Matthew Alper speaks directly about "the God part of the brain" and argues for a scientific interpretation of human spirituality and God.[6] In an extraordinary study Andrew Newberg and his colleague Mark Robert Waldman speak about new research that demonstrates "how God changes your brain."[7] A book by John Medina, a molecular biologist at the University of Washington, has translated brain research to a very accessible level in his book *Brain Rules*.[8] A recent book by David Eagleman entitled *Incognito: The Secret Lives of the Brain* is a fascinating study of the complexity of the brain.[9]

The goal in this chapter is to take these extraordinary research-based materials and the many other studies that are available and apply them to our understanding of lovescapes. In particular the intention is to draw upon this information as a guide for exploring the ways that our physiology, as well as environment, shape our capacity (or block our ability) to love, show compassion, and genuinely care for others. I also want to investigate how these findings might suggest ways of enhancing our capacity to be more loving people. It is not easy to pull this complex and large amount of material together in concise and well-ordered categories. This material draws upon an abundance of studies in diverse fields such as biology, sociobiology, evolution, neurology, physiology, behavioral psychology, psychiatry, psychotherapy, and religious practices. But, as I have done previously, I will use the goal of understanding our capacity to love as a way of classifying and describing this material. I will place it in three broad categories or models:

1. Love and the model of evolutionary biology and sociobiology, giving special attention to evolutionary theories of human development.
2. Love and the model of heart health based primarily on the work of the Institute of HeartMath.

---

5. *Healing the Hardware of the Soul*, on cover.

6. *The God Part of the Brain: A Scientific Interpretation of Human Spirituality and God*.

7. *How God Changes Your Brain: Breakthrough Findings from a Leading Neuroscientist*.

8. Medina, *Brain Rules: 12 Principles for Surviving and Thriving at Work, Home, and School*.

9. Published by Pantheon, 2011.

3. Love and the model of brain health, or how the brain functions in reference to our ability to care wisely and well for others.

## THE EVOLUTIONARY BIOLOGY AND SOCIOBIOLOGY MODEL

Most of the views about love in the category of evolutionary biology and sociobiology deal with that dimension of love having to do "with the relationships of humans to each other, and in particular with the dyadic relationships that two humans form."[10] The discussion of love in these disciplines tends to focus on romantic love.[11] The energy driving these relationships is a bias that serves evolutionary and genetic interests and in particular ones that facilitate reproduction and survival. It assumes that romantic love is an instinctive part of human nature linked to our physiology and present for the perpetuation of the race.[12]

Human beings come together in dyadic relationships and, as the two people who form the couple interacts, they face a variety of challenges related to reproduction and survival. At the beginning they face the decision of mate-seeking, and from there the problems move to mate retention and parental care, with each phase requiring a different form of love. For example, the love one feels for one's partner is different than the love one feels for one's child, and the love one has for another caregiver in the household may require an alternative type of love.[13]

Douglas T. Kenrick lists five aspects of love in what he calls "the dynamical evolutionary model."[14] They are:

1. At its core, love is a set of evolved decision biases, and these decision biases are designed to promote behaviors that enhance reproduction and survival.

2. These decision biases are not always the same and often differ between men and women. It is often the case that women make a higher investment than men in the relationship and sustaining the social bond.

---

10. Weis, *The New Psychology of Love*, 1.
11. See Fisher, *Why We Love: The Nature and Chemistry of Romantic Love*.
12. See Young-Bruel, *Where Do We Fall When We Fall in Love?*
13. Weis in *The New Psychology of Love*, 4.
14. "The Dynamical Evolutionary View of Love" in *The New Psychology of Love*, 16–17.

## Section III — The Development of Love

3. The human mind is sufficiently adept at selecting different decision biases in the several domains of social life. Various problems require different solutions. For example, mate retention may require a different form of love than caring for offspring.

4. The decisions one makes interact in a dynamic way with the other individuals within the social bond. There is often an "if-then" construct as exchanges with other individuals determine which option an individual may chose.

5. Cultural norms also have an influence on the decision biases with cross-cultural variation as, for example, in the case of the cultural approval of polygamy. However, even with the cultural differences, the decision biases still reflect the goals of reproduction and survival.

Another way of viewing these decision biases is through the lens of behavioral systems.[15] As one observes the dynamic interaction that takes place within the life of a couple, one observes at least three primary behavioral systems: attachment, caregiving, and sex. The goal of the attachment system, centered in the love within the dyadic relationship, is to provide maximum security by ensuring that one stays close to another who can provide a good support and protection system. It is worth staying attached for the sake of security. The relationship may be worth nurturing for a variety of reasons, but security will always be there; divorce is not generally a good option although at times necessary. Attachment ensures that there will be someone who can provide care when threats are encountered.

The goals of the caregiving system are designed to provide the support and care that are required when there are needs present in and threats to the offspring. The system may include others beside the parental couple, perhaps a grandparent or a baby sitter. In time, it will extend into the community in schools and other agencies that provide necessary support and learning. It may even be said that this component of caregiving has an altruistic motive in that it is focused on another person's well-being and development.[16]

The sexual system has as its primary goal the passing on of the genes of the couple to the next generation. So in mate selection, one carefully

---

15. Shaver and Mikulincer, "A Behavior Systems Approach to Romantic Love Relationships: Attachment, Caregiving, and Sex" in *The New Psychology of Love*, 35–64.

16. Others argue against the use of the word altruism, suggesting that the motivation is still driven by survival See Post, et al. in "Part II: Human Motivation and Action" in *Altruism and Altruistic Love*, 69–142.

"shops" for a mate whose characteristics are healthy and attractive. These traits may include such qualities as:

- Displaying reproductive potential
- Providing sexual availability
- Promising sexual faithfulness and commitment
- Showing signs of health and actions that lead to successful reproduction
- Demonstrating evidence of being an effective parent[17]

It should not be assumed in this brief summary of the discussion of love in evolutionary biology and sociobiology that there is a clear consensus among scholars about the unfolding patterns of evolution and their purpose, although there is little disagreement about its influence in shaping human behavior. There are many questions and issues that continue to be debated. One question that arises in terms of our discussion of love is whether there really is an element of altruism, freely chosen behavior for the good of another, within human relationships. The distinguished scholar Edward O. Wilson makes his position clear and focuses the debate. He claims: "Human behavior—like the deepest capacities for emotional response which derive and guide it—is the circuitous technique by which human genetic material has been and will be kept intact. Morality has no other demonstrable function."[18] Can ethical teaching be reduced to evolutionary biology? A related question that arises is similar in character. It is whether human behavior is genetically determined, and if so, does such a thesis rule out genuinely unselfish other-directed actions, especially as these actions extend well beyond the near and dear of the immediate family. A brief survey of these views and their implications for loving behavior may be helpful at this point.

Let's look first at Darwinian naturalism, which begins with the claim that all organisms including human beings are products of evolution and natural selection. There is a struggle for existence or more accurately for reproduction, and there is heritable variation or natural selection that promotes characteristics that aid in the battle to survive and reproduce. At certain times this behavior may take the form of cooperation and the behavior may be helpful to others. But it is a stretch to call this behavior

---

17. Buss, "The Evolution of Love" in *The New Psychology of Love*, 66. See also Sternberg, *Cupid's Arrow*, 53–57.

18. *On Human Nature*, 167. Quoted by Schloss in Post, et al., *Altruism and Altruistic Love*, 145.

## Section III — The Development of Love

altruistic in the sense of giving and caring without any thought of reward and because it is the good and right thing to do. It is better described as acting for the good of another because "it furthers one's own survival and/or reproductive ends. There is absolutely no implication of consciousness or intentionality, and often, of course, it is fully realized that the biological 'altruist' is anything but a thinker, or a free moral agent."[19] In short, when humans find themselves in a position when it pays to help others, a kind of loving behavior might be practiced. It has to have a pay-off and serve the individual.[20]

The current views of the place of loving behavior in the general category of evolutionary biology and sociobiology might be summarized as follows, knowing full well that there are different "spins" that may be given to any generalizations that might be stated:

1. The initial formulations in evolutionary biology and sociobiology were inclined to be reductionistic and deterministic, but current research suggests a more nuanced understanding of the place of loving behavior in these fields, allowing for a kind of "metaphorical" altruism.

2. But even with sacrificial actions on behalf of others that are not totally controlled by reproduction and genetic structures, there will still be the primary pattern of human behavior to act in ways that might be described in a broad-based evolutionary pattern.[21]

3. It follows that the human tendency to behave in a way that promotes reproduction and survival does not necessarily exclude genuine other-regarding motivations and patterns of ethical behavior.

4. In fact, there is a growing openness in evolutionary views that allow for and describe patterns of human behavior that are cooperative and extend beyond the family to others outside the circle of nearness. However, the moral teaching to love one's enemy is not as easily included in this trend unless "loving" one's enemy heals the conflict and the enemy ceases to be an enemy.

---

19. Buse, "A Darwinian Naturalist's Perspective on Altruism" in Post, et al., *Altruism and Altruistic Love*, 153.

20. It is interesting that John Rawls in *A Theory of Justice* leans in this direction with his view that justice is fairness.

21. Dowd in *Thank God for Evolution* moves easily to saying that there is no essential conflict between an evolutionary view of human development and altruistic behavior. See 209–30.

5. So we might say that what we call altruistic behavior in the context of biological evolution and sociobiology is complex, layered, and needs a range of disciplinary approaches to be fully understood and appreciated.[22]

## THE HEART HEALTH MODEL

It is interesting to observe that love and compassion have been associated with the heart for centuries. This association of the heart with love has existed and continues to be present in many cultures and religious traditions,[23] and it was certainly central to the biblical tradition. The word *heart* is mentioned 814 times in the Hebrew Bible and often in reference to the seat of motivation and the commitment to be a compassionate person. The Gospel of Matthew describes Jesus quoting the Hebrew Bible's command that we are to love God with our whole heart (Deut 6:5, Matt 22:27). The passage implies that a good heart is the oasis of love. In fact, the heart was viewed as the center of emotions, feelings, moods, passions, and even the center of our will and intentions. God is even said to have a heart, and it is frequently linked with divine love and compassion for humans who struggle and suffer. It was a metaphorical way, in biblical times, of speaking about the center or core of a person, and to have a good heart would lead to a happy, healthy, and loving life that would be pleasing to God. Again, Matthew's Gospel reports that Jesus says at the beginning of the Sermon on the Mount: "Blessed are those with a pure heart, for they shall see God" (Matt 5:8).

It is quite common in the lyrics of song, the scenes of the visual arts, and the literature of story and poem that heart and love are associated. "Love is the heart in blossom," Myrtle Reed reminds us.[24] The story of love and the heart in the arts is a long one, not possible to tell here, but it is possible to illustrate the point by referring to Carson McCullers' poignant

---

22. Schloss, in Post, et al., *Altruism and Altruistic Love*, 243–44.

23. It is profoundly present in the Buddhist tradition in form of compassion. See for example the Dalai Lama's book entitled *The Good Heart*. See as well the use of the term *heart* in Islam in the book by Nasr, *The Heart of Islam: Enduring Values for Humanity*, in which the author speaks directly about the centrality of love in Islam and points to one of the names of God as *al-Wadud*, best translated as love, 209–15.

24. Quoted in Stein and Neighbors, eds., *The Treasure of the Love*, 8. Henry Wadsworth Longfellow, quoted in the same volume, 37, reminds us "The heart hath its own memory, like the mind, and in it are enshrined the precious keepsakes, into which is wrought the giver's loving thought."

**Section III** — The Development of Love

novel, first published in 1940, *The Heart is a Lonely Hunter.* In this story we identify with a young woman and her contemporaries searching for love in many forms, some harmful and some helpful. Our "hearts" do search for a satisfying and lasting love.

Less profoundly and at times sentimentally, we see yearly the symbol of the heart, often a warm pink or a passionate red, as it has become the dominant visual expression of the day we devote to human love, St. Valentine's Day. It is not altogether a surprise that what was and is metaphorical language in the expression of heart-felt love in art, literature, song, and practice has now become a scientific orientation. From the earliest days of medical practice, the heart was understood as a central part of the body, central to the circulation of life-giving blood. With the rise of scientific research, this assumption about the heart was confirmed, and we now devote enormous amounts of money to heart research. Medical doctors counsel patients to take care of their hearts through healthy practices of diet and exercise.

In 1999, a book written by Doc Childre and Howard Martin with Donna Beech, entitled *The HeartMath Solution,* attracted a great deal of attention because it took the sound advice of the medical profession to take care of your heart beyond good physical health. It addressed the question of how the heart may also be related to our emotional and mental health. In this book, the heart is understood as more than just a physical pump supplying blood to the body, but the "core of our body and the core of how we think and feel."[25] It therefore should be viewed as not just an organ that is part of the solution to staying physically healthy, but part of the solution to staying emotionally healthy as well. Doc Childre and Howard Martin maintain that it is the central rhythmic force in our bodies, and, as we intentionally care for it, it can become a source of emotional health and well-being.

HeartMath places a strong emphasis on the interconnectedness, even integration of mind and matter. We care for the heart, not just by diet and exercise, but by the expression of positive thoughts and especially love, compassion, and gratitude, all of which improve our physiological condition. In turn, our healthy physiology contributes to our emotional health and our capacity to be loving and compassionate,[26] a point of view that

---

25. Stephan Rechschaffen in the Foreword of *The Heartmath Solution,* xi.

26. There is now an Institute of HeartMath that provides a range of services and information about pathways to emotional health. See http://www.heartmathstore.com. There are many other initiatives that are comparable to HeartMath, but this initiative is illustrative of the range of heart health endeavors.

informs our particular concern about the way that the human capacity to love is influenced by a healthy heart.

At the center of the research in this movement is the heart-brain connection.[27] The HeartMath proponents maintain that the heart is not passive and merely receives messages from the brain in the form of neural signals. They maintain that the heart may send just as many signals to the brain as the brain sends to the heart, if not more, signals which have the capacity to increase our cognitive faculties such as attention, perception, memory, and problem-solving. Not only does the heart respond to the brain, but the brain continuously responds to the heart. The research shows that different patterns of heart activity (which accompany different emotional states) have an impact on cognitive and emotional functions. For example, under stress and with accompanying negative emotions, the brain's high cognitive functions are limited. We think less clearly, do not remember or learn as effectively, and are less able to make wise decisions.

By contrast, the more calm and stable we are, the heart's input to the brain helps facilitate effective cognitive functions and reinforces positive feelings and emotional stability. Learning how to maintain stability and coherence with positive emotions not only improves our physical well-being but profoundly effects how we perceive, think, feel, and perform. The key or "solution" is to increase the normalcy of the heart beat rhythm (HRV or heart rate variability). The way this is done is learning how to adapt effectively to stress and environmental demands.

In general, it is possible to say that emotional stress—including emotions such as anger, frustration, and anxiety—causes the heart rhythm patterns to be irregular and erratic. The opposite is also the case; positive emotions send a very different signal throughout our body. A key term used by the HeartMath researchers is coherence, which they define as "the state when the heart, mind, and emotions are in energetic alignment and cooperation."[28] When we have positive emotions such as joy, love, and compassion, our heart rhythm pattern becomes ordered and smooth, or *coherent*. We feel positive emotions and our whole system works better.

The HeartMath approach to health and well-being is specific and practical. It has several steps that can be used by those seeking a more

27. I am dependent upon articles which are available from the HeartMath Institute, and in particular one entitled "The Science Behind the emWave, Desktop & emWave2 Products."

28. This definition or its equivalent is used frequently in HeartMath publications, and this particular version is provided in a "BePeace" publication that helps children to increase their learning abilities.

## Section III — The Development of Love

focused and coherent life. The first step is to become more aware of heart intelligence and practice reducing stress and increasing the expression of positive emotions such as appreciation, compassion, care, and love. We must learn to listen to our hearts and use the power tools of the heart, which in HeartMath are primarily love and its many cognates such as care, compassion, acceptance (being nonjudgmental), and forgiveness.

A second step is to acknowledge the partnership between the heart and the brain, and then consciously allow both to work in a complementary fashion. Positive feelings will increase our cognitive abilities, and clearer thinking and better decision making will reduce our stress and anxiety. One practice suggested in this partnership is called Freeze-Frame. It is a strategy of pausing before expressing an emotional impulse caused by conflict or frustration, and then selecting a more positive strategy for expressing the emotion and resolving the issue.[29]

A third step is to consciously develop coherence by reducing negative emotions such as anger and increasing positive emotions such as appreciation. This can be done in many ways; for example, paying attention to the positive guidance of the heart, managing our "energy accounts" (not wasting energy on the negative emotions and insoluble problems), and the common practice of breathing exercises.

Still another step to take or attitude to cultivate is commitment, called in *The HeartMath Solution* a "Cut-Thru to Emotional Maturity."[30] This chapter is followed by another one titled "Heart Lock-In" that also calls for disciplined intentionality in order to make progress.

A final point of guidance is to take this learning and emerging health insights and apply them beyond individual growth and development to social situations. These practices of love and appreciation can be applied in the family, the workplace, and in the associations and organizations to which we all belong. The practices can also be taught to children and applied in a school setting, and evidence indicates that children make dramatic gains in their learning abilities.

My initial tendency in my exposure to HeartMath was to be a bit skeptical. Was it a new fad that promised too much and did not demand the usual hard work required for genuine and lasting progress? Was it just another approach that sought to be a commercial success? I confess

---

29. *The HeartMath Solution* has a number of practical guides and worksheets that enable a practitioner to monitor progress. For example, there is a "Freeze-Frame Worksheet," an "Asset/Deficit Balance Sheet," and an "Overcare Inventory Sheet" among others.

30. Chapter Nine, 183–210.

to these early reservations about the HeartMath approach to increased health and well-being. It sounded a bit repetitive (practice the breathing practices found in Buddhist meditation), too simple and a bit "warm and fuzzy" (don't yield to negative emotions and practice positive emotions of love and compassion), and not really addressing deep emotional distress and illness (just do it). But I have come away, after my immersion in both the literature and the practices, as a supporter of a point of view and set of practices that can have a very positive influence on one's life. It does not do everything to heal us and take us to maturity, nor does it promise to eliminate life's problems. But it does have a solid research base, which increases its credibility, and there is a large group of people who openly speak about how they have improved their health and sense of well-being by using HeartMath strategies. It can help increase one's capacity to be a truly coherent person, one with inner serenity, a mature balance of head and heart, a keen sense of social responsibility, and a commitment to be a person for others committed to a life of love and compassion. The movement does provide one more glimpse of the vast geography of the lovescapes we are exploring.

## THE BRAIN MODEL

The heart research done by the HeartMath Institute and by numerous other universities and research hospitals has provided excellent guidance for an endless number of people seeking to live a healthier and happier life. We have learned that our care for the heart is an integral part of the nature component in the nature-nurture continuum that shapes our growth toward maturity. Equally informative, and perhaps attracting even more attention, has been the extraordinary developments in brain research, another part of the nature side of the equation. We have learned that the heart is more than just a physical pump supplying blood to the body but also a core ingredient in our quest for emotional health and well-being. So too we learn in the brain research of recent decades that the brain is not exclusively for cognitive functions, but also for improving the quality of life—in our work, in our relationships, and in our spiritual quest for meaning and values. For our purpose of exploring the geography of love, we learn that our heart and our capacity to love are interconnected; and we also learn that our brain can have a similar role, enabling us to be more loving and compassionate. It is to this topic we now turn.

## Section III — The Development of Love

Perhaps the best place to start is with a brief explanation of the various parts of the brain. One popular image of the heart is that of a sophisticated pump that receives, cleanses, and sends out life-giving blood, sustaining health and improving the quality of our lives. The popular image for the brain is that of a complex computer with several parts each ideally contributing to its smooth and efficient functioning and empowering our cognitive capabilities. Neither image is fully reflective of the many functions of these organs, but they do point us in the right direction as we seek to understand their many and varied contributions to our health and well-being.

Different starting points tend to influence descriptions of the brain, with evolutionary biologists viewing the development of the brain as "a story full of starts, setbacks, compromises, and blind alleys, as generations of organisms adapt to fluctuating conditions."[31] Other reputable scientists, not denying the evolutionary pattern of development, stress the remarkable ability of the brain to "house" the soul, that is, to be the means of guiding human beings in finding purpose in life, selecting foundational values, and enabling humans to love. They tend to side with Shakespeare, maintaining that "the brain is the soul's fragile dwelling place."[32]

Reputable brain scientists, regardless of their different starting assumptions, agree that the brain is made up of three major components or sub-brains, with each being the product of a separate age in evolutionary development. It is not uncommon to speak about the triune brain as a means of explaining how different love impulses arise from the ancient history of human development.[33] The oldest part of the brain is called the reptilian brain. It is an extension of the spinal cord and has basic functions. This part of the brain serves as the control center that supplies neurons that activate breathing, swallowing, heartbeat, the visual tracking system, and the reaction center. The reptilian part of the brain also ensures survival (enables swift reaction to danger) and sustains life. The name, reptilian, was chosen because we share this structure with reptiles, and it constitutes the complete brain of reptiles. They do not have a limbic brain which is the center of emotions, for example, and therefore reptiles do not have an emotional life. The reptilian brain does enable basic interactions such as displays of aggression, desire for mating, and defense, and

---

31. Lewis, et al., *A General Theory of Love*, 21.

32. Quoted by Amen in *Healing the Hardware of the Soul*, Chapter One, "The Brain is the Soul's Fragile Dwelling Place," 3–17.

33. *A General Theory of Love*, 21.

its various functions explain in part the battles over mates and territory common among vertebrates.

A second part of the brain is called the limbic brain because it is possible to see a line of demarcation between this part of the brain and the reptilian part of the brain.[34] The limbic brain sits on or drapes over the reptilian brain, and has a number components including: amygdala, hippocampus, hypothalamus, and thalamus.[35] These components of the limbic brain have specific functions as for example the amygdala which serves as the source of our emotions. The limbic brain evolved as mammals split off from the reptilian line, and it gave this new line of creatures the capacity to give birth to live offspring, and then to nurse, defend, and rear them in their immature state. It was a major step forward, indeed a social revolution. Vocal communication appeared and developed, and mothers could play with their offspring. Care, communication, and play evolved, although more primitive instincts of survival and aggression remained.

In evolutionary time, another part of the brain developed called the neocortex brain. It is the largest of the three parts of the brain, and is much larger in mammals of recent origin with the neocortex of humans expanding well beyond the size of the other parts of the brain. It fits across the top of the other parts of the brain and has extraordinary neural functions and capacities. It is in the neocortex that reasoning, speaking, and writing originate. It makes possible, for instance, what we humans assume is a simple function but what in fact is a quite complicated feat such as reaching for and drinking a glass of water. The neocortex sparks the intention of reaching for the glass, guiding one in filling it with water, and then raising it to one's mouth. It is also the neocortex that enables one to express appreciation with words about the satisfaction of a cool drink. It then sends the message for us to move on to the next item on the day's agenda, and we continue to function as a human being.

It is important to note that a brain composed of three parts with separate functions does not always act harmoniously and in synch. On occasion, it can function like a committee made up of three people with different points of view, one full of passion, one being very reasonable, and still another lost in thought and not persuaded that the passionate suggestions or the reasoned alternatives should guide the decisions and the report due next week. The brain, like the committee, swirls with

---

34. *Limbus* is the Latin word for edge, margin, or border. See Lewis et al., *A General Theory of Love*, 24.

35. Newberg and Waldman, *How God Changes Your Brain*, 43–45.

## Section III — The Development of Love

interactions, some growing out of those parts of the brain that evolved earlier and which might resist the force of reason articulated in the symbols of words. When it comes to the human feeling of love, the brain is central to its expression, but its parts are not always in agreement that this emotion and possible subsequent caring action are what should be expressed.

The structure of the human brain raises a variety of questions as we attempt to understand the value of love in human experience and how it can become a guiding force in our lives. One question is how love and the brain are related. From what part of the brain does the impulse of love originate? A second question arises from our understanding of love as a "many-splendored thing." What kind of love are we talking about when we link the emotion of love to the brain? A third question is how we might improve the health of our brains in order to increase our capacity to be loving and compassionate people. Let's take these questions one at a time.

If our brains are a network of neurons, with the various parts evolving across evolutionary time, then we answer the first question by saying that love may originate in different parts of the brain although the signals sent from different parts of the brain may not always be in agreement. The simple answer is that the source and sustainer of the various types of love come from both the limbic and neocortex parts of the brain, with the limbic sending messages about caring for offspring and feelings of attraction and attachment. Then the neocortex will come into play, enabling the loving response to be more complex, requiring reason and speech. The mating impulse, which may arise in the reptilian brain, in our judgment, should not be called a loving impulse; it is not driven by emotion and is basically instinctive.[36] We understand love as an expression of an emotion that cares for the other and one often guided by reason. We know that emotion stretches across the brain, and the various forms of love, as we use the term in English, are primarily rooted in both the limbic and neocortex parts of the brain.

This basic answer to question one leads directly, as we have already implied, to the second question about the meaning of love. We have described love as a range of attitudes, feelings, and actions that include both attraction and empathic care, and we observe these feelings originating in

---

36. There are those who might argue that the instinct to mate is a form of love. Freud, for example, might speak about love for humanity, love between children and parents and between friends as "sexual" and rooted in our instincts. See Nicholi in *The Question of God*, 16–186. Richard Dawkins attributes what we call love to our genetic structure. See *The God Delusion*, 184–87. Dawkins makes a similar point in his book, *The Selfish Gene*, New Edition, 140–65.

the brain. It is therefore possible to say that we are hardwired (endowed) for love, especially that part of love that is based in attraction and providing care and protection for offspring. As mentioned above, it would be hard to use the word *love* to describe the impulses coming from the reptilian part of the brain. Emotions do not originate in that part of the brain, and when we speak about love, we speak about an emotion and also possible actions of compassion that grow out of the emotion. Feelings of attraction and protection may emerge from the limbic brain, but sacrificial action on behalf of another may require a more reasoned and carefully articulated and understood value, intentionally chosen. This activity would occur in the neocortex.

This basic frame of reference can be used to answer our third question, namely, how we might improve our brain health in ways that will increase our capacity to be more loving and compassionate people. There are different strategies for improving brain health, and they might be categorized in two broad approaches, one that is focused in practices that keep our brain functioning well, and one more targeted to healing the brain. These two approaches frequently overlap, but motivations behind them differ slightly, with one aimed at preventative practices and one recognizing that through inheritance and environmental conditioning, the brain may not be functioning in ways that lead to health and happiness.

John Medina, a developmental molecular biologist, has written from both perspectives. He suggests positive practices that improve the health of the brain, but also writes about the challenges of aging, the debilitating affliction of depression, and the relationship of the brain to Alzheimer's and ways of treating AIDS. He has been a regular consultant in the field of education and given special attention to the relationship between neurology and education. His writing has a way of cutting through both the complexity of the subject and discerning between fact and hype. In his book, *Brain Rules*, he introduces the reader to "12 principles for surviving and thriving at work, home, and school." His list, which I have reduced to 10, includes the following:

1. His first observation is that exercise increases the health of our brains. He recommends that we engage in aerobic exercise at least twice a week, and as we do, it gets blood to our brain which channels glucose for energy and oxygen to absorb toxic electrons that are left over. Regular exercise can increase the efficiency of our brain and reduce the risk of dementia and Alzheimer's.[37]

---

37. *Brain Rules*, 28.

## Section III — The Development of Love

2. In addition, he suggests that we inform ourselves about how our brain evolved, acknowledge the three parts of the brain and their respective functions, and understand how conscious choice can help them work together in harmonious ways.[38] Impulses emerging from the reptilian brain may not lead to good decisions and need the guidance of the neocortex.

3. He suggests that we take into account that every brain is wired differently and develops at a different pace. We need to recognize that we and those around us learn differently and that there are a number of ways of being intelligent. We do not nor do others necessarily have a disability simply because we learn differently and operate in ways that vary from a certain norm.[39]

4. He underlines how important it is to keep the brain stimulated. The fact is that we get bored easily and cease to concentrate and therefore need to be self-conscious about ways to keep the brain active. He notes that emotional content helps the brain learn, and that this content, perhaps contained in dramatic and personal stories, needs to be included in our personal learning and in teaching.[40]

5. He explains that our brains have many types of memory systems and suggests that repetition of information helps us remember. We can improve our chances of remembering an event or information if we replicate the environment in which the event or information was put into our brain.[41] Our long-term memory is improved as we gather new information gradually and repeat the process in intervals. Re-learning is good learning.[42]

6. He explains what most of us have already learned the hard way, that lack of sleep adversely impacts our brain. The opposite is the key message; sleeping well and for an adequate amount of time improves the function of our brain.[43]

7. He speaks about the way that stress of various kinds impacts the brain and reduces our capacity to learn, think clearly, and make good

---

38. Ibid., 47. I have expanded his point in reference to the parts of the brain working in harmonious ways.
39. Ibid., 70.
40. Ibid., 94.
41. Ibid., 119.
42. Ibid., 147.
43. Ibid., 168.

decisions. Chronic stress, such as conflict in a family or at work, and the feeling of not being able to do anything about it can be very detrimental to the functioning of our brain.[44]

8. Brain health is improved as we stimulate more of the senses concurrently.[45] Vision is the most important tool in our learning kit, and we learn best as pictures illustrate the content, not just descriptions in written or spoken words.[46]

9. His research indicates that men and women learn differently, and once again we need to acknowledge that one way of learning does not work for all.[47]

10. Dr. Medina concludes his observations and recommendations with the reminder that our brains "are powerful and natural explorers"[48] and that we need to keep them healthy throughout life.

His observations and recommendations speak poignantly, although somewhat indirectly, to our thesis that it is the healthy and mature person who has the greatest capacity to be loving and compassionate. We learn from these "brain rules" ways to keep our brains healthy and functioning efficiently. As we keep them healthy, our cognitive abilities are increased, and our emotional lives in turn are more integrated and coherent. It follows that we can sense what is needed by those in our circle of nearness, and as our brains are functioning efficiently, we will have the inner resources to respond in loving and compassionate ways. We will be able listen with empathy as we are freed from the controlling influence of our inner conflicts, stress, and the demands of our own needs.

We can also apply these observations and recommendations as we participate in a variety of educational endeavors. Brain research has direct application in both in our families and also as we use our influence in our communities for improving the quality of learning in our schools. In addition, our awareness that we learn and process information differently will assist us in accepting those who are different from us, in learning style, emotional expression, and in the ways that they understand life. Cognizant of the differences, we are emancipated from our fear of the other, our need to exercise power and control over them, and are able to appreciate

44. Ibid., 195.
45. Ibid., 219.
46. Ibid., 240.
47. Ibid., 260.
48. Ibid., 28.

## Section III — The Development of Love

the differences of others and the contribution they can make to our lives and the common good. We can move toward being the kind of person who encourages others to flourish and live in a healthy and responsible way.

Dr. Daniel Amen, as a medical doctor, takes a slightly different tack in regard to brain health, stressing ways to heal the brain in order to increase its capacity and improve the health and happiness of his patients. His books, lectures, and television programs, all point in the direction of healing. Initially, his work was partially questioned by the medical profession, but increasingly his point of view is being respected, although not all of his opinions are being viewed positively. Dr. Amen does approach his research and teaching with religious convictions, and his suggestions for healing are occasionally filled with terms more commonly used in religious interchange than in medicine. For example, one of his widely circulated books is entitled *Healing the Hardware of the Soul*. The use of this metaphor is certainly acceptable, but there are those who have asked whether the soul, however it may be understood, has hardware, and if it does, is the hardware essentially the brain. With some caution, let's follow Dr. Amen in his recommendations about healing the brain (the hardware of the soul).

Daniel Amen fully utilizes the range of ways that science has developed to look at the contours of the brain, examine it, and make a prognosis.[49] These methods include:

- Electroencephalogram (EEG), an older technology that uses electrodes to record electrical activity that infer information about the brain.
- Quantitative EEG studies (QEEG), a more sophisticated version of the EEG, using computers to enhance electrical signals.
- Positron-emission tomography (PET), nuclear medicine studies that use minutes doses of radioisotopes to examine brain blood and metabolism. These studies provide excellent views of brain function.
- Single photon emission computed tomography (SPECT), a system that also evaluates cerebral brain flow.
- Functional MRI, used in psychiatry and which has the advantage of not using radiation.

---

49. *Healing the Hardware of the Soul*, 20–30.

The Amen Clinics use SPECT studies primarily in assessing the health of the brain and give special attention to the flow of blood to the brain and its metabolism. The information generated by these studies determines which of three categories the brain might best be placed: (1) those areas of the brain that work well; (2) those areas of the brain that work too hard; and (3) those areas of the brain that do not work enough. A patient in the Amen Clinic will have the different parts of his or her brain examined carefully, with a prescriptive analysis for improving brain health. Five areas of the brain are examined and treated. A full exploration of all five areas of the brain is beyond the scope of our study, but we will illustrate from two of them.

One area that is given special attention is what Dr. Amen calls "the thoughtful, compassionate brain" or the prefrontal cortex (PFC). This part of the brain guides and directs our thoughts and behaviors and gives us our ability to look into the future, to plan, and to guide behavior in a way that enables us to reach our goals.[50] When our "PFC is working properly, we are able to be thoughtful, empathic, compassionate, and appropriately express our feelings."[51] We can organize and be goal directed. We will be less inclined to engage in impulsive behavior, and be more inclined to sense right from wrong. It will help us to reflect on how to insure that what we say is appropriate, and fortunately to learn from our mistakes. It increases our ability to concentrate and focus on what is important in a conversation and filter out details that are less important.

In addition, this part of the brain enables us to express emotions such as happiness, sadness, joy, and love. The PFC translates the feelings of the limbic system to feelings that we can understand and about which we can be self-aware. We can recognize feelings of anger, joy, and love, reflect upon them and find ways to appropriately express them. But limited activity in this part of the brain will limit our capacity to express these emotions. It may lead to a decreased attention span, impaired short-term memory, apathy, moodiness, and poor impulse control. Even our ability to discern between right and wrong and how to express appropriate and inappropriate emotion is adversely impacted, and it may lead to unacceptable behavior.[52]

---

50. Ibid., 31.
51. Ibid., 32.
52. Amen lists positive PFC traits on Ibid., 38 and unhealthy PFC traits on Ibid., 41.

## Section III — The Development of Love

A second part of the brain that relates directly to our goal to see the connections between the brain and our capacity to love is the temporal lobes and the deep limbic system.[53] These components of the brain are often referred to as the emotional brain. Together, they generate and supervise our passions, desires, and even our sense of meaning, our values, and our spirituality. As a whole, they either give us our hope about life or, conversely, can drop us into despair. They essentially manage our memory, emotion, sense of social connectedness or community, moods, and anger control. These parts of a healthy functioning brain will generate the following positive qualities:[54]

- Good memory
- Mood stability
- Word retrieval
- Accurate reading of social situations
- Personality stability and coherence
- Control over temper
- Access to spiritual experience (meaning and values)
- Access to positive memories
- Ability to bond with others

The other parts of the brain treated in the Amen Clinics are equally important for brain health, but we will use the two above as illustrative of the analysis done in the clinics. The treatment for brain disorder, carefully discerned by the imaging techniques, takes many forms. One strategy is to invite the patient to engage in a self-report questionnaire that is relatively easy to score and reveals potential problems in the five areas of the brain.[55] It provides the basis for targeted interventions, although it is not used alone in determining the diagnosis. A second strategy focuses on exercises that assist the patient to discern his or her values and how these values guide thoughts and actions.[56] The goal of these exercises is to increase integrity and the capacity to achieve a life lived in harmony with one's deepest values and sense of meaning. Another strategy centers on finding ways to heal deeply painful memories. Again, through self-assessment and careful

---

53. Ibid., 59–83.
54. Ibid., 70.
55. Ibid., 129–47.
56. Ibid., 148–72.

counseling, the patient is invited to reflect on how important memories are, to remember good memories, employ a "directed memory" management technique, and then as necessary participate in psychotherapy.[57] The Amen Clinics also use techniques of prayer and meditation and encourages "soul to soul" connectedness and social bonding in order to remedy feelings of loneliness and isolation. In addition, as one might expect in these clinics, there is a careful use of a range of medications.

## IMPROVING OUR CAPACITY TO LOVE

A fundamental thesis of this part of our journey in our exploration of the geography of love has been to illustrate that our capacity to love is increased as we mature. Our mapping of lovescapes has focused on the ways that our interaction with the environment (nurture) and our physiology (nature) contribute to our ability to be a more loving person. In Chapter 5, The Nurturing Environment, we began to explore the ways that we might enhance our capacity to be compassionate by gaining insight into how we have been formed by and interacted with our environment. In the current chapter, "Endowed for Love," we have looked at research and theories that connect our capacity to love to our evolutionary development, the health of our hearts, and the care we give to our brains. In addition, we have discerned from this study some preliminary strategies about how we might enhance our unique qualities (our formation) and our "wiring" (our physiology) to be loving and compassionate people.

We build then upon the following foundational points:

1. The more nurturing and supportive our environment has been in terms of parental care, family life, friendships, education, associations, exposure to advanced learning and other cultures, and indeed an entire ecology of factors, the greater our potential to grow and develop into responsible and mature human beings.
2. The more mature and responsible we become (self-awareness, good self-esteem, self-acceptance, clear identity, values of honesty and respect for the dignity of others, deep integrity, well-informed, etc.) the greater is our potential for becoming a person who is loving and compassionate.
3. The better we understand our natural inheritance and evolutionary development, our genetic structure and the inherent needs in our

57. Ibid., 173–96.

struggle to survive and perpetuate the race, the better able we will be to factor in these elements of the human condition and to integrate them into our self-understanding and our growth toward maturity.

4. The more care we give to our health, and to our heart health in particular, the more coherent we will be. With this integrated coherence will come an increased capacity to extend ourselves into the lives of others and to be a person for others.

5. Further, the better we understand the way our brains function and the strategies for improving brain health, the more potential we will have to become responsible people who love. Also we gain the ability to assume responsibility for creating a more just and humane regional environment and a more caring and compassionate global context.

## EMPOWERED TO LOVE

There is one additional part of our journey in the exploration of this complex geography that we need to take. It is one that we have seen in our previous explorations on the signs that guide us as we come to the intersections of trails. It points us to the ways that we can intentionally cultivate our capacity to be more loving. It takes us on the beautiful but challenging lovescape of increasing our knowledge of the need for love and compassion both near and far. It will enable us to learn new skills and insights about how to respond to these needs. It will suggest strategies that can empower us to be loving and compassionate. And it will take us to the point of decision about whether or not it should be a priority in our lives. We move on to the topic of Chapter 7, empowered to love.

## STUDY RESOURCES

### Discussion Questions

1. Is it possible for us to be genuinely altruistic in our concern for others if our evolutionary development "programs" us to be primarily concerned about reproduction and survival in our relationships?

2. In what ways might a healthy heart contribute to our capacity to be a loving person?

3. In what ways might an active and healthy brain encourage us to be compassionate?

4. How does one manage and guide the signals that come from different parts of the brain in order to manage and integrate them and connect in loving ways with others?

5. What are some ways that we might improve the health of our hearts and our brains in order to be more loving and compassionate people?

## Key Terms and Concepts

- *The nature-nurture continuum:* a description and a way of assessing how both our natural endowments and our environmental conditioning contribute to our growth and development.
- *Decision-biases:* a way of defining love within the context of evolutionary biology as a set of choices that promote behavior that enhances reproduction and survival.
- *HeartMath Solution:* a book title and a movement that suggests a way of diagnosing the health of the heart and prescribing ways to improve the health of the heart in order to enhance the quality of life.
- *Coherence:* that state when the heart, mind, and emotions are in energetic alignment and cooperation.
- *Triune brain:* a way of speaking about the three components of the brain that developed in stages across evolutionary time, with different functions emerging in response to survival needs: reptilian, limbic, and neocortex.

## Suggestions for Reference and Reading

1. Amen, Daniel, *Healing the Hardware of the Soul.* New York: Free Press, 2002.
2. Childre, Doc and Howard Martin, with Donna Beech, *The HeartMath Solution.* San Francisco: HarperSanFrancisco, 2002.
3. Lewis, Thomas, et al., *A General Theory of Love.* New York: Vintage Books, 2001.
4. Medina, John, *Brain Rules.* Seattle: Pear Press, 2008.

**Section III** — The Development of Love

5. Sternberg, Robert and Karin Weis, eds., *The New Psychology of Love.* New Haven: Yale University Press, 2006.

# 7

# Empowered to Love

## BECOMING ONE WHO LOVES AND PURSUES COMPASSIONATE WAYS

WE HAVE EXPLORED THE ways that the settings of our lives have a profound influence on us. We are shaped by our environment, and as we move through life and look back across the years, we can identity those shaping influences that were positive and life-giving and those that were negative and life-denying. Some were healthy and nurturing, giving us integrity, a clear sense of identity, values that guide us, and meaning that sustains and moves us forward in hope. We can also point to many of the conditions in our environment that made us overly anxious, full of fear, insecure, plagued by stress, full of self-doubt, and often depressed. We maintained that the more positive our environment, the more potential we have to be those who are loving and compassionate, and the more negative our environment, the more likely we are to be driven by our needs and blocked in our capacity to express unlimited love; these negative influences have made it hard to be a person for others.

We also discussed the ways that our heredity and the maintenance of our health impact our capacity to be one who loves and pursues compassionate ways. We spoke about both heart and brain health, noting their interwoven connection and the ways that our physiology can increase our capacity to love or block our ability to be compassionate people.

## Section III — The Development of Love

We turn now to a third theme in our discussion of the development of loving and compassionate behavior, the ways that we can learn and be empowered to love and be compassionate. We will return to our discussion of both nurture and nature in reference to love, but at this point we will focus our attention on how we can take the initiative in cultivating a loving and compassionate lifestyle. We are more than our conditioning and our heredity; we are also those who have at least a measure of freedom to choose to place love as a central value in our lives. We can take the hand that we have been dealt, use it and transform it, and do our part in loving those who surround us, creating a more empathic culture, and working toward a more just and humane world. Again, I am aware that these value-driven goals can be seen as overly idealistic and not fully informed by the harsh realities of life. My response is, "Yes, they are idealistic, but in the best sense of lifting up our highest ideals and making them the focus of our lives." I would add as well in this response that these ideals are motivated by the "harsh realities of life" and the endless number of people who desperately need the touch of compassion.

Admittedly, to become one who loves and pursues compassionate ways is very difficult; it is a hard path to follow and one that we will often fail to follow as we seek to meet other pressing needs and pursue different goals. We are often distracted by other concerns in life, many of them good and important, although most of these endeavors may need to be motivated and seasoned by love. And not infrequently, we will also pursue the false consolations of power, prestige, pleasure, and possessions, pursuits that take us away from the life of love.

Our modest description of lovescapes and the geography of love, if nothing else, is an invitation to walk in the beautiful hills and valleys of love and explore the high mountains and deep oceans of compassion. No journey is more important and fulfilling. As we contemplate taking this bold journey, we realize that it will require preparation. At a minimum the following steps of preparation should be taken:[1]

1. One part of our preparation to become a more loving person and to pursue compassionate ways is to continue to learn. We know a fair amount about love already, but there is much more for us to understand. Love requires lifelong learning. In particular, we need to learn more about the nature of love, its complexity, and its many-splendored

---

[1]. Our preparation will not always follow a logical pattern and our best efforts will not necessarily endure. The steps will often be concurrent and mixed together, and we will need to return to them on a regular basis.

character. We are in the midst of that endeavor. In addition, we need to learn the skills of love and compassion, e.g., how to be an empathic listener, how to express unlimited and non-judgmental love, and how to care wisely and well for others. Further, we should learn how important loving and compassionate behavior are for a world in crisis. Love and compassion can guide and motivate all who have a part in building a sustainable infrastructure, the formation of just systems of law and security, the distribution of wealth and food, finding the ways we care for our threatened environment, and how best to address the many other problems of our earth community.

2. As we learn, we will be reminded again and again in direct and subtle ways that we need to change. The ways we are living as individuals, in corporate structures, in the regions where we live, as nations, and as a global community are threatening the world's sustainability. It is causing extraordinary suffering as the foundations of life begin to deteriorate. Water tables are falling, harvests are shrinking, soils eroding, deserts expanding, temperatures rising, and food is increasingly scarce.[2] The list of potentially failing nations grows, and governments appear to be inept and unable to lead and provide for the common good. As resources shrink, nations compete for land, water, and other resources, and as people become disillusioned by their government's inability to manage, there is the inevitable resort to violence in solving the frustrations and conflicts that prevail in many parts of the world.

3. As we learn and understand the need for change, we begin to ask ourselves what we might do to help. An inner voice whispers and asks us to commit, not to everything, but to something. In the immediate circumstances of our lives, in settings in which we live, across our states and nations, and in our global context, we discover ways that we might make a difference. As we look at the options, whether it is helping at a local food bank, or arranging for cargo jets full of food headed for Somalia, we find what we can do. We observe the pronounced need and then can commit in our own way to help.

We turn then to an exploration of the ways that we can be empowered to love, ways that will increase our motivation, educate us about the need, improve our skills, and begin the process of being transformed into more loving and compassionate people. We will look at ways to find a

2. Brown, *World on the Edge*.

supportive community and improve our environment, increase our physical and emotional health, and engage in practices that will change our inner compass and give us guidance to our destination—becoming a more loving person who pursues compassionate ways.

## THE SUPPORTIVE ENVIRONMENT

Our environment is profoundly influential over the years of our lives. Our biological parents give us our heredity, and our family structure and style shape our development through infancy and childhood. Our associations in groups such as school, faith-related affiliations, and extracurricular programs begin to give us a sense of identity and our initial values. Our intimate relationships and friendships in young adulthood form the way we relate to others. As we move into careers, we clarify our life purpose and chose a direction in which to use our abilities and education. We continue to be influenced by our environment as we become parents and assume leadership roles in work and community. In a specific context we establish ourselves as distinctive persons, gain competence in our chosen vocations, and build security for our senior years.

Our identity, meaning, and values reflect our exposures in the many environments of our lives. How is it possible, with this array of influences from these many environments, for us to become people who place love and compassion at the center of our lives? The distractions are numerous, especially in cultures that place such high value on accumulating wealth and surrounding ourselves with material possessions. We have maintained that certain conditions increase our potential to become loving and compassionate people. We have underlined that a supportive family life, the positive influences present in schools and associations, and an education that informs us about our society and the world increases our potential to become more compassionate. We have stressed that relationships of love and respect with life partners, friends, co-workers, and community groups will motivate us to be more caring for others.

All of these conditions point us in the right direction, but we need to say as well that many people become loving and compassionate whose environments are less than supportive and nurturing. In many cases, a person's struggle increases the feelings of empathy for those who suffer.[3]

---

3. See Simon Baron-Cohen's *The Science of Evil: On Empathy and the Origins of Cruelty*. It provides a persuasive argument and crucial information about evil as the absence of empathy.

What then are the factors that trigger the commitment to become a person for others?[4] Let me suggest five conditions that might spark moral transformation:

1. The first and most obvious one, as we have said, is a positive and supportive environment. An individual who has been exposed to the values of love in the critical years of development, supported in the family context by loving behavior, and has had altruistic attitudes and actions modeled by admired and important people is likely to internalize the values of love and pursue compassionate ways. Because of these supportive factors, such a person may move more easily into a pattern that places love and compassion as the guiding values of life.

2. A second way that one may be motivated to engage in the process of moral transformation is an exposure to an urgent sense of need. It may be triggered by a family situation in which a family member becomes troubled or ill and needs special care and attention. It might occur during a visit to a developing country, one in which there are starving people and many environmental refugees. The need for love is all around us if we have the eyes to see it.

3. It might happen because of active participation in an organization that places the value of altruistic love at the core of its purpose and activity. Often religious groups are active in causes that address injustice, world hunger, and children's education. To participate in the life of such an organization often causes an acceptance of and identification with the values of the group.

4. It might happen at a moment of personal crisis that causes a radical change of lifestyle, such as conversion from a life of indulgence and self-destructive behavior. It is not uncommon, for example, for a person in Alcoholics Anonymous to overcome addiction and then to become committed to assisting others with their addictions.

5. As a kind of summary, we might say that it often happens because of education, an exposure to those who suffer in our circle of nearness, and an understanding of the overwhelming problems of world

---

4. See Sorokin, *The Ways and Powers of Love*. While this work does reflect an earlier period of scholarship (mid-twentieth century), it nevertheless provides several categories that are helpful in describing the necessary moral transformation that must take place for an individual or a group to place altruistic behavior in our lives as a central motivating value.

## Section III — The Development of Love

hunger, poverty, global warming, terrorism, and other situations in which a compassionate response is so necessary.

Pitirim Sorokin, in his discussion of the ways of altruistic growth suggests three types of people who commit their lives to becoming a person for others.[5] These three types may be a bit obvious, but perhaps they will nevertheless deepen our understanding of the motivations of compassionate people and assist us in finding our own pathway to a life of love. His first type is called the "early fortunate," those who because of their nature and nurture are able to get beyond their own immediate needs and at an early age begin to respond to the most pronounced suffering and struggles of others. He highlights the lives of several gifted people who have used their emotional, intellectual, and spiritual gifts for the welfare of others. He mentions such people as John Woolman (1720–1772), the Quaker leader who led peace and justice movements in early American life. He describes the life of Albert Schweitzer (1875–1965), the great musician, theologian, and medical missionary who established a hospital in Africa and was so committed to nonviolence. Both, given their remarkable gifts and values, moved into life and career commitments that epitomized their motivations to love and show compassion.

He also identifies those whose conversion to the altruism came later in life and were precipitated by a personal crisis. He speaks of Gautama Buddha (c. 563–483 BCE) the prince who gave up power and fortune because of an exposure to human suffering (The Four Passing Sights), sought an alternative ascetic life, and then after the experience of enlightenment devoted his life to teaching the path of enlightenment and relieving suffering. Sorokin places St. Francis of Assisi (1182–1226) in this category as well. In his early years, he led a life of self-indulgence and was later wounded in warfare. It was during his convalescence that "the miserable emptiness of his life suddenly appeared before him."[6] As he healed, he committed his life to serving the poor and needy and lived with a spirit of humility and in abject poverty.

Sorokin's third category is what he calls "the intermediary course of self-identification," by which he means that transformation and commitment gradually emerge as circumstances require a response at certain times and places in life. In this category he places such people as Mohandas Gandhi (1869–1948). Sorokin describes the development of Gandhi's life from his time as a teenager, his education in the United Kingdom, his

5. Ibid., 144–74.
6. Ibid., 156.

experience of discrimination in South Africa, and his return to India to serve as the leader of his country's independence movement. These various stages contributed to the formation of Gandhi's commitment to love and compassion and his practice of nonviolent resistance. He also calls attention to St. Teresa (1515–1582), who grew up in a supportive and religious home, but sensed as a teenager that she was leading a "life of vanity." She entered a convent for her education, but the experience turned out to be more than basic education. As she was exposed to the Christian values of faith and love, she began a new life of dedication. In this context, even with some resistance from her father and a not an altogether passive and obedient spirit in the convent, she gave herself to the spiritual life characterized by prayer, love, and compassion.

In each of these illustrations, Sorokin carefully addresses the fundamental changes that occurred in these people and how their inner transformation led to lives of commitment to loving service. As we study the pattern of development and change in these lives, we see the variety of influences that led to moral transformation and dedication to loving service. In many cases, there was a supportive family; many had a superior education; they were positive influences in their associations or orders; there were precipitating incidents and circumstances in the environments that needed a compassionate solution; and in most cases there was a religious conversion and sense of vocation.

As we consider our pathway to the life of loving and compassionate service, we need not follow the exact path of another person, as inspiring as it might be; rather we need to find that path that is appropriate for us. It might mean living in isolation from the distractions of contemporary life, like Thomas Merton. Or it might mean living in the context of an organization or religious order that will cultivate the life of dedication such as monastic communities within the Sangha in Buddhism. But for most of us, it will involve living a much more ordinary pattern of life with job, family, and community responsibilities, while still finding ways of cultivating the life of love and compassion. Regardless, our environment will make a profound difference in our formation.

## THE HEALTHY LIFE

Increasingly, scientific research is demonstrating that heart and brain health are integral in achieving coherence, integrity, and equilibrium in life. The research is also showing that being a person who is integrated

## Section III — The Development of Love

increases one's inclination and capacity to be a loving person, one who has compassion for those who suffer, who can demonstrate empathic behavior, and be a person for others. We reviewed in Chapter 6 the work of the HeartMath movement and learned that the heart does more than supply sustaining blood to the body, but also shapes the way we think and feel. We take care of our hearts by staying physically fit, and our hearts in turn contribute to our emotional health and well-being. We care for our hearts, not just by diet and exercise, but also by the expression of the positive feelings of gratitude, joy, and compassion. These feelings increase the health of our hearts. Our hearts may in fact be akin to the metaphorical meaning of the heart in our common parlance, that is, the center of intuition, conscience, and loving behavior. It appears that if we are kind to our hearts, they are kind to us. There is a complementary relationship between our physical hearts and our positive attitudes about life. As we have the positive emotions of joy, practice the acceptance of others, and offer forgiveness, our whole system works better; our hearts in turn function in healthy ways that encourage these positive emotions.[7]

The HeartMath program recommends a strategy for health called "cut-thru to emotional maturity." It is a way to work toward inner coherence, which is called in the HeartMath program "the state of energetic alignment and cooperation between heart, mind, and emotions." Its goal is to facilitate emotional integrity and transform our emotions. It requires a sincere and intentional effort of reflection and contemplation and involves removing conflicting and negative emotions that drain our energy. We move beyond the feeling of being overwhelmed by the complexity and demands of life and move toward emotional balance based on reality rather than the projections of fear. Old "tapes" must be removed from our unconscious memory and neural circuity, a process that transforms our biochemistry, which influences our moods and behavior. As a result, we increase our emotional capabilities, become more sensitive and empathic, and are able to be more loving and compassionate.[8]

Still another strategy of the HeartMath solution is what is called the "heart lock-in."[9] This method helps us appreciate that we have within us the capability for regeneration. As we quiet our minds and focus on (lock in) our heart's power, we sense new energy flowing to our emotional center. We begin to realize, as our awareness increases, how we can be more

---

7. *The HeartMath Solution*, 183–210.
8. Ibid., 209–10.
9. Ibid., 211–24.

coherent and balanced by sustaining a loving and openhearted perspective. The more we maintain the spirit of joy, appreciation, and forgiveness, the more we are healed from the wounds of life and able to show acceptance and care for others. We become increasingly coherent as our systems align and integrate. As this happens, our well-being is enhanced and we have more resources and energy for loving behavior.

These strategies can have a profoundly positive influence on our lives. They are relatively simple in concept and application, and they can also be used by children, improving their capacities to have friends and to do well in school. These same strategies can be employed by those in the corporate and governmental sectors of our society and help to shape policies and programs that can point us in the direction of building a more caring society.

A similar case can be made for a conscious effort to improve brain health. Recent neurological research suggests that when our brain malfunctions as a consequence of traumatic or stressful emotional experiences or chemical changes, a variety of afflictions surface. We may fall into depression, our anxiety may increase, and we can easily lose our focus and resort to obsessive-compulsive behavior. In essence our entire life is adversely impacted and our ability to express love and compassion is dramatically reduced. New research is uncovering ways to increase the health of our brains and improve the condition of our lives.

Daniel Amen, whom we mentioned in Chapter 6, suggests a comprehensive approach to improving brain health and argues that a customized program will change the quality of our life.[10] He uses self-diagnostic tests and suggests a pattern of treatment and behavior that increase positive moods and facilitate our capability to engage in life-giving interpersonal connections. The treatments cleanse toxic memories and patterns of living and increase compassionate behavior such as forgiveness and empathy. He argues, as do the HeartMath proponents, that these positive emotions can actually have a physical impact on the health of our heart and the composition of our brain. As with the heart, there is also a complementary relationship between our brain and our behavior. Our positive thoughts and caring ways improve the functioning of our brains, and in turn, a healthy brain encourages loving behavior and a deeper spirituality.

---

10. *Healing the Hardware of the Soul*, 31–83. The three chapters in this section are entitled "The Thoughtful, Compassionate Brain," "The Flexible, Growth-Oriented Brain," and "The Spiritual and Passionate Brain."

## Section III — The Development of Love

Andrew Newberg, associate professor of Radiology and Psychiatry at the Hospital at the University of Pennsylvania, argues in a similar vein as Dr. Amen. He and his colleagues have done extensive research on the relationship of the brain and positive behavior and emotions at the Center for Integrated Study of Spirituality and the Neurosciences, at the University. He and his colleague Mark Robert Waldman build a theoretical foundation about the linkages between religion and the human brain and argue that the ways one perceives and experiences the divine can be either detrimental or helpful to one's stability and health.[11] They maintain that understanding God as loving and compassionate can improve how our brain functions. The case is also made that holding the conception of an angry and judgmental God can be harmful to us. Such a view of the divine might suggest and even encourage the belief that we, too, can legitimately engage in angry and judgmental behavior, as we follow what we believe to be the ways of God. This frame of reference is exclusive and judgmental rather than inclusive and it operates out of a "we-they" context.[12] Love is seldom present except in some cases for those in the in-group, and a person with this outlook is usually suspicious of those who are different in belief and behavior.

As much as we may try to eliminate anger, judgmental attitudes, selfish behavior, and in-group attitudes, we find that they continue to be our companions over the lifespan, possibly because of evolutionary reasons in reference to survival. But it is vitally important that we make every effort to transform our inner reality and remove these negative emotions. Newberg and Waldman suggest a number of tangible and concrete ways that we can lower our levels of anger and anxiety, enhance our social awareness and empathy, and improve our intellectual capacities.[13] In general they suggest that meditation and intensive prayer can strengthen our neural functioning, especially in those parts of the brain that are involved with feelings of anxiety and depression, and enhance love and cognitive functioning. These practices can help us to "remain calm, serene, peaceful, and

---

11. *How God Changes Your Brain*, 67–146. This book contains chapters that address such questions as how we view the "feelings" of God, how we understand the character and nature of God, and how we cope with the possible anger and judgment of God.

12. Ibid., 131–46, in the chapter entitled "What Happens When God Gets Mad: Anger, Fear and the Fundamentalist in Our Brain."

13. Ibid., 149–69, in the chapter entitled "Exercising Your Brain."

alert."[14] They suggest eight ways to exercise our brain, moving up from one to eight with increasing importance:

1. The first is that we must learn how to smile. There are days when we do not feel like smiling, days filled with stress and conflict, days that follow a poor night's sleep, and days in which one is overwhelmed because life feels out of control. But smiling is still important, even if it is not totally sincere. It can even be a spiritual practice, as it is, for example in Buddhism. The research teaches us that smiling stimulates the brain circuits that enhance social interaction, empathy, and a positive outlook. Conversely, frowning stimulates feelings of anger, disgust, and dislike. A smile is even better than laughter in that laughter can stimulate the amygdala, which controls feelings that are linked to discomfort and fear. Laughter can too easily become a defense against nervousness and shyness and even an expression of secret delight in the discomfort of others, as is often illustrated in the many comedies we watch on television.

2. In addition, we need to stay intellectually active. Here the phrase "use it or lose it" is appropriate. Intellectual and cognitive stimulation improves the neural connections in our frontal lobe, and this in turn increases our capacity to communicate, solve problems, and make rational decisions about life. In addition, for our purpose, staying in peak health in these ways increases our ability to care wisely and appropriately, be more loving, and express compassion.

3. We also improve our brain health when we consciously relax. This is not always an easy task, and sometimes the harder we try, the worse it gets; it requires practice. In time we can learn how to review all parts of our body in a conscious effort to reduce muscle tension and physical fatigue. There are some classical ways that this can be done, not the least of which is listening to calm music, a practice that does "sharpen our cognitive skills and improve our sense of spiritual well-being."[15]

4. Even such routine behavior as the yawn can reduce anxiety and hypertension. It has been shown that a yawn can actually stimulate feelings of empathy, social sensitivity, and increase cognitive awareness. A similar affect can occur with the practice of some forms of yogic breathing.

14. Ibid., 150.
15. Ibid., 155.

## Section III — The Development of Love

5. Still another way to improve our brain's health and functioning is to meditate.[16] It is an extremely important spiritual practice that enhances both our physical and emotional health. As we meditate, anti-stress hormones and neurochemicals are released, which have the effect of giving pleasure and reducing depression. Variations of meditation such as visualization and guided imagery may also help in maintaining a healthy brain.

6. Also important in our brain health is engaging in aerobic exercise. People of all ages can benefit from exercise and it will improve our health and lengthen our lives. A young athlete will obviously engage in exercise more frequently and more strenuously than an older person, but what is important is to find the right amount for our age and conditioning. It is similar in many ways to meditation in that it engages us in sustained concentration, movement, and regular breathing. It can heal us, rebuild damaged circuits caused by brain lesions and strokes, repair the neurological damage caused by stress, and reduce depression.

7. Still another very important activity to improve our brain health is to have regular dialogue with others. Our language skills developed hand in hand with the evolvement of our brains. They are interwoven, with language exercising large portions of our brain. The more interaction with others over the lifespan, the healthier our brain will be and the less our cognitive abilities will decline with age. Of course mundane conversations about the weather are much less stimulating and have less value for improving enhancing our social skills and improving our cognitive ability. But deeper conversations about all aspects of life can have a profoundly positive impact upon us. In educational settings in which the concerns about truth, justice, and peace are present, there is positive stimulation. Participation in a religious community often will lead to reflection and deep conversations about values, meaning, and spirituality, which can be positively stimulating as well.

8. This observation leads to the eighth and most important way of sustaining good brain health and our capacity to love; it is to have faith.[17] To have life-giving faith may not mean that all that you believe is

---

16. We will say more about meditation and other spiritual practices below.
17. Ibid., 163. Newberg and Waldman maintain that faith is the most important "exercise" for the brain.

necessarily true or that the way you articulate your faith is the only way to understand and connect with the divine. But people with faith, understood as a life-orientation rather than an acceptance of a set of beliefs, generally have a more a positive outlook about life; they believe that life can be good, or if there are problems, they can be solved. A faith commitment is intimately connected with hope and love, gives meaning to life, and assurance that a good future is possible. Even if our view of the divine and the religious life is partial and approximate, it nevertheless invites us into a pattern of life that pushes and pulls us toward becoming all that we are capable of becoming, or to say it more theologically, becoming all that God intends for us to be. Such an outlook or one similar to it without reference to the divine[18] is an essential for maintaining a healthy brain and increases our capability to empathic, loving, and compassionate.[19]

## EMPOWERED TO LOVE

The research done by Dr. Newberg and his colleagues at the Center for Spirituality and the Mind provide a natural segue into beliefs and practices within the religious traditions of the human family that empower adherents to become those who practice love and pursue ways of being compassionate. We have already introduced religious teachings about love and compassion in chapter four, but in this section we will be more selective and look specifically at practices that focus on ways for their adherents to be empowered to love. We will concentrate our attention on Buddhism, Christianity, and current trends in eclectic spirituality as a way illustrating the ways that a spiritual commitment empowers love and compassion. Other religious traditions also teach the practice of love; in fact love is an almost universal value in the religions of the human family and we will also draw upon insights from other traditions.

The Buddhist tradition, in its several forms over the span of history, has taught that compassion, and in particular the relief of suffering. is central to the Buddhist way of life.[20] In part it grows out the Four Noble

---

18. As for example in Buddhism or in more secular outlooks that encourage hopeful and positive attitudes.

19. The next few chapters in *How God Changes Your Brain* offer guidelines and practices that are aimed at increasing our serenity and ability to practice compassionate communication.

20. See, for example, the Dalai Lama's book entitled *The Compassionate Life*, and

## Section III — The Development of Love

Truths that were taught by Siddhartha Gautama (the Buddha), who lived approximately 2500 years ago, born about 563 BCE in the region of the Ganges River in northeastern India. The first noble truth is that life is filled with suffering (dukkha), and human sorrow is universal. The Pali word *dukkha* has the connotation of dissatisfaction because life is not all that humans want it to be. It includes the worry caused by the realities of disease, aging, and approaching death, but also the mental and emotional dimension of suffering as well. We suffer in large measure because of the second noble truth that we are sorrowful because of attachment and craving (tanha), our insatiable desire to have and possess. Buddhism teaches a third noble truth, that there can be an end to suffering if we let go our desire for possessions and eliminate our need for attachments. The fourth noble truth is that there is an eight–fold path that can lead us out of our suffering and to enlightenment.[21]

Buddha and his many followers who have followed and expanded his teaching and practices have devoted themselves to relieving this suffering and guiding people to enlightenment. As they have carried out this mission and continue to undertake it, they have been and are keenly aware of the need to follow the eight-fold path and to engage in a variety of spiritual practices that are essential to inner transformation. They begin with the sense that human beings have the potential to be enlightened, fulfilled, free, and to find a life of meaning. They become pilgrims (bodhisattvas) who are on the way to full enlightenment.[22] But as they go, there are aware of being caught in a larger system, that of karma or the cycle of cause and effect that is universal to the human experience and controlling. One's destiny is linked to karma and to the cycle of death and rebirth called samsara. Ultimately the goal of life is to reach nirvana, to escape the wheel of birth, death, and rebirth with the elimination of samsara, uncontrollable desires, and consequent suffering.

While on the path of the bodhisattva, there is comfort and guidance in the Three Great Jewels of Refuge. The faithful Buddhist will say, "I take refuge in the Buddha (the teacher), the Dharma (the teaching), and the Sangha (the community)." There are also a wide range of practices that cultivate inner spiritual formation and transform one's behavior.[23] At a

Thich Nhat Hanh's book entitled *Teachings on Love*.

21. The pathway includes right view, right intention, right speech, right livelihood, right effort, right mindfulness, right diligence, and right concentration. See Ferguson, *Exploring the Spirituality of the World Religions*, 100–17.

22. See Chodron, *No Time to Lose: A Timely Guide to the Way of the Bodhisattva*.

23. See Thich Nhat Hanh, *The Heart of the Buddha's Teaching*, 121–254.

very minimum they include having the right mental framework (right mindfulness) to begin down the path. It is essential that the pilgrim understands the origins of suffering. Then the pilgrim must strive to live a clean, moral life, treating others with compassion and fairness. Finally, one must practice meditation diligently in order to train the mind to move past the clutter of thoughts which lead to grasping and craving. As one matures spiritually, one is increasingly released from suffering and its cause, and becomes empowered to show compassion to others. However, empowerment is not a permanent state and it must be continually cultivated through other spiritual practices.

The Dalai Lama, in his book *How to Expand Love*, teaches that we should follow several stages as we seek to widen our circle of loving relationships. He suggests that before we begin this endeavor, however, we must make sure that we have a strong foundation. We do that, he says, by evaluating our lives, weighing options, and if persuaded, then committing to a life of "compassion and love, respecting the rights of others—this is real religion."[24] We also must recognize as we start our journey on this pathway that we will develop in our capacity to love gradually, in stages, and that we will need to have patience with ourselves as we grow; we will not arrive overnight. But ultimately movement through these stages will lead us to our destination, which is enlightenment. The stages are as follows:[25]

1. The first stage in developing a loving attitude toward others is to think and reflect about our relationship with our closest friends, whom we naturally love. Then, as we meditate on these relationships, we consciously expand these same feelings and attitudes to an ever-widening circle, which will eventually include strangers and even those who appear to be enemies.

2. A second stage involves practical reflections on the kindness shown to us by family and close friends, especially when we were children and needed support. As we reflect and meditate on this kindness, our gratitude increases and comparable kindness can then be extended to others, even those well beyond our circle of friends.

3. A third stage involves cultivating the spirit of reciprocity by developing a commitment to help others as we have been helped, an attitude of returning kindness and giving back to others what we have

---

24. *How to Expand Love*, 5.
25. Note: The Dalai Lama has seven stages, but I have combined steps 6 and 7.

## Section III — The Development of Love

received. We begin to understand that others, just as we do, long for happiness and relief from suffering.[26] They, too, are on the pathway to enlightenment and we can help them find their way as we have been helped in finding our way.

4. A fourth stage follows naturally; as we reach out to others, we discover that we are not always able to discern what the most appropriate form of compassion is. But as we reflect on how we have been wisely loved, we learn how to love others appropriately and purely. We respond to their needs, not in order to meet our needs but in order to meet their needs. As we better understand why people suffer, we feel genuine empathy and we can offer wise and adequate compassion. We gradually learn how to become "a friend to all beings, to have concern for their situation, and to be ready and able to help."[27]

5. A fifth stage is the cultivation of the feelings and practice of compassion and a deep desire to relieve others from suffering. We carefully develop our capacity to wish others to be happy, especially those who may be poor or sick or aging. We use a range of exercises that increase our ability to have mercy, one part of which is to imagine ourselves switching places with someone obviously suffering from poverty or illness.

6. The sixth step leads us to becoming fully committed to altruism. We turn this commitment to unlimited and unbiased love and compassion toward the highest aim of enlightenment—making compassion the central value of our lives and becoming more effective in offering love and compassion to all.[28]

Another highly regarded and helpful Buddhist teacher, Tana Pesso, with the help of Penor Rinpoche, offers guidance for cultivating the life of love in her book entitled *First Invite Love In: 40 Time-Tested Tools for Creating a More Compassionate Life*.[29] This volume is very practical and offers a range of meditation practices that can be incorporated into nearly anyone's life who sincerely wishes to become a more loving and compassionate person.

---

26. The Dalai Lama and Howard C. Cutler, *The Art of Happiness: A Handbook for Living*, 15–36.

27. The Dalai Lama, *How to Expand Love*, 11.

28. Ibid, 29–187. In each of the chapters, the Dalai Lama offers guidance for exercises and meditation to cultivate a life of love and compassion. Thich Nhat Hanh offers similar guidance in *True Love: A Practice for Awakening the Heart* and a more theoretical frame of reference in *Teachings on Love*.

29. I have personally used this book and found it quite helpful.

The practices are Buddhist in character, but can easily cross over into other religious traditions and more eclectic or secular outlooks. Ms. Pesso gives some initial advice in using the book and urges the reader to do the exercises in order, not skipping any steps, to practice them regularly, and to trust that one will improve even if concentration is difficult at first.[30] She goes on to suggest a pattern for laying the foundation for the compassionate life. It has four steps:

1. First invite love in,
2. Engage in the suggested meditation,
3. Then seal it with a vow and rejoice (a positive and hopeful outlook),
4. And finally send love out.[31]

One example of the meditative practices might provide a glimpse of Ms. Pesso's approach. It is called "Increasing Generosity by Imagining Giving All to Save the Life of a Love One." The goals of the practice are to:

- Increase awareness of and compassion for the suffering of others.
- Increase the aspiration to relieve the suffering of others.
- Decrease selfishness.
- Increase generosity.

Step one is to invite love in by mentally dwelling in a space of love, possibly by bringing to mind someone with the capacity for profound love, compassion, and peace of mind. Attempt to clear the mind of distractions, focus on receiving spiritual support, and then center attention on whatever compassion practice you are following (generosity). Step two involves thinking of five favorite objects that you own and how they might save the life of five people for whom you care deeply. Imagine yourself giving these objects to these persons and how relieved and grateful they are. Then imagine that there are an endless number of people who have deep needs that your generosity might help. Then seal this new understanding with a vow and rejoice in the good that is or can be done. Finally, send these insights out into the world and live in harmony with them.[32] Perhaps on the very day of engaging in this meditative practice, a need or an opportunity will come along that can be addressed by your generosity.

The Christian faith has placed love at the center of its ethical understanding. The word *love* is used more frequently in the Christian tradition

30. Ibid., 6–11.
31. Ibid., 16–24.
32. Ibid., 82–85.

## Section III — The Development of Love

than the Buddhist choice of the word *compassion*, although comparable meanings exist between the two words and the teaching of the two religions. More specifically, the early Christians selected the Greek word *agape* as expressive of the meaning for love, a word that means unconditional acceptance, unlimited care, and selfless compassion. It is the common word used to describe love in the New Testament, although several other words for love were available and in common use in the culture at the time that the New Testament took form.

The word was not entirely new and was used in the Septuagint and in some Jewish writings. It did have a different meaning than many of the others words that might have been selected such as *eros* or *philia*, and was most likely chosen because the early Christians wanted to stress a new idea about the essential meaning of love.[33] *Eros* was commonly used, but its meaning focused on the object of love as worthy (appraisal) and the lover's desire to possess. *Philia* was also commonly used, especially in reference to mutual and reciprocal friendship. The word *agape* moves in the different direction of giving love to others irrespective of merit (bestowal), and it is a love that seeks to give regardless of what might be returned in kind. Anders Nygren, the Swedish theologian of a previous generation fully articulates the differences in meaning between the words, especially between *agape* and *eros*, and maintains that agape is the heartbeat of Christian faith.[34]

The writers of the New Testament, describing the teaching of Jesus about love, use the word agape, although Jesus most likely spoke in Aramaic. Jesus is reported as using the concept of *agape* as he draws upon the Hebrew Bible when questioned about the law. He is asked by a Pharisee, "'Teacher, which commandment in the law is the greatest?' He said to him, 'You shall love the Lord your God with all your heart, and with all of your soul, and with all of your mind. This is the greatest and first commandment. And a second is like it: You shall love your neighbor as yourself. On these two commandments hang all the law and the prophets'" (Matt 22:36–40). The word chosen is the verb form of *agape*, *agapao*. The passage teaches that a follower of Jesus is to love God and neighbor fully and completely. Jesus also teaches his listeners and followers to not only love God and neighbor, but also one's enemies. The Gospel of Matthew attributes to Jesus the following: "You have heard it was said, 'You shall love

---

33. Morris, *Testaments of Love: A Study of Love in the Bible*, 123–28.

34. *Agape and Eros*, Part I, 41–48. His language in a section of the book is: "Agape as the Fundamental Motif of Christianity."

your neighbor and hate your enemy.' But I say unto you, love your enemies and pray for those who persecute you . . ." (Matt 5:43–44). Jesus goes on to say that anyone might give love to a friend, but follow the pattern of God who provides life-giving sun and rain to all, even those whose behavior is unlovable and unacceptable.

Such an expression of love does not come naturally and easily to us, and Jesus is careful in his teaching that this kind of unlimited love is given to us by the power and presence of God in our lives. The phrase used to describe this gift of empowerment is "the kingdom of God" or "the kingdom of Heaven." What is meant is that as we give ourselves in total love to God, we receive the presence of God in our lives, and we are empowered to love; God "reigns" in our lives and we begin to reflect the character of God who is Love. The Gospel of Mark is quite direct in describing this understanding as the central message of the teaching of Jesus. The author of Mark's Gospel describes the beginning and purpose of the ministry of Jesus in the following way: "Now after John was arrested, Jesus came to Galilee, proclaiming the good news of God, and saying, 'The time is fulfilled, and the kingdom of God has come near; repent, and believe the good news'" (Mark 1:14–15). Still another Gospel writer, the author of John, underlines that God is love as he writes, "For God so loved the world that he give his only Son, so that everyone who believes in him may have eternal life" (John 3:16).

The epistles and general letters also teach a comparable message. The Apostle Paul speaks of love (agape) as the essence of Christian ethics and practice.[35] He too acknowledges that unlimited and unconditional love is not an easy and a natural pattern of life for humankind. He even complains, "I do not understand my own actions. For I do not do what I want, but I do the very thing I hate" (Rom 7:15). He goes on to describe agape love as "a still more excellent way" and provides a full description of its content.[36] How is it that Paul and indeed any one of us can have this kind of love in our lives? Paul is clear to say that it is empowerment, a gift of God's Spirit who fills our lives as we invite God into our lives. In one of his letters, Paul contrasts two styles of life, one characterized by the "flesh" or self-seeking and the other characterized by the power and presence God's Spirit. He writes, "By contrast, the fruit of the Spirit is love, joy, peace, patience, kindness, generosity, faithfulness, gentleness and self-control.

---

35. See Vacek, *Love, Human and Divine: The Heart of Christian Ethics*, for a profound and persuasive development of love as the core of Christian ethics.

36. 1 Cor 12:31b—13:13.

## Section III — The Development of Love

There is no law against such things" (Gal 5:22–23).[37] It is interesting to note how many of the words chosen by Paul, in addition to the lead word of *agape*, are related to the broader understanding of love, for example, *patience, kindness, generosity,* and *gentleness*.

The author of the general letter in the New Testament known as 1 John underscores the same teaching and pattern of behavior about love. John of Patmos is again quite clear and direct. He underscores that God is love. He writes, "Beloved, let us love one another, because love is from God; everyone who loves is born of God and knows God" (1 John 4:7). He goes on to say, "So we have known and believe the love that God has for us. God is love, and those who abide in love abide in God, and God abides in them" (1 John 4:16). Once again, these early Christians are taught that love is the essence of the Christian life, and that as we love God with our whole being, we will be empowered to love, with the same quality of love that God loves the human family. In many passages of the New Testament, and over nearly two thousand years of history, patterns of Christian formation, varying in the different branches of the Christian church, have developed to guide Christians in deepening their spirituality and cultivating lives of love and compassion.

The importance of love within Islam is attested in many ways, although some have wondered about the place of love in Muslim teaching, given the attention in recent years on a radical and extreme element in Islam that has chosen violence as a means for social change. The same concern has been expressed by many regarding more extreme forms of Christianity and other religious traditions as well. But it is important to call attention to the fact that an international group of respected leaders and scholars within Islam, with representation from its different divisions, composed a letter which was sent on October 13, 2007 to Christian leaders around the world. The Letter, called "A Common Word between Us and You" invites the world Christian community to join the Islamic community in affirming and practicing the two love commandments, to love God with our whole being and to love our neighbor as ourselves. The letter underlines the common belief that God is Love and urges Christians to join with Muslims in finding ways to foster peace and justice in the world. The letter begins, "Thus in obedience to the Holy Qur'an, we as Muslims invite Christians to come together with us on the basis of what is common

---

37. See the book by John Levison, *Filled with the Spirit*, for a full account of the place of God's Spirit in human life.

## Empowered to Love

to us, which is also what is essential to our faith and practice: the Two Commandments of love."[38]

Space does not permit us to fully develop the importance of love in the beliefs and practices of Islam,[39] but such a letter of this magnitude indicates how central love is to Muslims. The same could be said of several other religious traditions as we have described in Chapter 4. One contemporary interpreter and medical doctor who represents the breadth of the Hindu tradition, Deepak Chopra, has written extensively on a range of themes related to health and well-being. His book, *The Path of Love: Renewing the Power of Spirit in Your Life,* shows how it is possible to be fulfilled by rediscovering the power of love in spirituality. In this volume, Dr. Chopra also stresses the need for empowerment in nurturing our capacity to love. He understands love as the primary expression of spirit or the divine in our lives. As we cultivate our spiritual lives, almost regardless of tradition, we can transform ourselves and our relationships, giving them depth and meaning, and enabling us to pursue lives of love and compassion.

He does place an emphasis in this volume on marriage and the committed relationship. The book deals more specifically with the love of attraction than it does with altruism. But his approach, drawing upon the great wisdom of the Vedic texts, could easily have expanded to include unconditional and unlimited love. In regard to the committed relationship, he suggests a pathway through the seven stages of love: attraction, infatuation, courtship, intimacy, surrender, passion, and ecstasy. With remarkable insight and practical wisdom, he melds Eastern wisdom and Western pragmatism, ancient knowledge and scientific research, and weaves them together through the use of classical meditative practices and the use of contemporary narratives from couples who have consulted with him. The book is helpful for those seeking a spiritual dimension and connection in their relationship.

Another author, Eckhart Tolle, eclectic in his approach, has written about the importance of renewal and empowerment as we seek to find true peace and happiness. As yet, no one of his books has love as its primary focus, but it is obliquely present in nearly all of them. Perhaps his best

---

38. Response to this letter has been overwhelmingly positive within the Christians community, although there are those who say that the differences between the two religions are too wide to cross. See my article in "Common Word, Common Ground: The Love Commandments and the Understanding of God," 26–35.

39. One thoughtful account of love within Islam is developed by Nasr, *The Heart of Islam: Enduring Values for Humanity,* 209–16.

## Section III — The Development of Love

known book, *The Power of Now,* offers a guide to spiritual enlightenment. Drawing upon insights from many religious traditions of the human family and from contemporary understandings of the human experience, he underlines that we are imprisoned by fear and by the ways that our minds work. We need to move away from the analytical mind and the way that it has created a sense of selfhood tied as it is to our ego needs, our guilt about the past, and our anxiety about the future. We must move toward the Buddhist (Zen) emphasis on living in the present and focusing our attention on the here and now. As we do, we will be able to surrender our fearful tendencies that drive us to do all we can to make life more secure. We need to pause and quiet our inner worry and turmoil. As we do, can then be receptive to the universal spirit and find peace of mind. He underlines that this surrender is not just for personal happiness, but to enable us to be transformed and used by the divine purpose. He writes in the front of his book, "You are here to enable the divine purpose of the universe to unfold. That is how important you are!"[40]

It is this last point that he fully develops in *A New Earth: Awakening to Your Life's Purpose.* Comparable themes that were articulated in *The Power of Now* are fully expressed in this volume. He points to the "flowering of the human consciousness" and to the ways that humanity is evolving to a higher state. There are ways of moving beyond ego needs and our fears, of breaking free, and being empowered to find our inner purpose. As we do, we will begin to find and accept our place in the world and be able with enthusiasm and enjoyment to show love and compassion in our relationships.[41]

Karen Armstrong, distinguished author of several books about the development of religious thought, customs, and traditions, has spoken directly about the need for compassion. She has joined with other religious leaders in developing an association of like-minded people committed to the compassionate life. Members of this association of religious and secular leaders recently came together to prepare a "Charter for Compassion,"[42] a document that will be useful to us in a later chapter. In her recent book, she makes the case for the compassionate life and outlines twelve steps to

---

40. Tolle, *The Power of Now*, vii.

41. Tolle puts more emphasis on human transformation than upon loving behavior and service, but his grand thesis certainly suggests that our transformation to participate in "a new earth" will have an altruistic component.

42. We will use this charter in our final chapter. It was launched on November 12, 2009 in sixty different locations throughout the world; in synagogues, mosques, temples, and churches as well as secular institutions.

*Empowered to Love*

follow in its cultivation. She stresses that compassion is natural to human beings and the fulfillment of human nature. Compassion is within us and must be drawn out. She maintains that it can be cultivated in our lives and that we can be empowered to act compassionately.[43] Her twelve steps are:[44]

1. We must learn about compassion. She points to the Latin word, *educere* (education) which means "to lead out," implying that compassion is inside of us, but can be drawn out of us through education. We can be empowered as we learn more about our makeup and the components of love and compassion.

2. We need to look at our own world. As we do, we will discover, as have great religious sages of the past such as Confucius, that the need for love is right in front of us and in our immediate surroundings.

3. She maintains that we should have compassion for ourselves as a foundation for understanding the need to express compassion for others. We can use our own self-knowledge and our need for compassion as an inspiration and a guide for our compassionate behavior with others.

4. It follows that we need to have empathy for others. As we learn about the needs of others, we find within ourselves a natural inclination and capacity to identify with them. As we get to know them and understand their struggles, we begin to care deeply for their suffering and their needs.

5. We need to cultivate right mindfulness, a concept important in the Buddhist tradition. We must learn how and endeavor to detach ourselves from the control of our own ego, a control which clouds our understanding of reality and prevents from seeing the present and caring for others. Mindfulness is a form of meditation that moves us beyond seeing the world through the lens of our own needs and gives us a better grasp of reality and the present. It enables us to observe and accept our way of living in order to discover how we interact with others and how to engage in interpersonal relationships that are honest, caring, and nurturing.

6. As we make some progress in our moral transformation, we learn that compassion is connected to loving actions. It is more than just feeling sorry for others. Gradually and incrementally, we become

---

43. *Twelve Steps to a Compassionate Life*, 11.
44. Ibid., 25–190. I will list her twelve steps and add my own words to them; each step is a chapter title.

## Section III — The Development of Love

more compassionate and commit to our version of the Golden Rule, to do unto others as we would have them do unto us.

7. We need to have humility and recognize how little we really know. With a humble spirit, we move out into the world to encounter others and the overwhelming challenges of our world in crisis. We go, knowing that we may not fully understand, but with an eagerness to learn how we might contribute wisely to the well-being of others.

8. As we go and encounter others, we begin to learn how we should speak to them; how to engage in mutual conversation, to truly speak and empathically listen to one another. We begin to learn the culture and customs of those who are different from us, and we acknowledge that our starting points may be different. But we assume that we share a common humanity, and that as we understand each other better, we learn ways to express wise and helpful compassion. We care adequately and appropriately.

9. We recognize that our responsibility is to show concern for everybody, not just those with whom we are comfortable. We give up our "tribal outlook" and learn how to express love across boundaries of culture and language, of belief and practice.

10. So, we seek knowledge about others, knowing that love and compassion imply responding with understanding, with appropriate feelings, words, and actions.

11. And as we do, we discover and begin to recognize the other as one who journeys on a comparable road of life. There is fear, anxiety, insecurity, grief, and pain. Others need understanding, compassion, and loving attention, even as we do.

12. At times, we will encounter those who are enemies, those who differ in outlook and values and see us and what we represent as a threat. We may see them as a threat as well as they seek to harm us. Again, standing back, we must look deep within in order to understand this behavior and search for ways that will bridge the gap between us. We learn about forgiveness and hope that the gap can be closed and we can extend compassion that heals the fear, the hatred, and the violence.

Compassion, understood in these many ways, is what is needed in our troubled world. And we need to be empowered beyond our natural inclinations to be able to demonstrate in tangible ways the love and compassion that is so needed.

## THE PRACTICE OF LOVE

The twelve steps of Dr. Armstrong lead us directly to a discussion of the practice of love, not that we have ignored the practice of love and compassion in earlier chapters. But our goal now will be to suggest ways of practicing love and compassion in the several arenas of life; in primary relationships such as spouse, parent, family, and personal friendships; in the regions in which we live in terms of responsible citizenship, community leadership, and care for those who are marginalized in some way; and in terms of national and global responsibility to be wise, thoughtful, informed and compassionate citizens of our nation and our earth community. We turn first to primary relationships.

## STUDY RESOURCES

### Discussion Questions

1. Do you think we can become more loving and compassionate by our commitment and efforts, or do you think we need to be empowered by an external source such as God?
2. Do you think that we are free to be loving and compassionate or are we so controlled by our heredity and environment that it is almost impossible to be "free" to love?
3. What role do heart and brain health have in enabling us to be more loving and compassionate?
4. What role does our faith, and the practices of our faith such as prayer and meditation, have on increasing our capacity to be more loving and compassionate?
5. What five steps should you take in order to cultivate your capacity to be more loving and compassionate?

**Section III** — The Development of Love

## Key Terms and Concepts

- *Empower:* To be enabled to take initiative and have the internal resources to accomplish a goal; as in empowered to love (inspired and transformed in order to love).
- *Enlightenment:* To be enabled to become aware and see clearly; to be fulfilled, free, and find meaning in life because you understand and are in touch with reality.
- *Meditation:* To reflect or contemplate deeply; to pause and quiet one's inner life in order be in touch with deeper and transcendent realities.
- *Empathy:* The ability to understand and feel the emotions, thoughts, motives, and suffering of another.
- *Mindfulness:* The ability to pay close attention to the present, what is currently happening within and around in order to grasp one's immediate feelings and context.

## Suggestions for Reference and Reading

1. Armstrong, Karen, *Twelve Steps to a Compassionate Life.* New York: Alfred A. Knopf, 2010.
2. The Dalai Lama, *The Compassionate Life.* Boston: Wisdom Publications, 2003.
3. Levison, John R., *Filled with the Spirit.* Grand Rapids: Eerdmans, 2009.
4. Newberg, Andrew and Mark Robert Waldman, *How God Changes Your Brain.* New York: Ballantine, 2010.
5. Pesso, Tana with Penor Rinpoche, *First Invite Love In: 40 Time Tested Tools for Creating a More Compassionate Life.* Summerville, MA: Wisdom Publications, 2010.
6. Sorokin, Pitirim A., *The Ways and Power of Love: Types, Factors, and Techniques of Moral Transformation.* Philadelphia: Templeton Foundation Press, 2002.
7. Thich Nhat Hanh, *Teachings on Love.* Berkeley, CA: Parallax, 1998.

## SECTION IV

# The Practice of Love

WE TURN IN THIS new section to the practice of love. We know from experience that love and compassion, although not simple, can be understood and that they have great appeal to many people. There is a tendency for people to claim them as values and attempt as they are able to practice them in the daily rounds of life. But it is all too easy to give lip-service to love, but fail in its expression. We have learned in our study of love and compassion that practicing them is quite difficult. We know that other concerns in life and competing values and needs can crowd out the best of our intentions to be a loving person. So the question is: how it possible to live congruently with our values and be a person of integrity? In this section, we attempt to answer the question. As we do, we take comfort in knowing that love and compassion are fundamental to our well-being and that we can be empowered to love and show compassion. With this hope, we explore the practice of love in primary relations, in the community and region in which we live, and in our national and global context.

> "Do unto others as you would have them do unto you."
> —THE GOLDEN RULE

# 8

# Love in Primary Relationships

## THE PRACTICE OF LOVE

WE HAVE DESCRIBED THE world we inhabit as being in crisis, faced with a range of overwhelming problems that are both regional and global in character. The problems are vexing and the solutions elusive. We have maintained that love and compassion provide hope and inspiration for many of us in this context and motivation and guidance for those who are directly addressing these demanding challenges. We offered a way of understanding love and compassion and their many cognates such as altruism, caring, and empathy. We explored the ways that these concepts have been understood and applied across history, traditions, and cultures. We proceeded to trace the way that love and compassion are central to the ethical systems of nearly all of the great religions of the world. We turned to the ways that love and compassion become a part of our identity and character, looking first at the influence of our environment. We also examined current heart and brain research in order to understand better how our heredity and health impact our capacity to love. We went on to discuss the many ways that are available to us for increasing our capacity to be more loving.

Our focus in this next section is on the practice of love. It is well and good to reflect about love and learn as much as we possibly can about its "many-splendored" character. These endeavors do contribute to our capacity to be more loving and motivate us to pursue compassionate

## Section IV — The Practice of Love

solutions in our troubled relationships. Further, they help us find just and peaceful approaches to the seemingly intractable problems facing the regions in which we live and the earth we call home. But it is too easy to pause at the point of reflection and not move on to action.[1] Action is difficult in part because of other demands on our time, demands which in themselves may be important and necessary to the well-being of those around us. In addition, we postpone practice because we do not know how to address the complex problems. We may lack access, resources, and the necessary connections that would give us the requisite tools to make a difference. Often, we simply do not have sufficient insight and skill to know how to love intelligently and appropriately. Section IV is about increasing our motivation, insight, and skills to enable us to be those who love in spirit and practice.

## THE SEVERAL PRIMARY RELATIONSHIPS

We most frequently reflect about and practice love in the domain of our primary relationships. As love and compassion come to our mind, swell in our emotions, and provoke our conscience, it is almost always in reference to those who are near and dear. At times, we are concerned about those who are distant from us and those who may be suffering in a different region of the world. We may worry about those who are unemployed or who have lost homes in a hurricane, and we attempt to find ways to assist them. We are often moved by stories and images of those who suffer from malnutrition and starvation, and we become motivated to support agencies that provide care for the people of Somalia and East Africa. But in the day-to-day rhythms of life, we are most concerned about the well-being of our spouse or life partner, our family, friends, and those whom we encounter on a regular basis at work and in the daily rounds of life.

Maintaining positive feelings and good communication in primary relationships is important to our well-being, happiness, and contentment. In many ways, these positive linkages constitute the heart of life. But these relationships are not always easy and can be quite complex and demanding. Maybe that is why there are so many programs on television about marriage and family life; they are filled with the twists and turns of difficult relationships which make for good comedy. There is no one way or

---

1. I have been moved by the example of Dietrich Bonhoeffer, the German martyr who resisted Hitler, who spoke often of his love for reflection, but gave his life for peace and freedom. See Eric Metaxas, *Bonhoeffer: Pastor, Martyr, Prophet, Spy*.

particular style to keep them positive and life-giving. In fact each of us has our own way of linking with those in our immediate circle. We often go about maintaining these relationships not fully conscious of the ways we function and what preferences and tendencies we may have. *Having a deeper awareness of our style and how we are perceived by those close to us can dramatically improve the quality of these relationships.*

There are several methodologies for assessing our ways of relating with others.[2] One that has been available a number of years and has been especially helpful to many people is the Myers Briggs Inventory.[3] This methodology does not intend to fully describe us or discern the factors that contributed to forming us. The goal of those who designed it is to help us understand our preferences and inclinations in the ways that we make sense of the world around us, the ways that we make decisions, and the ways that we relate to others. It is not intended to provide a method for counseling and psychotherapy nor is it a judgment made about the most or least effective styles and preferences for building and sustaining healthy relationships. It is more descriptive and aimed at self-awareness.

I have personally found the methodology very helpful, and it has increased my own self-understanding and self-acceptance. I have grown to appreciate my personality style and how this understanding points to my identity. The methodology has also enabled me to appreciate the styles of others and made me less likely to judge them because they have a different perspective about an issue and propose a different direction for action. In fact, I have become a much better team player because of the Myers Briggs Inventory. I value the perspectives and styles of others who contribute to the larger group's way of viewing an issue and the direction of a decision. More information is available as people with different perspectives contribute to the information pool. Not infrequently, a wiser consensus is achieved and a better decision can be reached. One fringe outcome of this kind of process is that there is an increasing sense of respect and bond between those who are involved in the process.

The Myers Briggs Inventory provides an orderly pattern for personality differences and draws upon the insight of Carl Jung in describing these differences.[4] Initially the Inventory describes two ways of perceiving,

---

2. The resources for building good relationships and maintaining a positive family life are numerous and range from the simple magazine article to the richly nuanced self-help book to the carefully researched scholarly article. Community classes are available and many therapists specialize in the field.

3. Myers and Myers, *Gifts Differing*.

4. Ibid., 2–3.

## Section IV — The Practice of Love

one by *sensing*, or how we become aware of the world around us through the five senses. The other is *intuition*, which is indirect perception by way of the unconscious, incorporating internal ideas and associations that frame perceptions that come from the external environment. As we move through childhood to adulthood, these tendencies become natural to us and shape the way we view the world around us. They often shape the sort of interests we have and the career we may chose.

In addition to the two ways of perceiving, there are also two ways of judging or making decisions. One way is by the use of rational thought (*thinking*), a pattern of logic beginning with first principles or universal truths and moving to understanding by way of the rational syllogism and reasoning from these universal truths. A second way has to do with the preference for *feeling*, a tendency to make decision more on the basis of empathy and the evaluation of how the decision might impact the feelings of those who are affected by the decision. We grow from childhood to adulthood with these patterns or styles as well, and they influence the way we relate to others.

Combinations of these patterns begin to give contours to our style of perceiving and judging. We may have the tendency to connect sensing and thinking (ST) or sensing and feeling (SF). Our pattern may be driven more by intuition to which we add feeling (NF) or thinking (NT). Our personality takes shape with these preferences.

The Inventory then adds two other categories, the *extraversion-introversion* preference and the *judgment-perception* preference.[5] The extravert tends to be more engaged by the external world and gains energy and satisfaction by being around and interacting with others. The introvert has a tendency to be more engaged with the inner world of ideas and concepts and gains energy and satisfaction by reflection. In the judgment-perception spectrum, those who lean toward perception are shaped by their external surroundings and respond to the input that comes to them. They make decisions and relate to others on the basis of what they perceive. Those who lean toward judgment tend toward making decisions and relating to others on the basis of feelings, values, and ideas that are already present. Once again, we get the combinations within the categories, an EJ or an EP, or an IJ or an IP. As we carefully assess these combinations, we begin to discern our pattern of relating to others and making decisions.

The outcome of the inventory is that one is given a description of a personality style that can be any of sixteen different types. As this is

---

5. Ibid., 7–9.

understood through a careful testing process and with informed and thoughtful interpretation, self-understanding, and an appreciation of the dominant style of those around you are increased. Those who use the Myers Briggs Inventory are careful to say that the styles are on a continuum, with a lean or dominant preference for one side of the opposite tendencies. A person taking the Inventory will be assessed on a scale of 1–10, and may be assessed, for example, as a 6 on the introversion-extraversion spectrum, with a more dominant 6 pointing to the tendency to be an extrovert. Each of the four scales then provides you with an understanding of your dominant pattern and your auxiliary pattern. As you receive your dominant patterns in the four categories, you are then judged, for example, to be an INTJ or an ENFP or any one of the sixteen combinations. Each combination includes a fairly comprehensive map of one's personality style.

It is also important to note that these dominant tendencies are not life sentences and may change over time and the exposure to different circumstances. A terribly shy young person may be a 1 or 2 on the Introversion scale, but with maturity and increased confidence around others may be reassessed as a 4 on the scale. My natural inclination has been to be a 4 on the introversion side of the scale, but because of several years of senior level administrative work involving meeting the public, I retested to a 6 with a lean toward extraversion. I began to think of myself as sort of a "professional extravert." As I returned to more scholarly pursuits, I found myself going back to a 4 on the scale. I also changed on the thinking-feeling spectrum. During my student years I was a fairly strong T (thinking) in part because of my exposure to logic and mathematics. As time went along, and I served as a chaplain and professor in a university setting, I discovered a gradual increase in my feelings of empathy. I began to care more about the personal lives of students and to identify with the pain and suffering of others. In time, there was an increase toward the feeling side of the continuum, not that rational thought was unimportant. It was not so much replaced as it was moved to a different place on the scale, with feelings of empathy gaining more importance. I now test as an INFJ, and I enjoy my inner life and find that I relate to others more cautiously (I or introverted). I trust my intuition and often make judgments based upon values that are present within me (N or intuitive). I tend to listen to others with empathy as they share their experiences with me, and I am less likely to process my inner life by talking and allow my thoughts and feelings to mature before I speak (F or feeling). In the conversations with others, I continue to listen well, but then suggest that a decision be made

## Section IV — The Practice of Love

(J or judgment). I often nudge those in my inner circle to move forward because the issue has already been discussed.

There is great value in the Myers Briggs Inventory as it increases our self-understanding. We gain insight about how we make sense of the world around us, assess information and make decisions, and for our purposes, gain insight about how it is that we relate to others. If we know our inclinations and tendencies (dominant and auxiliary styles), then we can use these insights to be sensitive to others, grow to appreciate their distinctiveness, and gain tangible skills that will help us to love and show compassion. Our caring can be wise, appropriate, and healing as we relate to those who make up our primary relationships.[6]

>  Summary of Four Preferences[7]
>  EI—Extraversion or Introversion
>  SN—Sensing or Intuition
>  TF—Thinking or Feeling
>  JP—Judgment or Perception

Learning about our style and tendencies and how they influence the ways that we love and show compassion will enable us to have more satisfying and healthy primary relationships. A review of the different kinds of love might also be helpful to us as we learn to synchronize our style with practice. We spoke earlier of the several different ways that love and its many cognates are defined, understood in history, and become a part of the ethical systems of the world's religions.[8]

An attempt was made to summarize these several meanings in the three Greek words, *eros*, *philia*, and *agape*. We defined *eros* as the attraction we feel toward that which is beautiful, good, true, and just, drawing upon the teaching of Plato. Our feeling of *eros* is drawn to that which is attractive, admirable, valuable, and lovable. It is an act of *appraisal* as we assess what comes to us as having worth and the possibility of filling our life with pleasure and meaning.

The Greek work *philia* was also mentioned and defined as the attraction and satisfaction one finds in friendship.[9] As we encounter those who

---

6. Another classic assessment of personality style is the Enneagram, going back into history and updated with the rise of the social sciences. See Helen Palmer's treatment in *The Enneagram: Understanding Yourself and the Others in Your Life*.

7. Myers and Myers, *Gifts Differing*, 9.

8. See Section II.

9. See Emerson, *On Love and Friendship*, for a thoughtful discussion of loving friendships.

## Love in Primary Relationships

have common interests and values, whose culture and heritage may be comparable to our own, and engage in conversation and activities which are mutually enjoyable, we have found friends. Aristotle maintained that true friendships are reciprocal and in them the parties have a concern for the well-being of those with whom they associate. He noted that there are false friendships in which reciprocity is not present, but more an attempt to exploit another for one's own gain or pleasure. A friendship exists when one is willing to come to the aid of another and help them with whatever need may exist. The great theologian of the Middle Ages, Thomas Aquinas, gave friendship the highest possible place in human life when he spoke of it as the essence of one's relationship with God.

The concept of *agape* was also introduced, and it was defined as a love that is unlimited and without conditions. It is a love of *bestowal* as we vest value in the other person, but are not necessarily drawn to the other person because of their attractiveness and lovable qualities. We may do so for a variety of reasons, but one that is persuasive is the conviction that every person is created in the image of God and therefore has divine qualities within them, even if they are not immediately apparent at first glance. *Agape* is the word that is used in the New Testament to describe the character of God's love for the human family, and indeed for the whole world. It is also the word chosen to describe the essence of the spiritual and ethical life. We are empowered and told to love God with our whole being and our neighbor as ourselves.[10]

We move into our primary relationships then with a personality style and tendencies, and we then add our understanding of the several meanings of love. It is from this base that we learn how to practice love in primary relationships. Let's look at these primary relationships one by one and discern how love and compassion might be present. Primary relationships are our connection with people within a circle of nearness, those whom we encounter on a normal and regular basis. Let's focus our attention on five types of relationships.

The most important relationship for many people is the relationship with one's spouse or life partner.[11] I am fully aware that there are many

---

10. Chapman in *Love As A Way of Life: Seven Keys to Transforming Every Aspect of Your Life* offers the following dimensions of love: kindness, patience, forgiveness, courtesy, humility, generosity, and honesty.

11. I have been helped by two older, but emerging classics in the description of spousal relationships: Scarf, *Intimate Partners: Patterns in Love and Marriage* and Bloomfield and Vettese, *Lifemates: The Love Fitness Program for a Lasting Relationship*. Sternberg in *Love Is A Story: A New Theory of Relationships* offers a number of models,

## Section IV — The Practice of Love

people who live alone, partly out of choice and often because of circumstances over which they have little or no control. Many of these people who live alone are content and find ways of living a fulfilled and productive life. They often speak of the ways that a return to a home in which they live alone can restore them and provide them with time to regain lost energy and perspective. They are free to rest, engage in enjoyable activities, and manage the daily tasks of life without having to focus on the needs of another person. But often these people and certainly many whose circumstances have forced them to live alone confess to feelings of loneliness.

Those with a spouse or a partner have the joy and challenge of sharing the pleasures and pains of life.[12] The day's activities can be shared in direct and honest conversation, negative as well as positive feelings about the day can be processed, a meal can be shared, and there can be mutual planning for the next day, the next week, and for all the days of one's life. In a trusting and open relationship, one's deeper life can be shared with another.[13] One can be heard and understood, hear and understand, and two souls can touch in healing and life-giving ways. Of course, it does not always happen that way; there may be fatigue and preoccupation that makes one partner less likely to listen with empathy, and there may be conflicts and the inevitable pain and distance that conflicts can create. There may be separation and divorce. But the potential for an authentic meeting at a deep and true level is present, and a connection can be formed and experienced that enriches one's life. Love and compassion can be expressed and received.[14]

---

expressed in stories that capture the patterns of many of our relationships. There are dozens of recent publication on love and marriage. I have consulted Gottman and Silver, *The Seven Principles of Making Marriage Work*; Love and Stonsy, *How to Improve Your Marriage Without Talking About It*, and several others.

12. The Biblical character, Ruth, from a different tribe than her spouse, reflects on her commitment in anticipation of a move: "Don't ask me to leave you! Let me go with you. Wherever you go, I will go; wherever you live, I will live. Your people will be my people, and your God will be my God. Wherever you die, I will die, and that is where I will be buried. May the Lord's worst punishment come upon me if I let anything but death separate me from you" (Ruth 1:16–17).

13. See Chapman, *The Love Languages: How to Express Heartfelt Commitment to Your Mate* for an introduction to five principal ways of expressing love in a committed relationship. This book has had wide circulation and has been helpful to many people. The five are: Words of Affirmation, Quality Time, Receiving Gifts, Acts of Service, and Physical Touch, 39–130.

14. As John Donne wrote in "The Anniversary": "All other things, to their destruction draw, Only our loves have no decay; This, no tomorrow hath, nor yesterday, Running never runs from us away, But truly keeps his first, last, everlasting day." Quoted

*Love in Primary Relationships*

Another primary set of relationships is with one's family. Initially, there are parents, in time there are children, and frequently there are members of one's extended family. In many cultures, the extended family often lives in the same household. Family relationships are often complex and have the same potential as spousal or life partner relationships to be healthy and fulfilling, complex and demanding, or difficult and hurtful. It depends on what we make of them and our capacity and our family members' capacity to be loving and compassionate.[15] As the number of family members who are part of our circle of primary relationships increases, so too do the challenges and complexities increase—not just numerically but exponentially. One person added to a group of three does not just add a fourth more complexity, but the amount becomes the challenge of the fourth person's linkage with three others and the change that occurs with and among the three others.

The challenge then is to find good ways of being present, authentic, and self-giving in a manner that is appropriate to all of the relationships of the family. A child or teenager will need a nuanced linkage appropriate to his or her age and needs, whereas the adult or the grandmother will need a connection that is appropriate to his or her needs and the challenges of their lives. Each person in the family, often stretching across the age span, will be able to contribute to the well-being of the family in proportion to each person's maturity and will do so out of their inclinations, personality, and roles within the family system. Almost inevitably there will be conflict in the family, members with profound needs will need attention, and some members will be unable to measure up to the expectations of one or more members of the family unit.[16] But in all of this give and take of family life, there is the potential for deep and profound loving relationships that stretch across the generations. Sadly and ironically, it is often the death of a family member that increases our capacity to fully appreciate them, a truth I feel about my deceased parents and an early passing of my brother.[17] Support, encouragement, sharing, guidance, gratitude, and

---

in Greeley and Durkin, eds., *The Book of Love: A Treasury Inspired by the Greatest of Virtues*, 131.

15. See Viorst, *Necessary Losses: The Loves, Illusions, Dependencies and Impossible Expectations that All of Us Have to Give Up in Order to Grow*.

16. See John Welwood, *Perfect Love, Imperfect Relationships: Healing the Wound of the Heart*. He provides several exercises for the release of grievances in relationships, 169–87.

17. The French Jesuit scientist and theologian, Pierre Teihard De Chardin writes on the death of his sister: "Her disappearance has created a sort of universal wilderness

## Section IV — The Practice of Love

joy in another's growth and achievement are all possible when love and compassion are the fundamental values of the family system.

A third kind of primary relationships exists within our circle of friends. At the heart of friendship is the enjoyment of another person. We experience happiness in this person's presence for a variety of reasons. We may have many interests in common and find pleasure in speaking about them and participating in these common interests. We may gain insight and new perspectives on life because of the wisdom of our friend. We may see in another a model for living, a person whose values and behavior invite us to change and become a better person. We may find another person who truly listens to us, understands our struggle, and demonstrates empathy and support.[18] And, as Aristotle says, in friendship we truly care about another person and find ways to help them and make life better for them.

As in all of our primary relationships, so it is with friendships that they can be demanding and complex. There will be times when we experience imperfect connections and suffer the inevitable feelings of disappointment and disillusionment. We may hope for a phone call that doesn't ever come, an invitation to a social, cultural, or sporting event, and it doesn't materialize. We may anticipate a conversation in which we can share a most important development in our life, but our friend cannot hear us because this person is preoccupied with his or her own life challenges. We may even feel hurt and betrayed because our confidence in the mutuality of the relationship has been broken or we are falsely accused of being unfair and uncaring. We do have to give up some of our impossible expectations.[19]

Even as we had to let go of some of our unrealistic ideals, we can still find in our circle of friends the connections that make life so rich and satisfying. We can truly enjoy others, listen and be heard, appreciate and be appreciated, agree and disagree for the sake of learning, and care and be cared for in healing ways. We can enjoy beauty, wisdom, extraordinary ability, courageous behavior, and uncommon insight with others. We can engage

---

around me; it affects every element of an interior world of which I had gradually made her a partner. The two of us thought together in everything that makes up spiritual activity and the interior life. I shall miss her physical presence terribly; on the other hand I think that her power of inspiring and watch over me has strengthened." In Greeley and Durkin, eds., *The Book of Love*, 200.

18. In American culture, and perhaps universally, deep friendships are often more easily formed between women than between men. Hunt's book, *Fierce Tenderness: A Feminist Theology of Friendship* speaks poignantly to this point. So too does Smith's book, *The Friendless American Male*.

19. Viorst, *Necessary Losses*, 175ff.

in mutual projects, work together for the common good, jointly participate in events that help others and inspire, and say "best wishes" at the end of a wonderful day shared together. Life is too short not to have good friends and be a good friend. As Ralph Waldo Emerson says about friendship,

> "What is so pleasant as these jets of affection which make a young world for me again? What is so delicious as a just and firm encounter of two, in a thought, in a feeling? How beautiful, on their approach to this beating heart, the steps and forms of the gifted and the true! The moment we indulge our affections, the earth is metamorphosed; there is no winter and no night; all tragedies, all ennuis vanish,—duties even; nothing fills the proceeding eternity but the forms all radiant of beloved persons. Let the soul be assured that somewhere in the universe it should rejoin its friend, and it would be content and cheerful alone for a thousand years."[20]

Still another domain of primary relationships is our acquaintances in our many associations and with colleagues in our work. These relationships may not be as intimate and close as those with our spouse and family nor is there necessarily the same bond as one has with friends. But they are nevertheless an important part of our social world. As we go to work, depending on the nature of our work, we will likely encounter a number of people with whom we associate almost daily. We may be a receptionist or be greeted by one. We may have a staff meeting in which we associate with a group of people with whom we associate almost daily. Some of these people may easily move to the category of friendship. On the other hand, if they are work colleagues, a certain set of conditions and expectations generally exist. For example, we may be cautious about a close friendship with the person who reports to us or to whom we report. A close friendship might make the exchanges about assignments and assessment more awkward and difficult. With others, there may be differences of opinion or perspective because of our roles within the company or institution. I well remember in my responsibility as an academic dean that occasionally, in the hiring of a faculty member, I had some differences with the people in Human Resources and with the Chief Financial Officer. As I hired faculty, I tended to reserve the right of other faculty members to have substantial authority in the choice and I often wanted to offer a salary at the highest level in order to recruit the best candidate. I didn't always get my way. It

---

20. Emerson, *On Love and Friendship*, 33–34.

## Section IV — The Practice of Love

was in these settings that I grew in my understanding of what it means to be a team player.

We also have many acquaintances apart from our work, the people whom we meet in grocery stores, in shops, in the post office, in organizations to which we belong, in social and cultural events, and in the daily circumstances of our lives. Many of these people, of course, remain strangers, but frequently we see these people on a daily or weekly basis, learn their names, find out something about their lives, and form a cordial relationship. We will speak in what follows about the qualities that should be present in these encounters, but we might say at this juncture that these relationships in our work and in our everyday life can be very important to us and to those whom we meet. If there is a smile, a sincere interest behind the question, "How is your day going?" or the comment, "Have a wonderful day," we express a form of love and compassion. We say that they are people of worth, affirm them, honor them as those created in the image of God, and that our interest in their well-being is sincere even though there may be some distance between us. If we are friendly, fair, honest, and congruent, we can make a difference in their lives and ours by our behavior. If we are treated in these ways, we have a deeper sense of our own worth and value. We should not underestimate the impact for others or for ourselves in the more casual contacts between acquaintances and co-workers. Love and compassion can be expressed in these encounters.

A final category of primary relationships are those interactions with people who are strangers. We meet these people in our daily pattern of life, and we often meet them as we go beyond the region in which we live. We meet them when we travel, on airplanes, in train stations, and hotels. Many of the same values that I suggested as fundamental in our connections with acquaintances should also be present in our exchanges with strangers. We would underline the need to be respectful of the other person, regardless of position, age, dress, ethnicity, culture and custom, sexual orientation, or even inappropriate behavior. The expression of offense at inappropriate behavior may in fact be an expression of caring if done carefully in that the one acting inappropriately may learn from a timely and sensitive comment. A part of being respectful is being cordial and, as we are polite, we show in this behavior that we honor the other person. With strangers, we must find good ways to demonstrate fairness, honesty, and good judgment about the norms of behavior in particular settings. Further, we may find ourselves in a position of being able to help a stranger who has a particular need, perhaps an elderly person who needs some assistance with their

*Love in Primary Relationships*

luggage or a person seeking directions who does not speak English. We may show gratitude in many settings by saying "thank you" or giving the appropriate tip in a restaurant. On occasion, an honest comment to the stranger such as the expression of gratitude about the service they provide or a particular skill or friendly demeanor they demonstrate can mean a great deal to the one who believes that what they do is often not noticed. Again, the expression of a caring spirit, a compassionate act, and empathic listening can affirm the stranger and communicate to them in subtle ways that they are people of worth. We know in our heart what it is like to be a stranger, and we also long for welcome and acceptance.[21]

Love and compassion can be expressed in the variety of ways, depending on the nature of these primary relationships. Each person will have their own style that reflects their character and personality, but there will be common values, attitudes, and behaviors inherent in the encounters when love is present. It is these common qualities to which we now turn our attention.

## THE CHARACTER OF MATURE ADULT PRIMARY RELATIONSHIPS

We have mentioned in our discussion of primary relationships a number of qualities that should be present if we are committed to make love and compassion central to the way we live our lives. We described the many characteristics of love at some length in Chapter 2, but love and compassion surface in many ways, especially in primary relationships, and so we return once again to the ways that love is manifested. Love, like a beautiful diamond comes in cuts, carats, colors, and clarity. Its proportions can be viewed from many angles, and its beauty is apparent from all perspectives as light is reflected and shines through the stone. So we turn to the precious gem of love to help us gain perspective on how to express it in primary relationships. We carefully look to the qualities that should be present in every human encounter and will attempt to articulate how these qualities should manifest themselves in our interactions with others. As with the diamond, endless expressions of light and color may be listed, but I will focus on ten qualities.[22]

---

21. As the author of Exodus counsels, "You shall not oppress a resident alien; you know the heart of an alien, for you were aliens in the land of Egypt" (Exod 23:9).

22 Richo in *How to Be an Adult in Relationships: The Five Keys to Mindful Loving*, 26–40, stresses five, although he implies several others. He lists attention, acceptance,

## Section IV — The Practice of Love

The first of these is *giving attention*, the choice to be present for and acknowledge another person. The need to be acknowledged and have the attention of another and especially those with whom we are close is universal. It begins as we come into the world. As an infant, we feel the need for our parents, and especially our mother, to be present for us and pay attention to our lives. We want to be fed, to be held, and to be made comfortable. We long for our parent to be focused on us and be sensitive to our comfort and feelings. This need for attention stays with us throughout our lives. If we missed that attention in our childhood (and many of us have), then our longing for attention will be quite pronounced as we become teenagers and move into adult life. As we grow and mature into adulthood and get in touch with our desire for attention, we can find healthy ways of being acknowledged. It may be through success in our life work or as we engage in responsible and creative ways to make a contribution to the common good. In these ways we may naturally receive affirmation and the attention we want. For some, the longing does not subside, and it may take expression in inappropriate and unacceptable ways.

As we encounter another person, we should search for those ways of giving attention that are appropriate. It may be different with a spouse, a family member, a friend, and someone more distant. Different practices in certain settings (e.g. urban or rural) or in different cultures (e.g. American or Asian) sometimes create norms for demonstrating the way we give attention to another. It can be so easily misunderstood if we are not sensitive to the context. There are many times as well that we are preoccupied and distracted and let those who need our attention pass by like ships in the night. The opposite of giving attention is to ignore, fail to listen, and remain distant. Often this behavior is the result of shyness and the fear of being unacceptable. We give attention to others best when our needs for acceptance are met and when we can be more relaxed about the burdens of our responsibilities. In moments of stress and anxiety, we find it difficult to be present for others. We do it best when we are at peace within; being "together" empowers us to focus on another person who wants to be acknowledged. It is more likely that we will be present for them when we are fully aware that it is as fundamental expression of love, our highest value. We then make it a priority and a commitment. We give attention to the one in front of us, call them by name, listen as they respond and comment, and show by eye contact, a facial expression, a thoughtful and caring word that they are a person of worth. My failure in these encounters is partly

---

appreciation, affection, and allowing.

my shyness, but more often it is being distracted by schedule and a desire to make contact with someone else who means more to me and whom I might miss if I don't get their attention. I begin to look away and lose my focus on the one in front of me. But I continue to work on focusing on the one in front of me. I am learning to love, to be mindful, and be present and attentive even in the passing encounter.

The need and desire for attention does not go away; it will be with us all of our lives. It is a legitimate need, one for which we need not feel ashamed and guilty. It is acceptable to value ourselves and to expect to be acknowledged as a person of value. Most of us find healthy and constructive ways to receive attention, and it frequently comes when we are generous with our attention to another. Further, the need to be thought of as valuable and worthy of attention is often met in one's religious faith. Nearly all religious traditions speak about the value of each human being and offer ways to move toward mature self-worth and self-respect. In the Abrahamic tradition, for example, there is the teaching that a personal God gives attention to all people, offering them a life of peace and purpose. The author of the Gospel of Luke has Jesus comparing the value of a human being in God's sight to that of a sparrow; Jesus points to the way God cares for the sparrows and is quoted as saying, "But even the hairs of your head are all counted. Do not be afraid; you are of more value than many sparrows" (Luke 12:7).

A second characteristic of mature adult relationships is the *unconditional acceptance* of another. This quality of love is implied in the expression of acknowledgement and attention given to another, but it is a more active response. It goes beyond acknowledgement to giving unlimited positive regard for another. This fundamental dimension of love comes more easily to us when we encounter those who are attractive and have endearing qualities. But it is especially difficult to demonstrate positive regard for those who are unattractive and have personal characteristics and behavior that are offensive. Showing unconditional acceptance for those most difficult to love does not mean that we approve behavior that is harmful, self-destructive, and hurtful to others. Nor does it mean that we necessarily overlook poor hygiene, rude behavior, out of control ego needs, harsh and offensive language, and threats to our own welfare. We take all of this into account, but in the moment or over time, we find a way to receive the person into our hearts and learn how to love them. As St. Francis reached out to the leper and as Mother Teresa washed the body of the dying, we recognize that the one in

## Section IV — The Practice of Love

front of us has the divine in them. We extend ourselves as we would if we were with our spouse or child.

This quality of receiving another unconditionally when we encounter them will require the same level of mindfulness as giving attention. It, too, needs practice, the cultivation of the spiritual life, attunement, and commitment. We may encounter those whose behavior cannot be tolerated, and as a commitment to the greater good, we may have to take action to control destructive behavior. We have military, law enforcement, and legal systems that can help us in these cases, but in the normal flow of our lives, we accept those who come our way and say "yes, I accept you" to them.

As we noted in Section II, our capability to express unconditional love is intimately tied to our levels of maturity, our heredity and health, and to our openness to being empowered. It is not necessary to review all of these observations, but a brief reminder might be in order, not just in reference to our capacity to give attention to and to accept others, but also our capacity to express the several other qualities of love that give health and richness to our primary relationships. We underlined the following:

- In Chapter 5, there was a description of the ways that our environment shapes us and enables us to grow and develop into those who have the capacity to express genuine love to others. We also said that a deprived environmental background may limit our ability to love others.

- In Chapter 6, there was a discussion of the ways that our heredity and health, and in particular the proper functioning of our hearts and brain can contribute to our capacity to be loving people.

- In Chapter 7, there was an introduction to the ways that we can learn about and be empowered to love. It is this point that is so central to our ability to express altruistic love, a love that does not set conditions to be received, but is selfless and unlimited. We spoke in this chapter about spiritual discernment and the ways in which we receive the divine Spirit, the very presence of the God of love into our lives. We stressed what the Apostle Paul writes: "the gifts of the Spirit are love, joy, peace, patience, kindness, generosity, faithfulness, gentleness, and self-control" (Gal 5:22–23).

A third quality of love in primary relationships is the demonstration of *appreciation for the other person*. Appreciation gives depth to acceptance, and the person we encounter can hear us say, "I admire you; I delight in you; I prize you; I respect you; I acknowledge you, and I appreciate you as a unique gift."[23] In order for us to sense our personal worth and increase our self-confidence, we need those around us to appreciate us, not in an idealized way, but as we actually are. What is said to us when we are appreciated is that we have value and the potential to contribute to the well-being of others and to our environment. A parent's expression of appreciation of the child is to say that the child has potential and can make a distinctive and valuable contribution. These affirmations engender in the child a sense of self-worth and self-confidence, which lead to developing qualities that mark a mature and responsible adult. To be excessively critical of the child, or in adult relationships, to be critical of those whom we encounter, is to send the message of rejection.

It is not just the child who moves in the direction of those qualities which are appreciated by another; it is all of us. As our talents and gifts are recognized, we gain confidence in their expression, give attention to their development, and refine them in ways they contribute to welfare of others and to the formation of a more just and humane setting. As a teacher at the university level, I had a number of students who were very gifted, but not always confident in their abilities. It was gratifying for me to express appreciation for the quality of their grasp of the subtleties of the subject under discussion, their ability to reflect critically about it in exams and essays, and then to move forward in their lives and careers in admirable ways. I am pleased that I showed appreciation for their intelligence, their use of language, and their contribution to the good of society. Appreciation provides a nudge forward toward maturity and responsibility.

These qualities of love are interwoven; or to change the metaphor, they are a diamond with different cuts, colors, and proportions of beauty. To show appreciation in our primary relationships leads to another essential dimension of love, that of *affection*. Affection is the tangible expression of caring for another, and its opposite is to act selfishly or abusively. There are many ways of showing affection, and it can be done in word and deed. An honest word of caring for another, expressed appropriately within the context of the relationship, can be healing and life-giving for another. What is appropriate for one's spouse or life partner may be quite different than its expression for a friend or acquaintance. It is natural to speak a word of love, to touch, and to kiss our spouse. The shaking of hands or a hug may be appropriate for friends and acquaintances. A word or a smile is more important for the stranger.

---

23. Ibid., 33.

## Section IV — The Practice of Love

One small way that the expression of affection for the acquaintance or the stranger occurs for me is in the midst of a church service when the congregation is invited to "pass the peace." The simple act of saying, "the peace of God be with you" can be done routinely and awkwardly at times, but I have learned to shake the hand of my sister or brother, look them directly in the eye, and with a warm smile, say the words of the passing of the peace. I do not always do it well, but in most cases, I find a warm response and glow in the other person when I am sincere and not clumsy or embarrassed.

The expression of affection is expressed in alternative ways in different settings and cultures. In some cases, it is simply inappropriate because the social norms dictate an alternative way of behaving. It may not have a place in the Board Room, for example, as business is conducted in a more formal way. There are different norms in different cultures as well. I learned this reality in an embarrassing way once in Japan as I visited one of my students in Tokyo. As I was leaving, ready to board the train, I made the gesture of offering a hug in a public setting. She was chagrined, stepped away, smiled and said good-bye. I learned in full color what I should have known, that the expression of affection, especially among non-family members in public settings in Japan is not normal behavior.

I believe that this brilliant young Japanese woman knew, without physical affection, that I cared for her because I had spent hours with her in conversation. What was present, I hope, was that next dimension of love so necessary in primary relationships, the *expression of empathy*. I listened carefully as she spoke about her family, the differences between the cultures, her desire to understand Christian faith in the context of her Buddhist heritage, and her desire to be a concert pianist. She spoke at length about the customs of her upbringing, the differences between the roles of her father and mother, and the ways that these differed between families in Japan and families in the United States. I did (or at least tried to) listen with understanding, attempt to see the world through her eyes, and to care for the inevitable tensions of becoming an adult and one who is at home in different cultures.

To have empathy for another is to listen wisely and to care deeply and profoundly. It is to demonstrate to another that their world, their struggle, their worries, and indeed their victories and their joys, their relationships, and their hopes and dreams matter. With care not to be sentimental, but to show a keen interest and to demonstrate that the other has been heard, is what it means to be empathic. It is to understand what the other needs in terms of emotional support and to find ways to provide it; it is to offer to the other person what is appropriate for them.[24] We all need others who have empathy for us, those who understand our inner life and its unfolding pattern. Empathy is a gift in the blossoming of primary relationships.

Even as we need and give empathy in our primary relationships, so too do they need another dimension of love, *a connection that is based on honesty, integrity, and openness.* Good relationships must have these qualities present or they will deteriorate and ultimately fail. Primary relationships cannot be sustained when there is deception or when artificial roles are played. A good primary relationship begins with honesty. This does not mean that everything one thinks and feels must be expressed, but it does mean that what one doesn't express does not mislead. What is important in sustaining the relationship is communicated, and the amount of information shared will depend on the nature of the relationship. More is revealed and spoken with one's spouse, and perhaps less with family members depending on the needs present in the circumstances of life. Diminishing amounts of information may be shared with friends, although there are times when a good friend may be the one who listens with empathy and can be helpful in providing balance, perspective, and insight. With acquaintances and strangers, even less needs to be communicated, but what is important is that what we communicate is truthful and accurate.

Being honest in relationships sounds easier that it generally turns out to be in practice. The exhortation "just be honest" may be quite challenging and difficult to follow, and there are several reasons for this challenge. It may be because we have needs to be liked and respected that cause us to shade the truth in order to impress. Or we may have fears about being judged or even rejected if we reveal too much about our lives. The test will be directly connected to the progress we are making in our quest to be a person of integrity, an "integer person," one who has a single identity, one who is clear about values, and one who speaks with congruence and authenticity. To be a person of integrity may also mean being one who is open about revealing one's true identity and not attempting to project an alternative false self that we hope will impress or increase admiration. Again, being open does not mean being open about everything; some things are better left unsaid, again depending upon the nature of the relationship and the circumstances. But the person who is revealed is the real

---

24. Sorokin in his classic work, *The Ways and Powers of Love*, calls this dimension of love "adequacy," 17–19.

## Section IV — The Practice of Love

person, one who is pure in heart.[25] Primary relationships will thrive when there is honesty, integrity, and openness.

When such relationships exist, then there is another essential component of love, the *presence of trust*. People will be open and appropriately self-revealing when they trust the one or those in a group with whom they are communicating. We need a safe haven. In my years of working with students, I soon learned that it was important for them to have a place in which they were not afraid, one in which they did not feel threatened or judged, but one in which they were affirmed even in their struggles. Not infrequently in these settings, students spoke openly about the most sensitive issues in life; their sexual identity, their changing religious faith, their intimate relationships, conflicts with parents, their struggle about a major and a career, and about the lack of financial resources to sustain their education. Some students were more open and self-revealing than others, but nearly all of them needed the security of a safe environment, one in which confidence would be kept and where there was the presence of others who genuinely cared about their welfare and had their interest at heart.

It is not always easy to create these safe havens or even the safety within personal conversation. Inevitably, there have been times when most of us have been hurt in relationships and the pain stays with us. Perhaps we have the courage to share a deep and true feeling and have either felt that we have not been heard or that the person with whom we shared a sensitive concern simply did not care. Worse yet, many of us have had the information shared come back to us in a second-hand way and often in a distorted way. So nearly all of us are careful and wisely share, because we know that not all of those who are part of our circle of primary relationships have the capacity to hold personal information in confidence. But there are times in our lives when sharing our deepest feelings is essential to our health and well-being, and it is most likely within the primary relationships that we find those with whom we can be open. Love creates settings of trust in which we and those whom we love can speak about pain, fear, joy, and aspirations.

It is in those settings when we have been hurt or when we have hurt another by our lack of compassion and understanding that there is the need for still another dimension of love to be present, that of *forgiveness and reconciliation*. The pattern of rebuilding a relationship that has been

---

25. Jesus says in the Sermon on the Mount, "Blessed are the pure in heart, for they will see God" (Matt 5:8). Implied is that the person with integrity and without falsehood is able to see the transcendent and ultimate reality.

damaged or broken by insensitive and harmful behavior generally takes time. The feelings of being hurt by insensitive behavior or a thoughtless comment, treated rudely or unfairly, being misunderstand or ignored, or not being shown respect do not go way quickly. I have learned that there is a pattern of reconciliation when a relationship is broken, and generally it has at least three components:

The first of these has to do with being heard and understood about what has felt unjust and the presence of words and actions to demonstrate the restoration of justice and fairness. The broken relationship is usually a product of not being treated fairly, of not receiving what we feel entitled to have in the relationship, and a resulting sense of injustice. To restore the relationship requires an acknowledgment of the mistake or harmful action, a sense of being sorry or regretful, and a willingness to make it right.

When this happens, it makes possible the second step in the pattern of reconciliation, that of forgiveness. It is hard to forgive those who have hurt us, but when we hear from them that they are sorry, it releases us from the feelings of hurt and resentment and we can welcome them back in to our circle of nearness and communication. To be forgiven enables us to feel pardoned and to not have our offense held against us. It has the power to shatter the law of the irreversibility of the past, not by changing the record of all that has happened but by changing its meaning for us here and now. Forgiveness goes beyond the economy of reciprocity and retribution. We are emancipated from the need to get even and realize that getting even will more deeply harm the relationship.

When there is forgiveness, a third step becomes available to us; we can give love in return or be loved in return. Love in such a setting extends beyond the normal limits of human interaction and selflessly reaches out to the other; it goes to the point of need with a caring and healing response. With forgiveness comes the capacity to restore trust and caring and seek the well-being of the other person.

Nearly all of our primary relationships will be faced with the need for there to be the restoration of justice, the expression of regret and the giving of forgiveness, and the sense of once again being in the family of love. To get through these occurring cycles of hurt, forgiveness, and reconciliation, there is still another dimension of love, the quality of *perseverance and duration*. Those who truly love do not stop just because the relationships become difficult or because they cause discomfort and pain. Those who love make the commitment to stay in relationships across time and to find solutions to the complexities and challenges that are present in every

## Section IV — The Practice of Love

relationship. Yes, some relationships do break down and separation occurs. But as far as possible, those who love find the personal and spiritual resources to sustain the commitment. Even in those situations in which the relationship appears to be irreconcilable, there can still be the presence of respect and helpfulness. Those who truly love "go the extra mile."[26]

Relationships with one's spouse or life partner and family relationships require the ability to love across time. With time comes growth and change; we grow and change as do those whom we love. Accommodation to these spurts of growth and the pace of change, particularly with a child, will require us to make adjustments of attitude and spirit. In the marriage relationship, we have made the pledge to love "in sickness and health" and to love our life partner especially in moments of fear and despair. In the last few years I have had the privilege of being close to people whose life partner was aging and in decline, or seriously ill and not expected to live. I have been present for the aging and death of my parents as well. In these situations, I have learned what it means to make a life commitment to one's spouse and to one's family. Love perseveres, has duration, and lasts.

As part of going the second mile, we usually are required to demonstrate one additional aspect of love, and that is *to allow those in our primary relationships to be themselves, to give them the freedom to realize their full potential as human beings.* Our responsibilities may take the form of empowering others, helping them grow, and providing resources for them to heal. But our responsibilities do not extend to changing another person to fit our needs and expectations. It is a temptation to want to change other persons and to control and manipulate them in order to meet our particular needs. Not infrequently, we have projections of an ideal that may be conscious, but often these ideals are buried in our unconscious mind, and we have little awareness of our patterns of control.

In the limited pre-marriage and marriage counseling that I have been privileged to do, I have discovered that many young people come to a marriage with an image of an ideal mate, perhaps going back to a positive and sometimes a negative memory of one's parents. There is frequently an expectation of what it means to be a good husband or a good wife, a good father or a good mother, connected in some way with our experience in our family. It can take the form of: "be like . . ." or "don't be like . . ." and often these norms can be below the level of awareness. What surfaces, then, is disappointment, disapproval, and in many cases the attempt to change one's spouse. A good marriage or relationship with a life partner will in

26. Matt 5:41.

time grow out of this phase and begin to be characterized by an acceptance of the other person and a genuine appreciation for who they are and an enjoyment, even delight, in their many positive qualities. Love provides an environment for the other person to be free to grow, to change, and to become a mature adult person. I know that I thrive in such a context, and as I have freedom, I am better able to grow toward maturity and become one who loves in return.

## MAINTAINING PRIMARY RELATIONSHIPS

The quality of our lives and those whom we love and for whom we have some responsibility depends to a large degree upon the health and life-giving character of primary relationships. Our happiness and fulfillment as persons are intimately connected to maintaining the many dimensions of love in these relationships. As we close this chapter and move to an exploration of applying the spirit of love and compassion to our local and regional context, we might remind ourselves again how we can maintain a loving and compassionate attitude. Although the list of ways of sustaining the spirit of love could be quite long, let me suggest five strategies:

1. The first is to make a conscious choice and commitment to continue to *learn* the ways of love, compassion, caring, empathy, and forgiveness. We can do so in our reading, in our exposure to fine films and plays, in classes on interpersonal relationships, in observation of others who regularly demonstrate altruistic behavior, and by practicing these qualities in everyday interactions with others. It is possible to learn how to love, although it is also a gift that we can be empowered to demonstrate. By being aware of our behavior, we can gain valuable insight, habits that are helpful, sensitive and kind, and life patterns of service.

2. A second way is to find opportunities to *model and teach* others the geography of love. Most of us will find ways of teaching others by being an example of one who again and again incarnates unlimited and selfless love. We do it by helping others, being sensitive to their needs, offering to help, and volunteering to serve. We may also have opportunities to teach the occasional class, perhaps in a nearby school or in a place of worship. I find that others do "catch on" and begin the gradual process of becoming one who loves and is compassionate.

## Section IV — The Practice of Love

3. A third way to maintain primary relationships is to consciously *keep the channels of communication open*. When these channels close, and they often do for a variety of reasons, then love will not be present. Love is a form of communication, and may in fact be fundamentally essential to effective communication. It is when two people communicate that they are able to express love, empathy, and caring. If the channels close, perhaps from neglect or from disagreements and conflict, then love is not expressed and one is deprived of the infusion of love that could otherwise enhance and enrich one's life.

4. Still another way to maintain primary relationships is to *keep physically healthy and cultivate emotional stability and spiritual vitality*. We spoke in Section II about the ways that our capacity to love was intimately connected to physical and emotional health and how a deep and abiding spirituality can empower us to be more loving and compassionate. It follows that if we intend to be those who love, then we need to give attention to how we feel, what we take in, what we are exposed to, and how we are influenced. Exercise and a good diet, keeping levels of anxiety and stress under control, building in sufficient time for rest and relaxation, exposing oneself to a steady influx of stimulating, informative and inspiring reading and cultural events, and giving care to the disciplines of the spiritual life can increase our capacity to love.

5. One final suggestion is that we *commit and re-commit ourselves to the life of love and compassion*. So much of what we do, think, and feel in a given day can be seasoned with the spirit of love and compassion if we make a conscious choice to live our days as a person for others. In no way does this diminish our need for self-love and self-respect, but really grows out of sense of well-being. As our needs are met, we become free to give ourselves to a life of caring and service and to give high priority to the maintenance and quality of our primary relationships.

These simple observations and suggestions have been helpful to me as I attempt to live a life for others. Primary relationships are the foundation of the life of love and we build on this foundation when we lend a hand to the many others who need love and compassion outside of our primary relationships. Love and compassion help to create a more just, peaceful, and life-giving region, country, and world. It is to these subjects that we now turn.

# STUDY RESOURCES

## Discussion Questions

1. What is my Myers Briggs inventory and how does it influence the way I related to others?
2. What are my best assets in building relationships of love?
3. What are my greatest challenges in building relationships of love?
4. In general, when relationships break down, whose responsibility is it to restore the linkage and how can this be done?
5. What are some ways that I might improve those relationships which are most important to me?

## Key Terms and Concepts

*Myers Briggs Inventory:* A tool and way of understanding our preferences and inclinations regarding how we make sense of the world, make decisions, and relate to others
*Primary Relationships:* Our connection with people in our circle of nearness with whom we interact on a regular basis
*Mature Adult Relationship:* One that is based on integrity, respect, reality, and fairness
*Forgiveness:* To have a harmful word or action be pardoned and not held against us or that we do not hold against another
*Empathy:* to be able to feel what another person is feeling, to listen and emotionally understand what another person is saying and experiencing, to care
*Trust:* Feeling comfortable in the presence of another or others, knowing that you are safe and that what you say will be held in confidence

## Suggestions for Reading and Reference

1. Chapman, Gary, *The Five Languages of Love: How to Express Heartfelt Commitment to Your Mate.* Chicago: Northfield Publishing, 2004 edition.
2. ———, *Love as a Way of Life: Seven Keys to Transforming Every Aspect of Your Life.* Colorado Springs: WaterBrook Press, 2008.

**Section IV** — The Practice of Love

3. Myers, Isabel Briggs with Myers, Peter B., *Gifts Differing*. Palo Alto, CA: Consulting Psychologists Press, Inc., 1980.

4. Richo, David, *How To Be an Adult in Relationships: The Five Keys to Mindful Loving*. Boston: Shambhala, 2002.

5. Sternberg, Robert J., *Love Is a Story: A New Theory of Relationships*. New York: Oxford University Press, 1998.

6. Welwood, John, *Perfect Love, Imperfect Relationships: Healing the Wound of the Heart*. Boston: Trumpeter, 2007.

# 9

# Love and Compassion in Region and Society

## THE CURRENT CONTEXT AND THE COMMON GOOD

THE EXPRESSION OF LOVE and compassion is foundational to the preservation of the quality of our primary relationships. As I write, we are just passing a Christmas season and moving into the new year. It has been a season of reconnecting, honoring, and appreciating the richness and life-giving qualities of primary relationships—with my spouse, my immediate family, and with friends. I have had cordial and pleasant conversations with acquaintances, colleagues, and several strangers. It is this last group, strangers, that was surprisingly nurturing as I participated in a Taize service in a regional church, one in which I am not a member. There was a time of fellowship following the service, not a usual practice for a Taize service, but because of the Christmas season, one was scheduled. I was greeted by strangers in sincere and affectionate ways, and I was sent a clear message that I am worthy of the attention and care of others.

I have been aware as well of those who find the holiday seasons difficult in large measure because they are alone, but also because the social structures in our culture have marginalized them. Driving through the city, one could those on the street asking for help and others standing in

## Section IV — The Practice of Love

line at a food bank.[1] I visited those who were ill and who needed assistance to pay for health care. I encountered those who were facing all the challenges of aging, one with the presence of hospice. It was easy to be grateful as I reflected about the community and larger region in which I live because it has so many services that are quite tangible expressions of compassion. For example, there is an excellent organization called Good Cheer that provides food and inexpensive clothing and needed household items. I am grateful as well that there is an excellent Senior Center that offers a range of programs and services that make life better for the seniors in our region.

As I pondered the meaning of these two conflicting pictures of the region, the one of the marginalized people who live without the basic comforts of life, and the other full of people who have excellent services which address their needs, my mind went immediately to the phrase, "the common good." I began to reflect again about how we might be more diligent in seeking the common good for all of the citizens in the region. By the common good, I mean *the endeavor to build a community that works toward the welfare of the whole, and not exclusively to secure a single individual's well-being and advancement*.[2]

These reflections took me immediately to the reality that our government systems are not responding all that well to the needs of the marginalized people in my region and across the country. Regardless of political affiliations and social philosophies, most will agree that the work of our governments and community services at all levels is to insure fair and equitable treatment, access to education and health care, an economy that creates jobs for the underemployed and unemployed, and a reasonably good quality of life for all of its citizens.

I also thought about the lack of trust in our national government and the Congress in particular, the horrendous debt of our state government, the charge by a national agency that our city's police often resort to unjustified violence and even racial slurs, and how the children and young people in my specific location are being educated in a school system that lacks adequate funding. I sensed that governments, national, regional, and

---

1. Even families of those in the armed services were standing in line. Their salary wasn't adequate for even basic needs.

2. Aristotle, *Ethics*, translated by Thomson, 27. Aristotle writes, "For even if the good of the community coincides with that of the individual, it is clearly a greater and more perfect thing to achieve and preserve that of a community; for while it is desirable to secure what is good in the case of an individual, to do so in the case of a people or a state is something finer and more sublime."

local, are at an impasse, unable to overcome differences, struggling with inadequate funding, and suffering from a lack of credibility. Some of the government and community systems are working well, but so many of them appear to be unable to take the decisive action that is necessary to insure our security, offer fair and just protection under the law, upgrade the way we provide health care and education, and assist those on the edge who are lonely, hungry, and homeless.

*Love and compassion are integral to the quest for the common good.* While they do not provide specific solutions to the complex and technical problems that we face as a nation and in our regions, they do supply the motivation and guide us in finding and shaping solutions in these challenging times. Love and compassion deepen and enlarge our vision of the common good and nudge us out of our comfort zones into the world of struggling and suffering people.

## THE COMMON GOOD AND THE ROLE OF COVENANT

Commitment to the common good is based upon a written and sometimes unwritten covenant or social contract between the people and their governments and the systems and structures in society that are designed to serve the common good. For those of us in the United States, the covenants are contained in the Constitution, the Bill of Rights, and the many other documents that were created to guide the work of the governments, their agencies, and the many organizations that exist in our regions and communities to serve the welfare of the people. I prefer the concept of covenant to that of social contract in that a covenant implies levels of commitment and trust that go well beyond the obligations of a legal contract. *A covenant is a formal agreement and a relationship between two or more parties with each assuming some obligation to sustain the terms of the agreement and maintain the relationship.* A covenant implies a relationship of care and compassion not fundamentally present in the notion of a legal contract. The concept of covenant suggests that between the partners in the covenant, there may be this personal relationship filled with trust and forms of love.

These implied feelings of connection have strong biblical roots in both the Hebrew Bible and the New Testament. The covenant defines the relationship between God and the human family, and especially the relationship of God to the Hebrew people and the Christian community. It is based upon the trust that these people have in the ways God has blessed

## Section IV — The Practice of Love

them and will continue to provide for them. What is expected in return is faithfulness to the divine will and way. On occasion the word covenant is used to describe the connection between a greater power and a lesser one, as is the case in the biblical use of the term. The greater power expects loyalty and obligates itself to the protection of the lesser one. This biblical understanding of covenant has crossed over into our common life as a powerful symbol. It suggests that we vest a measure of power in our governments and social agencies and trust they will serve the common good and be responsible for our welfare, even as we live as responsible citizens.

The covenant between the government (including its many social agencies) and the people has been in peril in recent years. In many ways it has become a devalued currency as citizens have questioned whether the government is truly living up to its side of the covenant.[3] A flood of questions has surfaced: Are we getting the best service from government agencies with our tax money? Are the wealthy paying their share of the tax burden? Are government agencies really serving all the people in a fair and equitable way? Does the government have the right priorities, such as serving the needs of those living in poverty versus the exorbitant costs of wars in Iraq and Afghanistan? Is the government too intrusive in our personal lives, limiting our freedom? Has there been a breach of faith? The questions go on and on, but have the same root—is the government living up to the covenant and serving the common good?

Even as there are questions about whether the government is fulfilling its obligations of covenant, so too are there questions about the meaning of the common good. Is there really a *common* good, a unified way of describing the well-being of all of the citizens of the country and a region? Or are there several different understandings of the good society, depending upon country of origin, ethnic heritage, status in the society, and the distinctive features of geographical locations? Is it possible to apply one ideal of education such as "no child left behind" to every region and child? Or might there be ways of educating special needs children and immigrant children in a way that differs from a national norm? How responsive, respectful, and encouraging of differences is the community that holds one understanding of the common good? And if defenses of racial prejudice, discrimination, and an unfair tax structure can slip in and follow behind the banner of the common good, we know that we must

---

3. Mount, *Covenant Community and the Common Good: An Interpretation of Christian Ethics*, 13.

exercise great caution and care as we take responsibility in government and vote in the elections of our leaders and the direction of our policies.[4]

Two authors of a recent book have suggested that the presence of the common good is a matter of degree, but at a minimum its presence must have four requirements:[5]

1. The community must contribute to the self-identity of the members, but not necessarily define that identity. (This requirement points to the need to respect differences of heritage and ethnic identity.)
2. Members must participate extensively in the decisions that direct the community's life.
3. The society as a whole must take responsibility for its members.
4. The diverse individuality of each member must be respected.

Each of these requirements needs expansion, and we will attempt to provide this development as we explore the several critical arenas in which we expect the common good to be present. These concerns must be given attention if the covenant is to be honored and the common good, at least in some part, is realized.

The contours and dimensions of a given community, state, or nation are innumerable. For our purpose of exploring the place of love and compassion within our communities, states, and nation, we will focus only on six arenas or domains: family life, the economy, the environment, health care, education, and security and justice. Our goal is to place these dimensions of community life within the framework of a guiding covenant and the degree of presence of the common good.

We turn first to the *family* and the need for families, which are the basic unit of our community life, to have a setting in which the common good is a clear goal. In such a setting, families flourish. One important observation about contemporary family life is that there are many patterns and expressions, not a single model that is universal and must be followed. There are those who argue that the ideal model of the family unit consists of husband, wife, and two to three children. This nuclear family model is often viewed as the God-given design and part of the natural ordering of life. While this pattern of the family unit may have merit, it is not necessarily the only one, and it never has been, even in biblical times. It is the case that the pattern of the family unit does shape its health and vitality,

---

4 Ibid., 31.

5. Daley and Cobb, *For the Common Good*, 172. Quoted by Mount in *Covenant Community*, 23.

## Section IV — The Practice of Love

but the more fundamental issue is how the values of love, compassion, care, support, and trust pervade the family system. The families may be extended and have many generations; they may be childless; they may be made up of partners of one sex; and they may consist of people living in a group context. Single people speak of family in reference to those relations who live elsewhere, and occasionally, as a circle of friends. In some cases, those who live in group homes call the others in the group members of their family.

There are many challenges to sustaining a family life that is nurturing and supportive of all of its members.[6] Several issues regarding family life have been "on the front burner," such as abortion, the marriage of gay couples, and adoption, and they are integral to the discussion of covenant and the common good. A full discussion of these issues is well beyond the scope of this volume, but two family issues are especially germane to the ways we see love, compassion, and care as central to the well-being of families. These two issues are divorce and death, and how a family manages these events in sustaining the quality of family life. We will use these two issues as illustrative as we address the question: In what sense does our covenant with the government and many social agencies and our society's commitment to the common good provide needed services for our families to help them thrive or assist them when they are threatened?

Let's look first to the issue of divorce, which is the severance of the marriage covenant and threatens the foundation of the family structure. When there is divorce and separation, how do and should social services respond to this circumstance? How do the covenant and the commitment to the common good motivate those who have the responsibility and professional competence to help citizens with the breakdown of a marriage and its wave-like impact on the family?

The general pattern for many of the citizens in our communities and in our country has been for two people to enter into marriage and family life, pledging themselves to a covenant based upon the promise to love one another and support one another in all of the joys and challenges of life, "till death do us part." The relationship is based upon a life partnership that has the foundation of trust and fidelity and promises a life of happiness and fulfillment. When the marriage is successful, then there is the possibility that there will be a family life that is good for all of its members.

---

6. There are numerous resources for the study of family life. One that I have found informative, full of fun and helpful is the children's book by Hoffman, *All Kinds of Families*.

## Love and Compassion in Region and Society

Often the marriage is sustained and flourishes because the conditions have been right, the partners have been faithful and responsible, and needed services have been available. The common good has been served.

But for a multitude of reasons having to do with changing values, life's unrelenting demands, and the level of maturity of the partners, the institution of marriage built on a covenant of trust and fidelity is endangered. Nearly 50 percent of marriages now end in divorce in our communities and nation. It may be wise for the couple to separate or divorce because communication has broken down, all traces of love and affection have gone, and events have occurred that have violated the trust and failed to meet the expectations of the commitment. But when the marriage breaks down, there is often great pain and suffering, the need for healing and recovery, and adjustment for other members of the family and especially the children of the marriage. It is at all points, but especially at the point of suffering, that the partners and their family need the support of others. They need covenant partners who will seek not just their own well-being, but the well-being of all those who suffer in the midst of a broken relationship.

The community, out of a sense of being in covenant with all of its members and having a sense of the common good, will surround those marriages that are successful, helping couples to increase their love for one another and to provide a secure and nurturing environment for children of the marriage. But the community also has a special obligation in the covenant to those who are in failed marriages, those who seek to rebuild their lives, and find new relationships that are based upon love, trust, and fidelity. The obligation goes beyond just the partners in the failed marriage, but to the children and the extended family that will suffer as well and will need the healing of love and compassion. Through its supporting agencies, counseling systems, religious bodies, and the friendship and support of all those who are close to the partners of the failed marriage, the community, out of covenant love, shows compassion and offers wise and intelligent care. The common good is served as families are restored.

A second illustrative issue in family life is the shattering experience of a death in the family.[7] This issue is especially poignant for the members of the community in which my wife and I live in that there have been two fatal automobile accidents in the past month at the time of this writing. The deaths were unexpected and the families and the community have had to adjust and respond. One involved the death of three healthy young

---

7. Kubler-Ross in her classic work, *On Death and Dying*, offers wise counsel to those facing death and to families dealing with death, 157–80.

## Section IV — The Practice of Love

men who had the potential to lead fulfilling and successful lives. They were college age, had been fine students and athletes, were well-liked by their contemporaries, and were deeply loved by their families. Part of the tragedy was that there was a young woman driving who survived and now has to live the rest of her life with the memories of her three friends and the tragic accident. Unfortunately, she had been drinking, and in trying to pass another car on a narrow road, she lost control and the car crashed into a tree. All four families are grieving and the entire community is reaching out in a variety of redemptive ways to help these families.

Within this past week as I write, there was also another tragic accident that caused the death of a young girl, just nine years old. She and her family, mother, father, and two brothers were driving to the grandparents' home for a Christmas event. They, too, were on a relatively narrow rural road, and a tree uprooted by severe winds crashed across the car. The other members of the family survived, although the father who is an artist and largely supports the family by his work was severely injured.

How does the community respond in love and compassion to these grieving families? Fortunately, there were a number of very caring and appropriate responses to these families. Almost immediately, counseling services were provided. Thoughtful and sensitive memorial services were offered by churches, services that were overflowing with people who offered support to the families. Fund-raising efforts were made to help these families. In the case of the young girl, the school arranged for her class to meet and to talk about the loss of their classmate. Government officials stepped in to assist with all of the details of the accidents and guide other family members in reference to insurance and legal issues.

These families will never be the same again, but because of the inherent sense of covenant and commitment to the common good, the community has responded in healing and compassionate ways. This community has been a model of helping families in crisis. The feelings of grief are beyond measure, and the memory of these beautiful young people will be with the families for all of their days. But so too will be the gratitude they have felt as they have been surrounded by caring people, able to listen and understand and be wise in their guidance and support. In the case of these two tragic accidents, there was an appropriate response by the community.

## Love and Compassion in Region and Society

A second major concern in our regions and our nation is the *state of the economy*. Currently, the national unemployment rate is hovering at about 9 percent, and even those who are fortunate enough to be working often feel underemployed and unable to use the full range of their expertise and acquired skills. Across the country, there are a number of demonstrations by people using the terms "occupy" and "99 percent to 1 percent" and who are calling for fair distribution of wealth and a fundamental change of values.[8] In the past year, the Congress has had great difficulty in finding an agreement about a national budget and reaching a consensus on how to sustain the federal government. Many of the citizens have lost patience. Many levels of government, federal, state, and municipal are making severe cuts in budgets at the risk of reducing basic services in health care, welfare, and education. As we face a national election, we are hearing a wide range of opinions about how to "fix the economy," but many citizens often find themselves cynical about all the promises.

It is somewhat encouraging that the federal, regional, and local governments are concerned about the financial well-being of the citizens and believe that it is their covenantal responsibility to address the slumbering economy and work toward a balanced budget as part of their commitment to the common good. But the number of people living below poverty level in our country is very high. Food banks are busier than ever helping people to have adequate food.[9] Vast numbers of people are adjusting to the new reality that their pattern of life is changing and they will have to live more frugally. These realities are inviting local communities to find practical ways of expressing care and compassion for people in need. Appreciative of government help in all of the ways that support the common good, these communities are realizing that local expressions of commitment to the common good must be a priority. Grateful to those with wealth who are willing to help, they know that these gestures will not ultimately change the economy, and new initiatives that are local and rooted in the local infrastructure must address the needs of communities.[10]

---

8. Kavanaugh, a Jesuit priest, has made a persuasive case for a shift in values and a more equitable distribution of wealth in *Following Christ in a Consumer Society: The Spirituality of Cultural Resistance*.

9. Sider speaks directly to the Christian communities about their responsibility to address issues of hunger in his book, *Rich Christians in an Age of Hunger: A Biblical Study*.

10 McKibben advocates for community action in his influential book *Deep Economy: The Wealth of Communities and the Durable Future*.

## Section IV — The Practice of Love

The issues linked to the economy such as poverty, hunger, and the inequitable distribution of wealth will not soon go away. There will be a continual need for our governments and their service agencies to find ways of expressing wise and compassionate care to the citizens whom they serve. As citizens, we must hold our government agencies to the obligations of a covenant of care that seeks the common good. Thoughtful and wise expressions of love and compassion are desperately needed in the form of programs and services to all people, and especially to those with pronounced needs such as those in poverty because of unemployment and those who go to bed hungry. In addition, every effort must be made to find ways to make our economy work for all of the people, not just the few.

A third concern in our nation, regions, and communities *is the conservation of our environments.* For too long, we have viewed our natural surroundings as a possession, one that we can use for our own selfish ends. We have viewed our forests, rivers, lakes, mountains, and plains as there for us to exploit. We have viewed the earth's resources such as coal, oil, trees, and fresh water as unlimited in supply and have not fully accounted for their finite quantity and quality. We have viewed the living creatures with which we share the earth as subject to our desires and have destroyed an endless number of species. Only in recent years have we begun to realize that we live in interdependence within the entire natural world. We share the earth with all of its inhabitants and have a special responsibility to be good stewards of our common home and to sustain the healthy but delicate ecological balance. We are living in a time when the hard questions are now being asked by many who are fully informed: Are we too late? Will other humans around the globe join us in an effort to conserve our good earth? What must we do to insure better management of the planet?

We are given some hope by the extraordinary ways that our governments and social agencies are now addressing the issues of ecology. With only limited dissent, there is a shift in policy and practice that is addressing the issues of global warming and environmental degradation.[11] It is encouraging that there are laws regarding the gas mileage that our automobiles must attain and the shift away from dependence on fossil fuel consumption to other forms of energy. Across the West, there are many wind farms that are generating nature's natural gift of energy. It is

---

11. A good example of what is occurring is the changes in the topography of Greenland where the ice sheets and glaciers are melting at an alarming rate. This condition, caused primarily by the burning of fossil fuels, will mean rising seas impacting many parts of the world.

## Love and Compassion in Region and Society

reassuring that most all communities have recycling programs and guidelines for "green" construction of new homes and buildings. Our schools make ecological understanding a centerpiece of the curriculum and new generations are coming along that are more sensitive to the risks of a society based on consumption and materialistic values ("affluenza"). Colleges and universities in partnerships with public and private agencies are leading the world in research regarding sustainability, the global economy, and the future of the earth.

A variety of religions are discerning the values within their teachings and traditions that intersect with economics and government policy and seeking a new commitment to an epochal birthing of bio-reverence. These gems of counsel are present in the indigenous wisdom traditions that have been intimately connected with nature from the beginning. It is present in the great religions of Asia, Hinduism, Buddhism, Confucianism,[12] and Shinto, all of which have teachings that reverence our mother the earth. Even the Abrahamic religions, in some ways part of the problem, have begun to realize that they really do believe in a good creation for which they must care.[13]

In the next chapter, we will address these concerns on the global level more directly. At this point, we want to underline the national and regional responsibilities and underscore the need for local communities to be sensitive to the ecological concerns. The responses are mixed across the United States with some areas exercising a more vigorous and responsible approach. Others, for a variety of reasons, some unwittingly and others over which they have little control, are doing less and facing a deteriorating environment. Again, we stress the need to live in covenant with our governments and social agencies and in partnership with those who seek the common good as an expression of commitment to be those who love and show compassion to all.

Our society is facing extraordinary challenges in the areas of family well-being, a struggling economy, and a deteriorating environment. New understanding and commitments to these concerns are necessary.

---

12. See the volume edited by Joseph Runzo and Nancy M. Martin, *Ethics in the World Religions* and in particular the article by Mary Evelyn Tucker, "Confucian Cosmology and Ecological Ethics: QI, LI, and the Role of the Human," 331–45.

13. See the book edited by Coward and Maguire, *Visions of a New Earth: Religious Perspectives on Population, Consumption, and Ecology*. The Abrahamic religions have been criticized for the abuse of the biblical injunction to be "fruitful and multiply, and fill the earth and subdue it; and have dominion over the fish of the sea and over the birds of the air and over every living thing moves upon the earth" (Gen 1:28).

## Section IV — The Practice of Love

We turn to still another concern of our nation, regions, and communities, which is that *of providing high quality and affordable health care*. Historically, the United States has been a leader in providing excellent and affordable health care for its citizens, but more recently this excellent service has declined. The reasons are many. One is that the costs have increased exponentially, and there are many United States citizens who simply cannot afford it. An alarming percentage of people are opting not to see a doctor or obtain needed drugs because it would just add to their indebted state. Federal programs such as Medicare and Medicaid are only available for certain target populations such as the aging or profoundly poor. Health care insurance programs are quite costly and only a certain percentage of people have them as part of their employment benefits. A life-threatening disease or a complex surgery can be so costly that even those in the middle class with some coverage cannot afford the care.

One Presidential administration after another has attempted to address the "adequate and affordable health care" problem, but has found it very difficult to navigate through the maze of lobbyists, pharmaceutical companies, the insurance industry, and the broader field of medicine. President Obama has had a measure of success in getting health care legislation through Congress, but many of the features of his program are now being challenged in the courts. The challenge has had a political overtone as well. Some are calling the program to require people to be covered by health care a "socialist" encroachment and infringement of freedom. A further complication has to do with the move towards specialized medicine by medial school graduates. Fewer doctors are offering general family medicine. Rural regions of the country are not always able to attract medical doctors. Health care in the United States is considered the most advanced in the world yet accessible only to those with considerable wealth or good health care insurance. Health care in the United States is characterized by the extremes of brilliance with people from all over the world coming to the United States for specialized treatment, and by limited access for those who have low incomes and live in rural regions.

There are some encouraging signs as local doctors and other health care providers are finding new ways of offering medical services. New health care legislation is enabling those without coverage to qualify for both public and private programs. The high level of research continues and progress is being made in the treatment of such diseases as HIV AIDS and many forms of cancer. But the issue of quality care for all citizens remains a central issue for the government, the medical profession, the health care industry, insurance companies, and for local and regional health care providers. Once again, we return to the notion of our covenant and its application to the government and the medical profession to find ways of serving the needs of all the citizens, not the just those who have the financial resources or the coverage that enable them to receive high quality care. The common good is a healthy citizenry, and in many cases, it is a matter of life and death.

A fourth issue facing our society is the need to *provide excellent education for all of its citizens*. As with medical care, the United States has historically been a leader in its unique partnership of public and private education that has given its citizens the best possible education. Recently, however, the statistics and rankings show that our students are not performing as well as students in many other countries.[14] Our frame of reference once again is the covenant between the people and governments at several levels and the many private educational programs. High quality education for all of the people is seen as a common good, good for individuals, but also good and necessary for a healthy society. A democracy will work and thrive in proportion to the level of education of its people, and education drives prosperity.

This subject, as all the subjects on our list of arenas needing the renewal of commitment to the social covenant and the common good, is one which needs extensive analysis well beyond our purposes. But a few observations may help us to place the subject of education in context and see its relative importance. As with the medical profession, those with responsibility of providing high quality education have the challenge of finding the financial resources. The recessed economy has reduced the revenue stream of state and local governments that provide the lion's share of financial support. As the population ages, especially in some regions which are ideal locations for retirement, there is a decline in the number of school-age children and the school districts receive less money, based on the number of students, from funding sources. Course offerings and services have had to be reduced. Our schools have had to deal with diverse populations of students, many from immigrant families for which English is a second language at best. There have been the challenges, especially at the middle school and high school levels of increasing drug usage by

---

14. For example, *The Guardian* has the following rankings for success in reading, math, and science: South Korea, Finland, Canada, New Zealand, Japan, Australia, Netherlands, Belgium, Norway, Estonia Switzerland, Poland, Iceland, the United States. See Jessica Shepherd, "World education rankings: which country does best in reading, math, and science?" *The Guardian*, December 7, 2010.

students, absenteeism, and the increase of bullying. Teaching is a very challenging career and it does not pay as well as other professions, even though the educational demands are quite rigorous. Finding high quality teachers, dedicated to student learning, continues be a challenge for many communities. Buildings are aging, it has been difficult to keep up with the most current technology and software systems, and special needs children require the expertise of those well-trained in the field. Education has become life-long, and communities, companies, and professions have had to find ways to provide continuing education to the adult population.

Are there encouraging signs? The answer is yes and no, depending on a variety of factors such as location, level, and the quality and vision of the leadership. There continues to be pockets of excellence at all levels, but this quality is not universal. For example, Parent Teacher Associations in middle to upper class neighborhoods are successfully raising money to fund programs and resources that have been cut from school district budgets; unfortunately low income areas do not have these resources. There is an increasing awareness in the domain of education that the country's vitality and future will depend upon a full commitment to the covenant between the educational providers and the public, and a dedication by both the providers and the public to pursue the common good. Perhaps in all the arenas being discussed, but especially in the field of education, there must not be a compromise in providing high quality education. Our country, our well-being, and the future of our children depend upon the excellence of our education.[15]

There is one more arena in which I want to illustrate the crucial nature of our society's covenantal status and its commitment to the common good. It is the domain of providing a *fair and just social order*. Americans pride themselves on having the oldest ongoing democracy in the world, one whose government is "of the people, by the people, for the people" and one, hopefully, which "shall not perish from the earth."[16] Our Constitution and Bill of Rights protect all of the citizens of the country and imply that the values of safety, fairness, and justice for all people shall be foundational for the life of the nation. The governments, the court systems, the several layers of law enforcement, and in many ways the cultural norms do attempt to approximate a fair and just system for all of its citizens,

---

15. There are a multitude of excellent books about the current state of education, but I continue to be informed by the recent book by Ravitch, *The Death and Life of the Great American School Systems: How Testing and Choice are Undermining Education.*

16. Abraham Lincoln's Gettysburg Address, November 19, 1863.

non-citizens who live within its boundaries, and in the structures and practices of international diplomacy.

There are endless exceptions to and violations of these values of fairness and justice. We observe them on a regular basis and many have personally experienced them, but the exceptions and violations do not undermine the conviction that justice must prevail in order for there to be integrity within the social covenant and perseverance in the pursuit of the common good. The ideals will always be out in front of performance and represent our aspirations. These ideals represent the core values of love for others, compassion for their hardships, and care for their well-being. Professor Michael J. Sandel of Harvard University explains in his book entitled *Justice: What's the Right Thing to Do?* that justice has been understood and preserved in three primary ways:

- The *utilitarian* or the greatest good for the greatest number: he maintains that this approach makes justice a matter of calculation, not principle, and that trying to hold that the common good is a single measure of value does not take into account the qualitative differences and shades of meaning for different populations.
- The *libertarian*, or the respect for free choice: this view, he argues, does say that certain rights must be respected, but it too easily accepts people's preferences without question or challenge.
- The *moral* or cultivating virtue and reason about the common good: This point of view brings serious debate and reflection to the needs of society and makes informed judgments about values and the common good.

He maintains that "to achieve a just society we have to reason together about the meaning of the good life, and to create a public culture hospitable to the disagreements that inevitably arise."[17] As we attempt to resolve disagreements, approximations and judgments will be made as we endeavor to be fair to all and find good ways to distribute wealth and opportunity. We make value judgments, and these judgments are made in reference to our deep and abiding concern for the well-being of all of our citizens, as individuals and as a group. The just society will cultivate a sense of belonging, a commitment and even a sacrifice and a willingness to serve as a way of achieving the common good. It will resist all forms of inequality, live in solidarity with those on the margins of justice and

17. Sandel, *Justice*, 261–62.

## Section IV — The Practice of Love

opportunity, and engage in a politics of moral engagement.[18] And fully aware of the risks, we are willing to take our deepest values of love and compassion, often rooted in our religious faith, to the life we share with those in our communities, our states, and our country.[19]

We expect our national, regional, and local governments which make laws, our court systems which adjudicate complexities and conflicts inherent in the justice system, and our law enforcement agencies to maintain law and order with integrity. There must be justice for all and respect for the law that we hope will closely approximate justice. It almost goes without saying that justice is foundational to our social covenant and essential to the common good. At all levels, national, regional, and local, the challenges are very real. Recently, we have observed corruption at the national level in financial institutions and global companies. Closer to home, we or someone near to us has been affected by the increase of assaults, the use of narcotics, property theft, robbery, threats and harassment, shop lifting, fraud, and property damage. Our part of the covenant in securing and maintaining the common good directly intersects with maintaining a fair and just social order.

## THE CHANGING STRATEGY

There is a growing consensus that we can and must do better in living up to the social covenant and striving to increase the common good. This perspective is highly visible at the several levels of our concern, local, regional, national, and global. There is urgency about this concern in that our problems are so threatening and overwhelming in scope and complexity that they challenge our capacity to find solutions. Our government systems seem unable to cope with the speed of change and the magnitude of the problems. As a result, informed citizens are nearly unanimous in calling for our government systems and structures to be assessed, changed, and made more responsive to the challenge of creating a more humane and compassionate social order. It is comforting and encouraging to see this growing awareness in leaders at all levels. National and regional governments, local communities, and non-governmental agencies increasingly understand that they must do more to make life better for everyone.

18. Ibid., 265–69.

19. See the book by Marty with Moore, *Politics, Religion, and the Common Good: Advancing a Distinctly American Conversation about Religion's Role in Our Shared Life.*

## Love and Compassion in Region and Society

In some cases, the vision and energy of this movement has been channeled through current governance systems and structures to make social change. In other cases these changes have been brought about by grass-roots and community initiative, direct challenge, and intervention. There are those who are asking, "What is more important, doing things the 'right way' or doing the right things?" The strategies for change are direct and often take a different form than those used in a previous era, and are driven by a new configuration of values and strategies. A brief glance at current history provides the context for the changing strategies.

The latter half of the twentieth century brought fundamental challenges to unjust laws and conditions that discriminated against great numbers of people. In the United States, and in many other parts of the world, there was the quest for liberation, equal rights, and access to education and better careers for large groups of people who suffered from discrimination and lack of opportunity. For example, there was the liberation of India from Great Britain and the formation of a new nation state led by Mahatma Gandhi. This pattern of liberation from a colonial past occurred in many parts of the world. There was the quest for racial equality led by Martin Luther King, Jr. and many other courageous people that brought about increased fairness and justice for all citizens. There was a new government formed in South Africa, led by Nelson Mandela, who challenged apartheid and gave opportunity for voting rights and access to better education and employment, all of which led to a better quality of life for more people. Recently, we have observed the freedom movements across the Arab world, in the Middle East, in Tunisia, Egypt, Libya, and the less successful quest for freedom in Syria. It is interesting to note that the relative success of these movements come about in some measure because of the use of social media, pictures, videos, and the use of digital communication through email and texting. People were able to see firsthand the suffering and oppression. Almost globally, there has been the increasing freedom and enhancement of the life of women. The outcomes of these quests for freedom and a better life have been mixed, and the goals have not been universally reached and probably never will. But their very presence has given those living on the margins a measure of hope.

The results of these movements and the many that have not been mentioned point to a trend that cannot be ignored. The trend is toward more freedom, equal opportunity, justice under law, and an increased commitment to the common good. One might ask, is there one ideal, one understanding of a social covenant, and one definition of the common

## Section IV — The Practice of Love

good? The clear answer is no. There are bitter feuds about these definitions at all levels, perhaps epitomized in our time by the revival of a worldview within Islam that is at odds with many in the Islamic world and which challenges the values of Western world.[20] Some might interpret this Islamic revival as a threat, and in its more radical form, it has been a threat. But it has also been filled with clear goals to improve the lives of millions of people.[21] Within Islam there are enduring values for humanity.

A case can also be made that this trend toward a more just and humane world is not just a passing fad, but a fundamental shift in global understanding. Illustrations of this shift are taking form in the day-to-day life of people in communities around the world.[22] This trend has many forms, is elusive and hard to describe, and competes and runs concurrently with the opposite tendencies of tyranny, persecution, violence, and destruction. Resistance to reform in Syria, a very complex issue, is an obvious example of the ambiguity within the movement. The power of the drug cartels in Mexico points to the power of the opposite tendency. I want to highlight several dimensions of this positive but mixed and ambivalent movement, and in this chapter, focus on trends that are regional and national, and then examine in the next chapter those trends that are more global in scope. In most cases, the same values are present. At the national and regional level, there are many dimensions of the trend and the following examples are merely illustrative and do not represent a comprehensive analysis. For example, there is a new moral vision, a different leadership style, a committed political will, an alternative form of governance, and an increased participation and involvement of people in those issues that affect their lives. Let's look at each of these trends.

First, there is increasing evidence of a *new moral vision* in our nation, our states, our regions, and our communities. While not always described as an emergence of a new social covenant, it has fundamentally taken that form. At the national level, and especially in the election season during

---

20. See the description of this revival of an Islamic worldview in Esposito's book, *Islam: The Straight Path*, 165–69.

21. I am keenly aware of the differences within Shari'ah Law and Western understanding of law, but we do not all have to affirm the same vision if different visions lead to a better quality of life. See the books by Nasr, *The Heart of Islam: Enduring Values for Humanity*, 113–56 and Imam Feisal Abdul Rauf, *What's Right with Islam: A New Vision for Muslims and the West*.

22. See the book by Rifkin, *The Empathic Civilization: The Race to Global Consciousness in a World in Crisis*. See as well the book by Pinker, *The Better Angels of our Nature: Why Violence Has Declined*.

which I am writing,[23] we are seeing articulations by presidential candidates of the way to frame our national life in the context of a moral vision. These visions are being stated as a way to approach the *crisis* in which we find ourselves. These views of the several candidates differ, ranging from the libertarian, the evangelical or conservative Roman Catholic, the mixed but leaning toward conservative, and the progressive outlook of President Obama. There was a measure of change ("flip-flopping") in the views that were expressed depending upon the direction of the political winds, and a trace of cynicism was justified. But by giving the benefit of the doubt, it was fair to say that nearly all of the candidates had a moral vision. They sincerely wanted to give leadership to the building of a better society, not that presidential candidates in previous years have not had similar goals and convictions. But clearly this group of people came with deeply held convictions about the covenant between the government and the people and the ways to improve the common good. With only one or two exceptions, it was clearly evident that each of these candidates had a moral vision, although not always substantial and persuasive.

It is my judgment that the stronger moral vision, and one less controlled by the harsh realities of how to succeed in a presidential election, exists at the regional and local levels. More people enter into regional and local politics and give themselves to social causes out of a commitment to a moral vision and not primarily to further their personal ambitions. Many of the people engaged in serving the regional common good could easily begin a description of their involvement with the statement, "I believe that if we . . . then our lives and those we care about will be better." My good friend, a County Commissioner, undertakes her complex and often thankless work because she has lived in this region all her life, her children have grown up in the region, and her dearest friends are in the community. She wants a better life for them and gives her time, talent, and energy to creating a caring, just, and compassionate setting for all of us. I see it all around me as I observe business leaders, those involved in local government, artists, authors and musicians, lawyers, educators, and staff and volunteers in a range of agencies caring for the needs of those who have less income, who are aging, or who face and live with debilitating illnesses. The Habitat for Humanity program in our region is a glowing example. A moral vision inspires these people and guides and motivates them in their work.

---

23. We now have to assess the wisdom of our voting.

## Section IV — The Practice of Love

I am sensing as well *a different style of leadership* at the national and regional level. It is more principled and less self-seeking and cynical.[24] This shift is far from universal and not always motivated by the noblest aims. In many cases, the shift has come about because it contains within it a more effective way of leading and achieving the desired goals. There has been a steady stream of movements, often stimulated and guided by a thoughtful book containing new theories of leadership and governance. New movements (for example, total quality, re-engineering, etc.) have come and gone, although the more universal principles that provided the foundation for them have remained in the accumulated wisdom of effective leadership. In a slightly more popular vein, the well-known author Steven Covey has spoken about *The Seven Habits of Effective People*[25] and followed this thesis in several other books. As a reminder, his seven habits of leadership are: be proactive; begin with the end in mind; put first things first; think win-win; seek first to understand, then to be understood; synergize; and sharpen the saw (continuous improvement and self-renewal).[26]

I have learned about this style of leadership from these several authors and the many who have continued to write and teach in this field.[27] I would like to focus more on the values which are espoused rather than on the needed steps for personal success, an emphasis that creates in me a trace of discomfort in that it has the ring of self-centeredness and a less compassionate tone. A survey of these volumes and movements suggests an emphasis on the following principles regarding leadership:

---

24. This new style of leadership may not be totally new, but it has been identified by many observers as a shift, and Jean Lipman-Blumen in *The Connective Edge: Leading in an Interdependent World*, 3–110, identifies it as a new style of leadership. The shift was pointed to at least obliquely in the widely circulated volume in the 1980s by Peters and Waterman, Jr., *In Search of Excellence: Lessons from America's Best-Run Companies*, 81–86. Toffler in *Future Shock* and in *Power Shift* also spoke of the emergence of principle-centered leadership in this era.

25. New edition published in 2004.

26. Listed as a reminder in his book, *Principle-Center Leadership*, 40–47. Another volume by Stephen Covey is entitled *The 8th Habit: From Effectiveness to Greatness*.

27. I am somewhat overwhelmed by the number of current books about styles of leadership and pathways to personal and business success. One widely circulated book by Welch and Welch, *Winning: The Ultimate Business How-To Book* represents that trend. Over the past few years, I have served as a consultant, gradually shifting my consulting strategies to current trends. I have been influenced by Organization Development (see Anderson's recent book, *Organizational Development: The Process of Leading Organizational Change*, and Bossidy and Charan, *Execution: The Discipline of Getting Things Done*). I am now drawing from scenario planning. See Chermack, *Scenario Planning in Organizations: How to Create, Use, and Assess Scenarios*.

1. Find ways to balance personal and professional areas of life in the middle of the constant crises and pressures. There is a clear sense that we lead best when we are centered and focused rather than driven by our fears, anxieties, and stress.

2. Learn how to be genuinely pleased for the successes and competencies of others. There is an increasing emphasis on the recognition of the wisdom of others and the need to listen, be open, and to encourage and nurture others to be creative.

3. Learn how to be firm in leadership, but give others the freedom and autonomy to take responsibility and design their own work. There is a strong emphasis that we perform best and find satisfaction in our work when we are given the freedom to shape our goals.

4. Learn how to internalize principles of excellence and continuous improvement at all levels and nurture these same values in others. There is an increasing concern for personal growth and the development of the abilities of others. Fulfillment in one's work makes one more effective and increases one's personal contentment.

5. Learn how to move to listen to one's conscience, cultivate character, follow clear ethical norms, and focus on the common good. There is a keen sense that we give leadership not just for our own success, but for the well-being of the organization we serve and society.

6. Learn how to lead from our center. Again and again, there is a return to the leader's integrity, trustworthiness, the goal of empowering others, and the need to serve in a way that creates a better society for all.[28]

Coupled with this new moral vision and principle-centered leadership are growing convictions, awareness, and clear articulations that changes occur for the benefit of our society when there is a *strong political will*. Making change to create a more just and compassionate society is incredibly difficult. Generally and ironically people tend to be comfortable with "the way things are" even when the way things are does not enable a high quality of life. It is not uncommon for those who are on the margin in our society to strongly resist change, and it is especially difficult for those who are privileged and have vested interests to allow and seek change. As we mentioned, there are encouraging signs, but the resistance to change, as for example in the improvement of health care, is still quite strong.

---

28. See a partial listing of these principles in Covey's *Principle-Centered Leadership*, 13.

## Section IV — The Practice of Love

We are fortunate to have extraordinary and exemplary models of those who have created change for the common good. Mother Teresa in a humble and simple way gave her life to the improvement of conditions for those who suffer the most ("the least of these..."). In 1948 she founded the Society of the Missionaries of Charity in the Calcutta slums and worked faithfully across the years of her life to bring aid and dignity to the destitute and dying both in her adopted country of India and later in twenty-five countries worldwide. She took to heart the words of Matthew's Gospel and the cry of those who live on the edge. She served those who "are the least of these who are members of my family" (Matt 25:40). She heard the Gospel challenge: "I was hungry and you gave me no food, I was thirsty and you gave me no drink, I was a stranger and you did not welcome me, naked and you did not clothe me, sick and in prison and you did not visit me" (Matt 25:42–43).

She did the difficult with remarkable conviction and strength of will, as so many others have even at the risk of their lives. We are reminded of people like Mahatma Gandhi, who fasted to the edge of death in order to bring Muslim and Hindus together in the new nation of India and Nelson Mandela, who spent the best years of his life in prison because he dared to challenge apartheid in South Africa. It is from these models that we can learn about courage and the political will to make change for the creation of a more humane society.

Often these changes for good come about because of the use of a better or at least a different strategy for change. We are also seeing alternative *strategies for governance* that are bringing about needed social change for the common good. As circumstances change in our common life, different strategies emerge to deal with these changes. A hundred years ago, the human family was less focused on ecology and finding solutions for global warming. The particular challenges of dealing with terrorist groups such as Al Qaida were not at the forefront of government attention, although other forms of violence and tyranny were certainly present. There was less concern about the power of global companies that have influence on the flow of energy and the stability of the global economy. As our society and the world change and bring with the change a new combination of issues and problems, the way of thinking about reality and the means of governance to manage these new realities also changes. Old forms of thinking and governance remain such as autocratic tyranny and discriminatory structures that marginalize people and keep them in poverty. But increasingly, new strategies are being developed that are designed both to deal with a changing environment and to seek the common good.

One branch of sociological study speaks about "memes," usually defined as core intelligences that impact our way of functioning, often without our full awareness. These patterns of thinking transpose themselves into "a worldview, a value system, a belief structure, an organizing principle, a way of thinking, and a mode of living."[29] As developed by Don Beck and Christopher Cowan, memes function in the following ways:

1. As our core intelligences, they form systems of thinking, feeling, and valuing that profoundly impact our behavior. They represent our way of viewing reality, our motives, and how we make decisions and prioritize the values in our lives.
2. It follows that they impact all of life's choices.
3. They express both healthy and unhealthy qualities.
4. They can shed light on or create blindness to the conditions that surround us.

In *Spiral Dynamics*, Beck and Cowan call attention to eight memes that have been characteristic of human behavior across the centuries and which exist in some form today. Each meme is assigned a color and describes a worldview and resulting attitudes and behavior. Let me attempt to summarize a quite complex pattern of describing human behavior:

- Beige: the thinking is automatic, almost instinctive; the structures are loose; and the pattern is motivated by survival. It might be described as actions taken to stay alive and perpetuate life. It represents life at the most basic level.

- Purple: The thinking is animistic, the structures are tribal, and the processes of life tend to be circular. One obeys the spirits, shows allegiance to chiefs and elders, preserves and utilizes sacred objects, and observes rites of passage, seasonal cycles, and tribal customs.

- Red: The thinking is egocentric, the government structures are empires, and the means to realize goals is exploitive. The world is full of threats and predators and only the strong and forceful will survive. Violent action is justified as a means to an end.

- Blue: The thinking tends to be absolutistic, the structures are pyramids of power, and the process of achieving desired ends is strategic

---

29. Beck and Cowan, *Spiral Dynamics: Mastering Values, Leadership, and Change*, 40.

in character. One sacrifices for the great Cause, the code of conduct is based on eternal principles, and one lives obediently to the dictates of law and a disciplinary code; they build character. The leadership guides and controls using challenge and guilt. It functions with a sense of having eternal truth and leads with an authoritarian style.

- Orange: The thinking is filled with a range of viable options, the structures of organization tend to be hierarchical, and delegation is a common pattern. The process of decision making is strategic in character, and there is a strong belief that progress is possible. Societies will prosper and be successful through strategy, technology, and competitiveness.

- Green: The thinking is relativistic, the structures are egalitarian, and the mode of decision making is consensual. The human mind must be freed from greed and dogma, the goal of life is a universal spirituality, and life should be lived in harmony with others.

- Yellow: The thinking is systematic, the structures of decision making are interactive, and the process followed is integrative in character. Life is a kaleidoscope of systems and forms that should be valued. Flexibility and spontaneity are appropriate styles and differences can be integrated into an interdependent whole.

- Turquoise: The thinking is holistic and the structures are global in character. The process involves a sense of the ecology of the earth, the world is a single, dynamic organism, and we think, behave, and manage within the earth's ecological alignments.[30]

Those who work within this understanding of memes also point to a new emerging meme, coral in color, and it remains to be seen how this new pattern will take shape. If in fact there is an evolutionary pattern of thinking and functioning in response to our environmental challenges, and organizations are shifting from one color to the next, then there are clear implications for finding the best ways to shape governance systems that serve the common good. All of these memes continue to exist in the world and in our regions and communities, and there is much to learn from the different memes. What is encouraging is that there is a pattern of development that is moving toward the formation of a more participatory, loving and compassionate way of creating a society that is characterized by justice and peace.

30. Ibid., 44–47.

This understanding of social evolution leads to one final characteristic of the changing strategies of governance that are emerging in our common life. It is that there is an *increase of participatory forms of governance*. More people are involved in shaping the national government, their state and regional systems, and there is increased engagement in creating a community that empowers its members to flourish. In fact, there is a trend toward both partners of the covenant (those who govern and provide services and those who live within the forms and government and receive a range of services) to step up to the expectations of the covenant and to jointly work for the common good. Every day, there are many exceptions in the communities in which we live. People are selfish and rude and unable to engage in civil discourse. Decisions are made that discriminate against those who are powerless and give special privilege to the decision-makers. People go hungry, are denied access to education and adequate health care, and are not treated justly in the judicial system. My point is not to deny how far we have to go, but to suggest that we are on the way and need to be engaged with others in the formation of a community that is filled with justice and love.

## THE CULTURE OF COMPASSION

We have been describing the geography of love, the contours and dimensions of the most enduring and life-giving value in human life. In this section, we are focusing on its expression in the primary relationships, its manifestation in our national and state governments and agencies, and regional and local organizations, and community initiatives. The images and pictures we have given to these lovescapes have suggested a very complex map, only partially explored in our trek. Some sightings are very discouraging, but others give us hope for the new vision and energy focused on creating a culture of compassion. We now take these signs at the national, regional, and local levels to the larger frame of our world and will attempt to trace the ways love, compassion, and their related values might play a part in painting a global lovescape.

## Section IV — The Practice of Love

### STUDY RESOURCES

### Discussion Questions

1. In what ways are love, compassion, and their cognates relevant and applicable to the formation of the "good society"?
2. Are you essentially despairing or hopeful about the future of your country and the region in which you live? Is the cup half full or half empty?
3. Do you think national and regional leaders of governments and social service agencies really sense that there is a covenant with the people to serve the common good?
4. Do you think that our current patterns, designs, structures, and organization in government and social service agencies are designed in ways that make possible the betterment of our lives?
5. What are some ways that you might serve the common good?

### Key Terms and Concepts

- *Covenant:* a formal agreement and relationship between two or more parties with each assuming some responsibility to sustain the terms of the agreement and maintain the relationship.
- *Common Good:* the endeavor to build a community that works toward the welfare of the whole, and not exclusively to secure one individual's well-being and advancement.
- *Requirements of the Common Good:*
  - The community contributes to the self-identity of its members but does not define that identity;
  - Members of the community participate in decisions which shape community life;
  - The society takes responsibility for its members;
  - The diverse individuality of each member must be respected.
- *Justice:* the application to society of an understanding of virtue (the good) and the use of reason (the right) to make informed judgments about the common good.

- *Meme:* our core intelligence and worldview that impacts our way of functioning, our value and belief system, and our mode of life.

## Suggestions for Reference and Reading

1. Beck, Don Edward and Cowan, Christopher C., *Spiral Dynamics: Mastering Values, Leadership and Change.* Malden, MA: Blackwell Publishing, 2006.
2. Covey, Stephen R., *Principle-Centered Leadership.* New York: Free Press, 1991.
3. Daley, Herman E. and John B. Cobb Jr., *The Common Good.* Boston: Beacon, 1989.
4. Marty, Martin E. with Jonathan Moore, *Politics, Religion, and the Common Good.* San Francisco: Jossey-Bass Publishers, 2000.
5. McKibben, Bill, *Deep Economy: The Wealth of Communities and the Durable Future.* New York: Times Books, Henry Holt and Company, 2007.
6. Mount Jr., Eric, *Covenant, Community, and the Common Good: An Interpretation of Christian Ethics.* Cleveland: The Pilgrim Press, 1999.
7. Sandel, Michael J., *Justice: What's the Right Thing to Do?* New York: Farrar, Straus and Giroux, 2009.

# 10

# Love in the Global Context: Creating a Culture of Compassion

## CLARIFYING THE MEANING OF COMPASSION

There are many ways to live our lives, and we are not absolutely bound to any one way. We generally have a certain amount of freedom within the limitations of our life circumstances and more as we mature and less as we remain driven by conscious and unconscious needs. In addition, as we travel through life, there is a wide variety of values that compete for our allegiance and these values guide us on our way. Our choices about how we respond to these options and how we choose to live our lives are profoundly influenced by our time and place in history, our family and relationships, our health, our culture, our education, our religious heritage, our talents, our access to opportunities, and the standard of living that is possible for us. Our choices, loyalties, and commitments are also influenced by our dispositions, our inclinations, and an "inner voice" that speaks to us in quiet moments. This inner voice may whisper many messages, and we need to discern which suggestions lead to a life of integrity, responsibility, and compassion and which ones may lead us into a self-centered life and even to self-destructive behavior. We have within us, as the Noble Indian Chief told his son, two wolves, a good wolf and a bad wolf, and our behavior depends upon which one we feed.

## Love in the Global Context: Creating a Culture of Compassion

Across the years, I have been shaped by the myriad circumstances that I was given at birth and that have come my way across the years. Within this context, there have been many voices and I have listened and followed a variety of them. Some have led me in good directions and have nurtured me and enabled me to mature and become more responsible. Others have led nowhere, and still others have led to situations that have been harmful and life-denying. My family life as a child was not all that positive, even dysfunctional. The culture I grew up in invited me to pursue possessions, power, and prestige. The messages I heard were that happiness consists in the abundance of things possessed, that control over others makes life better and easier, and that being important in the eyes of others can erase the discomfort of a poor self-image and insecurity and provide a sense of power and control. Fortunately, I was privileged to receive a good education and was exposed during my years as a young adult to a spiritual way of life. I did have modest talents, good mentors, and many opportunities, and there seemed to be enough money to enjoy the good life available in American society. I am grateful that the decades have been filled with a measure of peace and purpose as I fed the good wolf most of the time.

I continue to hear many voices calling me in diverse directions. I am more discerning now about their message, and the ones leading to a life of peace and purpose are the most persuasive and compelling. I try to follow the inner voice that invites me to a life of service to others, gives me a disposition that calls me to try to help others, provides the challenge to relieve suffering in all of its diabolical forms, and emphasizes the need to do my small part in building a more loving and compassionate community, society, and world.[1] I have been lured away by the values of a materialistic culture, a way of viewing others that exploits them and meets my needs, not theirs, and have sought the approval and attention of others. But no one of these inclinations has won the day. What has been telling in my decision-making and life commitments is the inner voice of God that has called me to a life of love and compassion. Biblical faith calls this voice the image of God or the Spirit of God and nearly every religious tradition speaks in its own way about this inner nudge and conscience. This divine voice has been clear: there are no borders, just horizons as we live out the vocation of compassion.[2] I have learned that love is "the threshold where

---

1. See my "The Way of Compassion: An Invitation," *Convergence*, 8–22.
2. Doctors without Borders, an association of physicians who serve around the world, uses the phrase, "not borders, just horizons."

## Section IV — The Practice of Love

the divine and the human flow into each other."[3] It is this threshold that I seek to make my dwelling place.

It is this call to love and compassion and its application to the global context that will be the focus of the final chapter. We have attempted to define love in its many expressions, but move more directly now to love's expression as compassion, which is the best word to describe the ways that love reaches out to the world. *Compassion is that capacity to identify with and feel the suffering of others; it is the inner awareness of shared suffering.*[4] This capacity leads to a sense of caring, a commitment to ease the suffering of others, and an engagement in responsible action to improve the lives of others. In many ways, compassion is something that you become, not just something you do on occasion. It becomes deeply rooted in your identity and a natural expression of your inner character.

I am influenced in my understanding of compassion by the way comparable concepts and words are used in the Bible.[5] In the Hebrew Bible, for example, the word most comparable to compassion is *hesed*, and it is often translated as loving-kindness. Other cognate words such as *grace* and *mercy* appear in the context in which *hesed* is used. The word *hesed* frequently refers to God's grace. It describes the way that God comes alongside to support and sustain. It gives hope to those who live on the edge of society, who are poor and hungry, and who have no access to privilege and power. The word is linked as well to God's covenant with the human family. God will show mercy and grace because of the promise inherent in the covenant. God will remain loyal and faithful and show loving-kindness regardless of our circumstances and behavior. God's steadfast love is unconditional in character.

In the New Testament, compassion is often associated with love, mercy, and grace. It is especially available to those who live with undeserved suffering, those who never had a chance, and those who got left behind at birth. The biblical bias is toward those in need. Compassion is the wise and caring action that reaches out in redemptive ways to the sick, the uneducated, the unemployed, and those who are marginalized. The

---

3. John O'Donohue, quoted in "Journeying Through the Days," a calendar published by Upper Room Books, Nashville, TN, 2010, between January 15, 2011 and January 16, 2011.

4. The Dalai Lama's small volume, *The Compassionate Life*, provides a succinct description of the compassionate life, and particularly how it is lived out in the context of Buddhism.

5. I am profoundly influenced by many other sources as well, and particularly by the understanding of compassion in Buddhist thought.

## Love in the Global Context: Creating a Culture of Compassion

essence of compassion in the New Testament is expressed in the passage that culminates with the Golden Rule: "But I tell you who hear me: Love your enemies, do good to those who hate you, bless those who curse you, pray for those who mistreat you. If someone strikes you on one cheek, turn to him the other also. If someone takes your cloak, do not stop him from taking your tunic. Give to everyone who asks you, and if anyone takes what belongs to you, do not demand it back. Do to others as you would have them do to you" (Luke 6:27–31, NIV).

Compassion is central to the ethical teaching of nearly all of the great religious traditions.[6] Confucius articulated the Golden Rule by saying, "Do not unto others what you would not have them to do unto you."[7] Hinduism understands that all human beings are in some sense one, and the creation is one, and any part is connected to the whole. So, linked as we are to the whole human family and the good earth, we treat all with respect, kindness, justice, and compassion. The Buddha encouraged those seeking enlightenment (the *Bodhisattva*) to dedicate their lives to teaching the way of enlightenment and the relief of suffering rather than to retreat to a monastic life of exclusive contemplation. Rabbi Hillel, an older contemporary of Jesus, said, "That which is hateful to you, do not do to your neighbor. This is the Torah; the rest is commentary; go and learn it."[8] The compassionate life is central to the teaching of Islam. Among its many teachings about compassion, the Quran teaches that we must share our wealth (*Zakat*) in order to create a society in which the poor and vulnerable are protected and respected.

---

6. Templeton, *Agape Love: A Tradition Found in Eight World Religions*.

7. Analects 15:23. Other religious traditions have different forms of the Golden rule. For example, Baha'i: "Blessed is he who prefers his brother before himself" (*Tablets of Bahaullah*, 71); Buddhism: "Hurt not others in ways that you yourself would find hurtful" (*Udana-Varga*, 5:18); Hinduism, "This is the sum of duty: do naught unto others which would cause pain if done to you" (*Mahabharata* 5:1517); Islam: "No one is a believer until he desires for his brother that which he desires for himself" (*Sunnah*); Jainism: "In happiness and suffering, in joy and grief, we should regard all creatures as we regard our own self" (Lord Mahavira, 24th *Tirthankara*); Native American: "Respect for all life is the foundation" (*The Great Law of Peace*); Sikhism: "Don't create enmity with anyone as God is within everyone" (Guru Arjan Devji 259, *Guru Granth Sahib*); Zoroastrianism: "That nature only is good when it shall not do unto another whatever is not good for its own self" (*Dadistan-i-Dinik*, 94:5). Compiled by Temple of Understanding and quoted in Joel Beversluis, ed., *Sourcebook of World Religions*, 172–73.

8. This quote is often called "The Great Principle." It draws upon Leviticus 19:18, and may be found in the *Babylonian Talmud*, Shabbat 31a.

## Section IV — The Practice of Love

### CONSTRUCTING AN ETHICAL NORM

Even as we suggested the construct of social covenant and commitment to the common good in the discussion of the place of love in national, regional, and local settings, so we suggest a similar although not an identical construct for the application of love and compassion to the global context.[9] We noted earlier that there are several views of ethics and the ways that justice is understood as a primary expression of an ethical theory. There is the theory of natural law, a view articulated by Thomas Aquinas in his *Treatise on Law* in *Summa Theologica* and developed by many others in its application to the modern world.[10] The first premise of Aquinas was that all laws governing human behavior must be determined by reason. Secondly, he argued that these laws must serve the common good of the whole society. By reason, we discern these laws and then follow them in order to secure our happiness, the fundamental aim of life, but they are only valid if they also serve society as a whole and insure that it is functioning well. He then says that these laws must be made by the people as a whole or by those who have the good of all as their clear motivation. And finally he argues that these laws must be enacted openly and not in secret. The underlying assumption in the argument is that human beings and their reason are part of the divinely created order of the universe. The natural law, according to Aquinas, consists of the way our minds operate when we are reasoning about what we do to achieve our ends. In essence, Aquinas says that we discern the natural law, what is right and good, through reason, and then we live in accord with it.

This view is persuasive and compelling in many ways, and reason is foundational in understanding and shaping ethical norms. But the risk is that even those who are most reasonable are limited in their capacity to discern what is right and good. They may have some self-interest in their reasoning and only be able to approximate what is right and good.

Immanuel Kant proposed an alternative view in his classic works, *Foundations of the Metaphysics of Morals* and *The Critique of Practical Reason*. He argues for the use of "practical" reason rather than purely theoretical reason in the attempt to know what is just. He says that the way to discern what is good and right in human behavior is linked to duty, and that our duty in essence is a categorical imperative, to "act as if the maxims

---

9. See Chapter 9. I am influenced by Rawls, *A Theory of Justice*, in this construction as I was in suggesting the ethical construct of the social covenant and the common good.

10. See for example O'Connor, *Aquinas and Natural Law*.

you choose to follow always became universal laws of nature."[11] Following a long and carefully reasoned argument, he maintains that these universal laws have a double edge: they must be maxims that we are willing to have everyone follow; and ones that treat everyone as an end rather than as a means to an end. Humans are not objects to be exploited, but should be treated with respect and in ways that promote the person's free rational choices.

This Kantian view has been quite influential and has many contemporary expressions. It too is persuasive and compelling. But if there is a tiny crack in it, it might be that human beings are not always able to be rational and fully understand what "duties" should be made universals. We may be too much the product of our limitations as human beings and inadvertently subject to the norms of our culture. Too often we see what is superficial and even self-serving, and not what is ultimately true and good. Further, our views may be shaped by our language, customs, and habits. We may name them as universal, but they may be controlled by our limited moral eyesight.

Still another view in the mix with natural law and Kant's categorical imperative is utilitarian ethics. This view was expressed in its classical form by John Stuart Mill in *Utilitarianism,* published in 1861. Mill's point of view also has contemporary expressions. It is developed by Mill and others in expanded and nuanced forms, but might be summarized as: "the good is that which is best for the greatest number." Mill notes that it is not possible to prove this assertion and recognizes that it is a practical judgment about the view that all people seek happiness, and that it follows that which brings general happiness to the aggregate of all persons is what is good and right. The risk in this view of course has to do with the reality that what makes some people happy may not make everyone happy, and it may inadvertently hurt others.

All of these views have elements of truth and value. Still another view, with classical expressions,[12] but given a more modern application is the understanding of justice proposed by John Rawls.[13] It is a view that argues that the good and the right, and justice and fairness are discerned in careful and reasoned debate. The aim is to achieve an egalitarian end and the treatment of all people fairly and with neutrality or "disinterest."

---

11. Beck, ed., *Kant Selections; The Critique of Practical Reason,* 316–17.

12. For example, the view of ethics in *Leviathan* by Hobbes and the writing of John Locke in the *Second Treatise on Government*.

13 *A Theory of Justice.*

## Section IV — The Practice of Love

In addition, to achieve a just society, there must be an effort to correct the imbalance that exists in nature and society and a public culture hospitable to the conflicts that will inevitably arise in this endeavor. We help to correct the imbalance by living in solidarity with those who suffer and engage in action to change their circumstances. It is a life of moral judgments and engagement, a view that has many of the risks of the other views, but adds a loving and compassionate component. This view is an invitation to the challenges and rewards of the life of compassion, and it suggests the need for a culture of compassion.

Those more deeply rooted in the biblical tradition would want to add both the foundational assertion that the life of love and compassion is rooted in the will and way of God, and that its application is given to us in the teachings of Torah and the New Testament.[14] It is not possible to insist that a particular country or indeed the many countries of the world should adopt a biblical point of view. But to be informed by it, given its extraordinary wisdom, does add to the depth and subtlety of human understanding. Following the biblical mandate to love God with our whole being and our neighbor as we love ourselves is to choose a life filled with great demands and extraordinary fulfillment. It is to follow the life that Jesus epigrammatically describes: "Whoever finds his life will lose it, and whoever loses his life for my sake will find it" (Matt 10:39, NIV). It is to live a life on behalf of others or as Dietrich Bonhoeffer said, live as "a man for others" and in so doing, to find true life. It has many challenging dimensions.

It requires, first of all, that *we pursue a spiritual way and give up a preoccupation with our own needs and desires* (not that these are unimportant in our lives).[15] What is needed is to be free from viewing the world through the lenses of one's own personal quest for happiness, again, not that a deep inner contentment and sense of well-being are unimportant. The life of compassion requires that we need "to forget ourselves on purpose"[16] and then we will find true happiness. It is how we find inner peace that matters and we begin to travel there by seeking the divine will and way. It is only when we are free from our own self-centeredness that we can truly identify with the needs of others. And it takes a lifetime, with continual

---

14. See for example, Hauerwas, *The Peaceable Kingdom: A Primer in Christian Ethics*, and the two volume work by Gustafson, *Ethics from a Theocentric Perspective*: Vol. One: *Theology and Ethics* and Vol. Two: *Ethics and Theology*.

15. In fact, it is when we have reached that point of maturity when our needs are no longer dominant, but managed wisely and well.

16. Mahan, *Forgetting Ourselves on Purpose: Vocation and the Ethics of Ambition*.

## Love in the Global Context: Creating a Culture of Compassion

and constant nurture, to reach a measure of this freedom. The life of compassion does ask us to pursue a spiritual pathway and be filled with the divine spirit however we may understand the divine presence within us. It is a process that means the cultivation of love, compassion, wisdom, and empathy through a variety of spiritual practices such as prayer, meditation, contemplative reading, and the support of a loving community.

Further, the life of compassion asks us *to get involved with others and live in solidarity with them.* As we do, we begin to realize how "messy" and demanding such involvement can be. It takes time away from our own concerns, uses our energy and resources, and is often an irritating interruption of our plans for the day and week. Our tendency is to judge ourselves as too important for the petty interruptions of others. It often causes stress and fills our lives with conflict and frustration. Early on in this endeavor, we often catch on to how important we think we are, and how difficult it is to change the behavior and circumstances of others. We soon get sick of the rhetoric of superficial piety and wonder why change is so difficult.[17] We begin to discover how easy it is to try to help others for the wrong reasons (e.g., to meet our own needs) and in inappropriate ways (e.g., to attempt to change others into the pattern in our minds). In time, with patience, discipline, and clear intention, we begin to make progress. We become more liberated and less driven, develop helping skills, cultivate generosity, and increase in wisdom. We discover it is possible to make a difference in the lives of others. We begin to ponder the reality that what we do does make a difference, and we need to know and decide what kind of a difference we want to make. So, using our gifts and talents, we respond in compassion to those in our circle of acquaintances. We also give ourselves to causes that create better lives for those who live in areas of the world where poverty, hunger, injustice, and lack of access to health care and education are the norm.

The life of compassion asks us *to make a caring and intelligent response to those in need.* Often our inclination is to assume that we know what is best for another individual or how to solve a particular social problem. We may make judgments too quickly, based on our own experience, and then discover that our own experience does not always cross over to other situations. The hard reality is that finding the right response will require study, reflection, consultation, and time with those whom we are called

---

17. Books such as Joyce Meyer's *The Love Revolution* may help those in the evangelical tradition who are beginning to follow the way of love.

## Section IV — The Practice of Love

to serve. We may assume we know, but then discover that the situation is more complex than we realize.

I remember a conversation from my recent past that taught me how wise we must be to truly help others and to change the infrastructure and social systems that either harm or heal and help others. This experience grew out of my work with the racial ethnic schools and colleges related to the Presbyterian Church (U.S.A.). For a wide variety of reasons, these institutions were profoundly challenged in their effort to sustain their financial stability and their educational quality. Often, in the pursuit of these goals of stability and excellence, the leaders of these institutions would approach the leadership of the Presbyterian Church with requests for financial assistance. After all, the presidents of these institutions argued, it was the Presbyterian Church that founded us, and the Church has a clear obligation to sustain us and the mission that our institutions represent. Such conversations were taken seriously by the leadership of the Church, but were often frustrating, even irritating, because of limited resources and intense competition for the mission dollar. One day, a person to whom I reported, reflecting about the complexity of such demands, partly with humor but also with some frustration, said to me, "Fix it." Of course my colleagues and I tried, but I also thought to myself that there is no way I can fix over two hundred years of racial injustice. I could only help as I attempted to find wise and thoughtful strategies to strengthen these institutions.

There is one other point that needs to be made as we attempt to more fully understand the life of compassion, and it is *that as we commit to the life of compassion, we choose a vocation and we need to assess the rewards and costs of such a decision.* A vocation is to hear the divine voice and respond. It is to take up a holy calling and be set apart for a special and divine purpose. The particular form our vocation takes will vary with each of us, but it asks that we invest our lives in building a more just, loving, and peaceful world. It will require the best we have to give, but it will also bring us profound fulfillment. There are costs, but so too are there great rewards in pursuing the selfless life of service. The rewards are not what motivate us to the life of compassion, and they are certainly not rewards in the way our culture generally thinks of rewards. The benefits are internal, and they often take the form of "fringe benefits." Jesus speaks directly to this point in the beatitudes when he begins them with, "Blessed are . . ." by which he means that blessedness is the highest state of inner peace and well-being possible for humans to experience. We are fulfilled as we

## Love in the Global Context: Creating a Culture of Compassion

show compassion; doing the will and way of God is deeply gratifying in the following ways:

- It centers us and gives a strong sense of *identity*. It helps us understand who we are and why we are here. It helps us find our best and purest self and sets us on the pathway to a life of authenticity and integrity.

- It gives our life *meaning and purpose*. We know what our life is all about and what our priorities should be. There will be many questions and struggles, but the broad outline is in place. We have a map, a sense of the big picture, and can find our way. Love and compassion become our Rosetta Stone.

- It clarifies the way we should live our lives and provides us with the *values and ethical principles* that guide us along life's way. We learn that a life of love and service is both right and fulfilling. We also learn that "a threat to peace and justice anywhere is a threat to peace and justice everywhere,"[18] and that our guiding values lead us to address these threats.

- As already mentioned, it leads to *inner peace and joy*, a sense of well-being and confidence in our ability to manage the stresses and strains that continually come at us. We will not be free from stress, frustration, worry, and fear, but we have resources within to guide us through these feelings.

- Our sense of vocation will lead us to *a sense of community and belonging*, knowing that we are with others who are on a similar journey. We are intricately linked to all of the human family, and indeed to the whole earth, but have a special community that surrounds us in love and support.

## CONNECTING TO A WORLD IN CRISIS

We began this discussion of lovescapes, exploring the geography of love, with a description of a world in crisis. It was suggested that love and compassion, and the several values associated with love and compassion, need to enter into our deliberations on how to address the harsh realities which humankind faces in the first quarter of the twenty-first century. We argued

---

18. A phrase often used by Martin Luther King, Jr. It can be found in the "Letter from a Birmingham Jail."

## Section IV — The Practice of Love

that this crisis is challenging, perplexing, and alarming. We acknowledged that these values do not provide the technical solutions to issues such as global warming, natural disasters, insoluble wars, insurgency and violence, religious intolerance, widespread poverty, and failing states, but increase the motivation to find solutions and shape the direction of these solutions. For example we ask, how do the values of love, compassion, caring, empathy, justice, and forgiveness influence the ways that multi-national associations such as the United Nations, or a regional group of nations in the Americas or Europe, or in Asia or Africa, attempt to solve global and continental problems that reach beyond the scope and resources of any one country? How do philanthropic agencies and non-governmental organizations pursue their goals of improving the life of the human family and the emerging global community? And how do divided countries, torn apart by religious differences and years of suffering, find a way to live in cooperation and collaboration, putting away resentment and forgiving one another for the centuries of conflict and oppression?

Finding solutions has and will require the best minds and the finest spirits within the global human family cooperating across all boundaries to seek a way forward at this critical moment in the earth's history. It is a time when we must not let the future happen to us, but choose a preferable future. It is a time to recognize that the world is in great peril and increasingly interdependent and fragile. We must come together, draw from the marvelous diversity of the world's many cultures, join hands as one earth community, and commit ourselves to a deep respect for nature, the protection of human rights, the quest for economic justice, and the building of a just and peaceful world.[19] Let's examine then how love and compassion and their related values can guide us as we seek to find our way in the following domains:

- Creating an earth community of care and respect
- Creating an earth environment with ecological integrity
- Creating a global culture of social and economic justice
- Creating a global context of democracy, nonviolence, and peace[20]

19. I am influenced by and will draw upon "The Earth Charter" published by the Earth Charter Secretariat, and adopted at the UNESCO Headquarters in Paris in March, 2000.

20. "The Earth Charter" suggests four overarching goals. The ones I am suggesting are somewhat different, but I do want to acknowledge how this Charter influences my thinking and what I am writing. The original Charter is now over a decade old, but its principles remain viable and their expression is being continually updated.

## Love in the Global Context: Creating a Culture of Compassion

We turn first to the profound need and the daunting task of *creating an earth community of care and respect.*[21] It is of fundamental importance to our future that we learn how to care for the earth and respect all those who call it home. The steps in achieving the inherent goals within this vision will meet strong resistance by powerful groups with vested interests, whole cultures with destructive habits and prejudices that have existed for centuries, and individuals who have become accustomed to patterns of life that harm the earth and members of the earth community. Part of the challenge becomes educating countries, creating new cultures, changing the mindset of groups of people, and focusing especially on ourselves and our need to change our outlook and practices. We need to internalize the realization that we live in and have a responsibility to an interdependent world. The following goals should guide this larger vision:

- It is essential that we learn how to respect our mother, the earth, in all of its diversity. We need to grasp the reality of our interdependence and recognize that all of life has value and that we live in a sensitive ecological system, even if we have grown accustomed to killing parts of life and harming its most fragile components in order to meet our own needs. The immediate challenge and perhaps the best place to start is to recognize the inherent dignity of all human beings and the ways that our diversity as a human family can enrich the whole family. We are in it together. As Martin Luther King, Jr. said, "We are caught in an inescapable network of mutuality tied in a single garment of destiny. What affects one directly affects all indirectly."[22]

- It will mean a fundamental shift of understanding about the human family. It is so easy to fall into the pattern of viewing humankind as made up of "us and them," of friends and enemies, and then proceed to violate and harm those who differ from us. We will need to learn how to respect the rights of others, acknowledge their beliefs and ways as acceptable and insure their rights to a good life. Inevitably there will be conflicts such as we now face with the development of nuclear power in Iran or reform in Syria, just to name two. It is essential that we find ways of peacefully resolving these conflicts. Part of the challenge is to affirm the truth: That increased freedom and knowledge of all people leads them to responsible living and the

---

21. I have found the books of Lester R. Brown of the Earth Policy Institute very informative about the challenges we face. See *World on the Edge* and *Plan B 4.0: Mobilizing to Save Civilization*.

22. In the "Letter from a Birmingham Jail."

## Section IV — The Practice of Love

promotion of the common good. In this affirmation we become a part of the solution, not a part of the problem. Others need not be like us and follow our way as long as their way is peaceful and just.

- Then we give ourselves to becoming advocates of democratic forms of governance that are participatory in nature and promote justice and peace, allowing for different expressions of these governance systems in different cultures. In our differences, especially with autocratic governments with policies and the language of threat, we negotiate firmly and wisely, reducing threats and increasing security. What is needed is to encourage peaceful solutions that ensure security and economic justice that enables an acceptable standard of living for all.

- We understand the earth and its resources as a wonderful gift and therefore seek to sustain it in its marvelous diversity and richness, and then make sure that it is available to generations that follow us. We use practices that encourage the sustainability and the flourishing of the earth.

This only becomes possible as we seek to *create an earth environment that has ecological integrity*. Once again, moving toward this grand vision will meet strong resistance. Not only will it challenge vested interests and call into question habits and patterns that have existed for centuries, it will also be met by strong and articulate voices maintaining that certain patterns of food production, its movement, and distribution are necessary to feed all of the people of the world. In addition, there are those who will maintain that we need to preserve entrepreneurial initiatives and freedom inherent in them if we are to make progress. These voices must be heard, and they do make sense in the short run, but we should not adopt these approaches at the cost of the exploitation of the earth's resources. Our future will require that wise and knowledgeable people in charge of governments and companies will need to be able to find ways of achieving and maintaining ecological integrity while overcoming the growing poverty and hunger in certain parts of the world. Together, as countries and regions, we will need to:

- Recover and then sustain the integrity of the earth's delicate and sensitive ecological systems with special attention given to biological diversity and the natural rhythms that sustain life. This will require educating those who farm and mine its resources, teaching them that environmental conservation is a "win-win" in that it preserves their livelihood and protects all of life. There will need to be regulations and safeguards that protect wilderness and marine areas that provide support systems for wildlife and preserve our natural heritage. Initiatives must be taken to restore endangered species and find ways to control the introduction of foreign and harmful organisms. It is important that we use our renewable resources in ways that do not exceed rates of regeneration and manage the use of non-renewable resources such as fossil fuels in ways that reduce depletion and do not cause damage to the environment.

- All of these efforts suggest policies of care and caution. We are at the point in our development when fundamental choices must be made or we will do such serious damage to our environment that it cannot be restored. We must find ways to sustain the expanding human family while at the same time preserving our good earth. New strategies and approaches will have to be tested in order to ensure that the ways we sustain the earth and care for its inhabitants do not pollute and build up dangerous toxins and hazardous substances. The avoidance of wars is critical to this care and caution. There are no winners in war; it destroys both human life and the environment that sustains us.[23]

- As far as possible, we need to prevent the harm to the environment that so many of our current practices are causing. Some of this harm may in fact be irreversible, and studies must be undertaken to assess the long-term consequences of certain practices, not the least of which is storage and build-up of radioactive substances. We will need to adopt patterns of development that protect the regenerative powers of nature.

- This shift will require an extensive study of ecological sustainability, and the knowledge generated from this research must be shared widely. There is a pronounced need to harness global science and empower it to focus on food production, the improvement of health, and the management of the environment. It will need to be a worldwide effort, shared with research agencies and universities, and with governments and private industries in every corner of the earth.

In addition to the grand vision of creating an earth community of care and respect and of creating an earth environment with ecological integrity,

---

23. The work of McKibben in *Deep Economy: The Wealth of Communities and the Durable Future* is especially poignant on this point, as are his other books.

## Section IV — The Practice of Love

we must also *move toward the creation of a global culture of social and economic justice*. Each of these components of our vision are interrelated; there will not be a global culture of social and economic justice if there is not the care and respect of all those who call earth home and if we do not have ecological integrity. For example, if we do not have care and respect for the community of life and if we do not have ecological integrity, then there will be shortages of food and those who do not have sufficient influence and wealth will continue to go hungry. We speak here of a global culture of social and economic justice, and as we do, we are keenly aware of the many ways that the word culture is used. Our use of the term suggests *an integrated pattern of human knowledge, belief, and behavior, and a set of shared attitudes, values, and goals*. Because different regions of the world have varying cultures, it is hard for there to be a single world culture. But because the larger good of our shared earth is so crucial to all of humankind, it is important that every effort be made to find ways within a regional culture to endorse the fundamental value of social and economic justice. Ways can be found in regional contexts to affirm this global value and to implement it, although the task is a daunting one. But alternative ways are possible within diverse customs, beliefs, attitudes, and norms of particular regions. It is possible for both China and the United States to say yes to a culture of social and economic justice, although a different means of achieving this goal will be followed. However the goal is pursued, it must have some of the following components:

- A primary goal of this larger vision must be to eradicate poverty with all of its damaging consequences.[24] This means finding ways to ensure that all people have access to clean air and water, sufficient food, a dignified way to make a living, educational opportunities, and adequate health care. As we move toward realizing these objectives, it is essential that we find ways to help those who are most vulnerable.[25] Bold steps should be taken to utilize the resources UNESCO, the World Bank and the International Monetary Fund in overcoming poverty.

---

24. The writing of Sachs, *The End of Poverty: Economic Possibilities for Our Time* and *Common Wealth: Economics for a Crowed Planet* speak profoundly and directly to the issues of global poverty.

25. For example, 42 percent of the children of India are malnourished and do not have a diet with sufficient nutrients. See Associated Press, "42% of Indian Children Under 5 are Malnourished," *The Seattle Times*, January 10, 2012.

- Every effort must be made to shape economic and tax policies to insure that all people have access to a dignified livelihood. Without removing the motivation to create wealth, we must find ways for a more equitable distribution of wealth both within countries and between countries. Attention must be given to provide resources for developing countries and to relieve them of debilitating debt. Basic to this endeavor is to encourage equitable trade practices and ensure fair labor practices. Attempts must be made to provide economic laws that require multinational corporations to be accountable and serve the public good and not yield to the temptations of greed and excessive profit.

- We must affirm, even in the face of strong traditional resistance, racial and gender equality. To accomplish this goal, we will have to seek to find ways to provide high quality education for girls in the developing and ethnic minorities that will enable them to pursue satisfying careers. Ways must also be found to open all of the channels of employment, decision making, governance, and cultural life to all citizens. There must be an attempt to strengthen the family as the unit of support and nurture so that every child will know they have value and are loved.

- Of course we must eliminate all discrimination based on race, color, religion, sexual orientation, language, or national origin. We need to give special attention to indigenous peoples, young people caught in the plight of poverty, and citizens of nations and regions plagued by drought and war and those with few natural resources.

Finally, to round out this vision of a better world, motivated by love and compassion, we will have to work toward creating *a global context of democracy, nonviolence, and peace.*[26] There are leaders in the world who argue that democratic forms of government, and especially those forms imported from Western Europe or the United States, will not work in their countries. They point out that their citizens are not sufficiently well-educated or trained in the ways of democracy and more localized decision making. Others argue that nonviolent means of preserving security are naïve and unrealistic in their part of the world. One listens to these arguments with respect, knowing full well that democratic and nonviolent practices are learned over decades and centuries, not weeks, and that even countries such as the United States must protect itself from the attacks

---

26. These words are borrowed directly from The Earth Charter.

## Section IV — The Practice of Love

like those of September 11, 2001. The vision to "move toward" remains, as we attempt to find every means possible to increase participation in governance, reduce violence, and secure a more just and peaceful world.[27] We move toward our goal in the following ways:

- Efforts should be made by all countries and within regions to establish and encourage democratic institutions and processes by increasing transparency and accountability, inviting participation and sharing in the process of making decisions that impact the quality of life for people and insure justice for all. Those who are impacted by a decision should be able to participate in shaping its direction, although not necessarily to control the outcome. Countries and regions must learn how to encourage the free expression of opinions and the right to gather in groups for education and action. Provisions need to be made to provide access to those in positions of power and insure that there is accountability in order to prevent any form of corruption or abuse of power.

- In addition, efforts should be made in all parts of the world to introduce into the curriculum at all levels of education the values and ways of the democratic process. Our schools should enable children to experience and participate in forms of decision making and the execution of local justice. It may be wise to introduce into the curriculum as well the forms and models of nonviolence, using the lives of Mahatma Gandhi and others as examples of major change through nonviolent means. Students need to be exposed to the mission and goals of the United Nations and other global and regional agencies that work in ways that encourage democratic practices and the pursuit of peace.

- Part of this vision of moving toward nonviolence and peace is to find ways to reduce the violence and cruelty to animals. Here we might learn from Muslim countries that have the protection of animals as a value of their religious tradition. The value of *ahimsa* (non-injury to all living things) in Jainism and Hinduism has wisdom for the whole human family. As policies are formed to control animal populations, hunting, and fishing, it is important that as far as possible we

---

27. A good example of movement in the direction of democracy, nonviolence, and peace and the means used to achieve an approximation of these goals is South Africa. See the accounts of this development in Chapman and Spong, eds., *Religion & Reconciliation in South Africa* and Helmick and Peterson, eds., *Forgiveness and Reconciliation: Religion, Public Policy & Conflict Resolution*.

eliminate animal suffering. Especially we need to develop and support ways to protect threatened species. Policies should be developed that are based on humane treatment and the sustainability of the creatures of the earth.

- Once again, to use the word culture, we will need to create a culture that affirms and even celebrates the differences within the human family. We must find ways to resolve conflicts, and when necessary to resist harmful intrusions by foreign powers, and explore the options of negotiation and nonviolent resistance. As far as possible, we need to eliminate nuclear, biological, toxic weapons, and all weapons of mass destruction. If they are not in the arsenal, they will not be used. So we pursue peace in every form, within oneself, with other persons, among different cultures and nations, other life forms, and throughout the world. We must make our home, our mother the earth, a peaceful place to live, to work, and to express all forms of love and compassion.

## COMMITTING TO A LIFE OF COMPASSION

At the risk of some repetition, I want to return to some of the material in Chapter Two on the many ways of understanding love. In particular, I would like us to relook at the meaning of commitment and categories used by the great sociologist of an earlier generation, Pitirim Sorokin.[28] He calls them "The five-dimensional universe of psychosocial love." They have special relevance for the ways we are speaking about compassion as the attitude that should inform policies and approaches to addressing the problems faced by the human family in the first quarter of the twenty-first century. We are speaking about this quarter and perhaps beyond it as a time of crisis, a critical moment in which we must make strategic decisions about planetary management and choose a preferred future to the one that our current behavior and practices are pointing us. We note again that love and compassion are not detailed and technical solutions to the overwhelming problems of our time, but these values provide the motivation and spirit with which they should be approached.

The first dimension of compassion articulated by Sorokin is *intensity*. It is that quality of love that is deeply felt and to which we are profoundly

---

28. *The Ways and Powers of Love: Types, Factors, and Techniques of Moral Transformation*, 15–35.

## Section IV — The Practice of Love

committed, not just a passing emotion stirred by the beauty of nature or a romantic film. Some expressions of love and compassion take the form of being polite as we might do by giving up our seat on the bus for an elderly person. We sense that a life of love and compassion also asks that we respect the privacy and customs of others, to be friendly and to listen attentively, and to avoid the many forms of rudeness that have become all too commonplace in our culture. This behavior is one level of showing regard for others. But many situations and certainly the ones we are dealing with in our time and our immediate future will require more than respect and etiquette. Those who were involved in the clean-up operations in the destruction caused by hurricane Katrina or by the earthquake in Haiti or by tsunami and the related nuclear tragedy in Japan have had to care more intensely; they had to care sufficiently to give up comforts and immediate contacts with family and to live with conditions of discomfort that required an unusual sacrifice. These conditions, and the many others caused by natural disasters in other parts of the world, exposed those who helped to the suffering and death of fellow human beings, an exposure that created the gut-wrenching feelings of sadness and grief. Only those who love intensely and who are committed to compassion will engage in behavior for a grand or needy cause such as relieving suffering or pursuing a more just social order.

Another concept chosen by Sorokin to describe a dimension of altruism is *extensity*. Not only do we need to feel deeply in our care for those who suffer, but we also need to think wisely about what caused the suffering and how the cause might be eradicated. We may not be able to prevent hurricanes, earthquakes, and floods, but we can build more substantial buildings and manage the land in ways that control the flow of water. The restoration of the city of New Orleans required action at every level of that city's infrastructure. Solving the problems in Haiti has been more difficult even with the two billion dollars that have been contributed. It points to the harsh reality that the problems of poverty and world hunger require a comprehensive global strategy that ranges far and wide and cuts across nearly every dimension of human organization. There are times when an act of love and compassion can be simple and direct such as providing a meal for another. It may mean that we do as the Good Samaritan did and help someone who has been robbed and injured. But there comes a time when the Good Samaritan must go to "city hall" and make sure that there is security on the road from Jericho to Jerusalem. It may mean extending our activity and engaging in the political process of changing the social

## Love in the Global Context: Creating a Culture of Compassion

structures. Our work in relieving suffering is extensive, reaching out in a multitude of directions to conditions that are both near and far.

A third dimension of compassion suggested by Sorokin is *duration*. The Apostle Paul notes about *agape* love, "Love never ends" (1 Cor 13:8a). Other qualities and gifts may cease to be, but true compassion continues, even in the face of obstacles, diminishing resources, and fading energy. Love finds a way of regrouping, finding alternative strategies, renewing one's own spiritual center, and responding in love to those to whom one has a commitment. It is certainly true that relationships come and go, and our emotions change by the hour, the day, the week, and our stage in life. The focus on particular social problems changes from era to era, and the needs of one group of people may seem to be more urgent at one time than the needs of another group. But many of the problems we face as a human family are sufficiently threatening in character and universal in scope that we cannot give up. The challenging issues of global warming will not just fade away, but continue to challenge the best minds and problems-solvers within the human family. Nor will the challenges caused by an increasing world population with all of the related problems of poverty and hunger. Our compassion must motivate us to stay engaged in the task of finding solutions as we are able. We will need to support those with the expertise and training to find solutions as elusive as they appear to be, and to vote for people and policies that that care about the welfare of the human family. Love and compassion have duration.

The next quality of love that is integral to Sorokin's description is the quality of *purity*. Inevitably, the ways we express love and compassion are mixed with a tangle of emotions and motivations, often linked to our needs. Even our ability to express love to our spouse and children is connected to the events and demands of a given day and our developmental needs at a given point in our lives. But we love more perfectly as our energy and attention is free from self-preoccupation, from the demands of our own needs, and our distortions of the reality of the particular circumstances in which love is required. We grow in our capacity to show compassion as we nurture a spiritual center, become people of integrity, and demonstrate empathy and care with a pure focus on the needs of the one or the many in front of us. In Richard Bernstein's mass, God is described as "the simplest of all" meaning that God is one and *is* pure love. Jesus teaches, "Blessed are the pure in heart, for they will seek God" (Matt 5:8). The pure see God clearly because their eyes are not full of the sands of distraction. We love others well when we have pure motives.

## Section IV — The Practice of Love

Finally, Sorokin speaks of unlimited love as having the quality of *adequacy*. This quality implies that our love must be appropriate for the ones needing love. On occasion, our heart is full and we are well-intentioned, but our offering of compassion does not meet the need of the person or group that we are trying to help. In some cases it may meet our need to be needed or our desire to be liked and thought of as a kind person. In these cases, some of our expression of caring may be helpful, but it may also be misunderstood and create some confusion and even suspicion in the ones we are trying to help. True compassion means that we learn how to love smart; we find ways to help others by discerning the adequate response. What is the adequate and appropriate expression of compassion as we lend a hand in Haiti or Somalia? How do we help those who do not trust us or what we represent, as for example members of the Taliban or those who are suspicious of the motivations of the U.S. presence in Iraq or Afghanistan? Compassion may motivate us, but its expression must be based on in-depth analysis, a sense of history and culture, the use of language that is filled with cultural connotation, and behavior that must cross cultural divides. For our love to be adequate, it must be filled with careful listening, cultural sensitivity, and an empathic grasp of the context. Paul reminds us that "Love does not insist on its own way . . . but rejoices in the truth" (1 Cor 13:5a, 6b). The expression of love and compassion must be adequate and appropriate.

### CLOSING CHALLENGE: CREATING A CULTURE OF COMPASSION

It is not always easy for an individual to fully grasp what it means to live a life full of love and compassion. It is even more difficult for larger groups of people to share a commitment to the values of love and compassion. Individuals may have a sensitized conscience that calls them to be caring, but groups of people do not have a conscience in the same sense as a person. In most cases these corporate entities function out of self-interest.[29] But corporate groups, communities, towns, regions, states, and nations can be guided in their policies and actions by values. These values are often expressed in founding documents and then re-expressed and interpreted as corporate entities select their leaders, plan for their futures, and

---

29. See the classic works of Niebuhr, *The Nature and Destiny of Man* and his book, *Moral Man and Immoral Society* which speak directly to the issue of a personal conscience and the self-interest of corporate structures.

## Love in the Global Context: Creating a Culture of Compassion

engage in implementing policies and programs for the common good. It often takes bold and visionary leaders to call groups of people to address the pressing needs of those whom they serve and to function in altruistic ways. We long for these leaders in our time.

Such leaders generally begin by asking those whom they serve to be *converted to see reality clearly and face it fully and responsibly.*[30] It often takes a 'conversion' whether in the context of an immediate crisis that shocks us into a deep understanding or by a growing awareness that comes gradually over time. A conversion is needed because we become so blasé, engage in selfish behavior, and are driven by greed and self-interest; these attitudes and actions have such a powerful grip on us. Individuals and the groups in which individuals function in their work, associations, and in their governance of region and country need to see the world as it really is and become more aware of how to live responsibly in reference to the realities of their regions, countries, and the world. All of us must begin to look beyond the assumptions of our culture and society, beyond the prejudices and biases of a world that is no more, and beyond an outlook on our culture and world that exclusively preserves our place of status and power. To stay put leads us into a life that can easily become careless, intellectually lazy, and potentially harmful to the life of others in our immediate circumstances, our society, and our world. Gradually, as I have had the privilege of traveling to many parts of the world, including many developing countries, I have had my eyes opened and been disabused of my provincial outlook and the all too prevailing view that my country is always right, has special privileges, and the right to control other countries. I have been motivated to read extensively and to take advantage of lectures and conferences in order to inform myself about the realities or our world. From trip to book to conference, over the past several decades, I have been intellectually converted and sought ways to live more congruently with what I have learned. I have also sought to share these perspectives with others through teaching and in my participation in a variety of groups.

Because of my increased understanding of the challenges we face at this moment in history and the harsh realities of the world, I have gradually changed my outlook associated with my place of privilege and had a *moral conversion*. I then had to raise the question of how to wisely share my new insights and commitments to larger communities and groups

---

30. I choose the word "conversion" knowing it may have negative connotations for some because of a less than satisfactory religious heritage, but it says what I mean. We do need to change directions.

## Section IV — The Practice of Love

and join hands with contemporary prophets to move this ethical vision to nations and to the world community. But *first I knew that I had to have integrity and act on my insights*; I had to live authentically. I continually sense that I am not doing enough, especially when I take account of my comfortable way of life. But what I have tried to do is to use my modest abilities, range of experiences, and limited resources and put my vocation of compassion into practice. Each of us will find different ways and levels of commitment in our expression of the call to compassion. We take into account the pattern of our lives, our obligations to family, and the unfolding of careers. Within this intricate network, we seek to express compassion and to influence the culture in which we live and find ways to make it more compassionate in nature. I have been converted, and need to be converted daily to fulfill my obligations to "do good," to be kind and caring, morally responsible, ecologically sensitive, and generous with time and resources. Then, in humble and caring ways, help and influence other individuals and corporate structures; they too need a moral conversion and to put their convictions into practice.

In addition to being educated to the realities of the world and being converted to a life of compassion, I find I need, and the organizations in which I associate need, to have an *emotional conversion* as well. I need continual inspiration to find the energy and commitment to extend myself in caring ways into the lives of others. My motivation to increase their well-being comes from *feeling love* for them. Our emotions twist and turn in the winds of life, and I cannot count on always feeling love for those around me; I get tired, frustrated, and need to focus on the tasks that life brings my way. But I need to find ways to be inspired, to grasp a grand vision of love for others, and to develop a compassionate spirit. As this internal spirit is alive and well, I will accept and affirm those whom I meet, and I will pursue policies and actions that are altruistic in nature within the several groups in which I participate.[31] I try in my own small way to be active on behalf of others by improving their lives through education and the cultivation of leadership skills. I fail daily, but press on and try to find in relationships that are open and honest the inspiration I need from others to be more loving.

There is a need for individuals to be informed, then to be converted to action on behalf of others, and subsequently to sustain these

---

31. For example, I currently participate in local causes such as the educational and social mission of a local church and committees linked to these missions. I also help Bread for the World and serve in more global causes with Board support for educational institutions in Pakistan and in the region of the Galilee in Israel/Palestine.

## Love in the Global Context: Creating a Culture of Compassion

commitments by intensely feeling the call to be loving and compassionate. In these ways, I hope to avoid what Mahatma Gandhi called the "Seven Deadly Social Sins:"[32]

1. Politics without principle
2. Wealth without work
3. Commerce without morality
4. Pleasure without conscience
5. Education without character
6. Science without humanity
7. Worship without sacrifice.

I conclude with the Charter for Compassion.[33]

> The principle of compassion lies at the heart of all religious, ethical and spiritual traditions, calling us always to teach all others as we wish to be treated ourselves. Compassion impels us to work tirelessly to alleviate the suffering of our fellow creatures, to dethrone ourselves from the centre of our world and put another there, and to honour the inviolable sanctity of every single human being, treating everybody, without exception, with absolute justice, equity and respect.

*It is necessary* in both public and private life to refrain consistently and empathically from inflicting pain. To act or speak violently out of spite, chauvinism, or self-interest, to impoverish, exploit or deny basic rights to anybody, and to incite hatred by denigrating others—even our enemies—is a denial of our common humanity. We acknowledge that we have failed to live compassionately and that some have increased the sum of human misery in the name of religion.

*We therefore call upon all men and women*—to restore compassion to the centre of morality and religion—to return to the ancient principle that any interpretation of scripture that breeds violence, hatred or disdain is illegitimate—to ensure that youth are given accurate and respectful information about other traditions, religions and cultures—to encourage a

---

32. These words of Gandhi are listed on a poster used by Sojourners.

33. This document was prepared by an association of good and gifted people and written by Karen Armstrong, the well-known British author of several important works on the history of religion and its place in the contemporary world. She has invited many people to join her in this work and several organizations have pledged their support. See the Charter for Compassion web site. Note that I have kept the British spelling and the sections in bold.

## Section IV — The Practice of Love

positive appreciation of cultural and religious diversity—to cultivate an informed empathy with the suffering of all human beings, even those regarded as enemies.

> *We urgently need* to make compassion a clear, luminous and dynamic force in our polarized world. Rooted in a principled determination to transcend selfishness, compassion can break down political, dogmatic, ideological and religious boundaries. Born of our deep interdependence, compassion is essential to human relationships and to a fulfilled humanity. It is the path to enlightenment, and indispensable to the creation of a just economy and peaceful global community.

## Love in the Global Context: Creating a Culture of Compassion
## STUDY RESOURCES

### Discussion Questions

1. How much freedom do we really have to choose our values and the course of our lives, and how much are we bound by our genetics, circumstances, and environment?
2. How might love and compassion be incorporated into the thinking and decisions made by those in government and other positions of power and influence?
3. What is the best way to discern what is right and good? How do we know what is just and fair?
4. How might I cultivate the ability to be more loving and compassionate? In what ways should I begin to express these values?
5. Am I really my sister's and brother's keeper? Do I have some responsibility for the well-being of others?

### Key Terms or Concepts

- *Compassion:* that capacity to identify with and feel the suffering of others; the inner awareness of shared suffering.
- *Culture:* an integrated pattern of human knowledge, belief, and behavior; a set of shared attitudes, values, and goals.
- *Hesed*: a Hebrew term meaning loving-kindness and steadfast love, often associated with God's love for humankind.
- *Natural Law:* a term generally used in contrast to the human laws of the state. It refers to that which is universally valid. It is discovered by reason alone, and in the thought of Thomas Aquinas, it is placed within humans and the universe by God.
- *Categorical Imperative:* to act as if the maxims one chooses to follow may always become universal, and then to express behavior toward everyone that views them as an end rather than a means to an end. Developed in the thought of Immanuel Kant.

**Section IV** — The Practice of Love

- *Utilitarianism:* the good which is best for the greatest number. Developed in the thought of John Stuart Mill.

## Suggestions for Reference and Reading

1. Brown, Lester R., *World on the Edge: How to Prevent Environment and Economic Collapse.* New York: W. W. Norton & Company, 2011.

2. Gustafson, James M., *Ethics from a Theocentric Perspective, Vol. One: Theology and Ethics; Vol. Two: Ethics and Theology.* Chicago: University of Chicago Press, 1981 & 1984.

3. Hauerwas, Stanley, *The Peaceable Kingdom.* Notre Dame, IN: University of Notre Dame Press, 1983.

4. Niebuhr, Reinhold, *Moral Man and Immoral Society.* New York: Charles Scribner's Sons, 1932.

5. Rawls, John, *A Theory of Justice.* Cambridge, MA: The Belknap Press of Harvard University, 1972.

6. Sachs, Jeffrey D., *The End of Poverty: Economic Possibilities for Our Time.* New York: Penguin, 2005.

7. Sorokin, Pitirim A., *The Ways and Power of Love: Types, Factors, and Techniques of Moral Transformation.* Philadelphia: Templeton Foundation Press, first published in 1954, republished in 2002.

# Bibliography

Ackerman, Diane. *A Natural History of Love*. New York: Random House, 1994.
"A Common Word Between Us and You," October 13, 2007. A Muslim document and letter to the Christian world community. Online: www.acommonword.com.
Afsarudin, Asma. *The First Muslims: History and Memory*. Oxford: One World, 2008.
Ali, Ayaan Hirsi. *Nomad, From Islam to America: A Personal Journey Through the Clash of Civilizations*. New York: Free Press, 2010.
Alper, Matthew. *The God Part of the Brain: A Scientific Interpretation of Human Spirituality and God*. Naperville, IL: Sourcebooks, 2008.
Amen, Daniel G. *Healing the Hardware of Your Soul*. New York: Free Press, 2002.
———. *Change Your Brain Change Your Life*. New York: Three Rivers, 1998.
Anderson, Donald L. *Organizational Development: The Process of Leading Organizational Change*. Los Angeles: Sage, 2010.
Aristotle. *Nicomachean Ethics*. Translated by J. A. K. Thomson in *The Ethics of Aristotle*. London: Penguin, 1955.
Armstrong, Karen. "The Charter of Compassion." Online: http://charterforcompassion.org.
———. *Twelve Steps to a Compassionate Life*. New York: Knopf, 2010.
Augustine. *The City of God*. Translated by Marcus Dods. New York: The Modern Library, 1950.
———. *The Confessions*. Translated by E. B. Pusey. New York: Everyman's Library, 1913.
Aurelius, Marcus. *Meditations*. In Whitney J. Oates, *The Stoic and Epicurean Philosophers*. New York: Modern Library, 1940.
Baer, Greg. *Real Love: The Truth about Finding Unconditional Love & Fulfilling Relationships*. New York: Gotham, 2003.
Barasch, Marc Ian. *The Compassionate Life: Walking the Path of Kindness*. San Francisco: Berrett-Koehler, 2009.
Baron-Cohen, Simon. *The Science of Evil: On Empathy and the Origins of Cruelty*. New York: Basic, 2011.
Bassett, Thomas and Alex Winter-Nelson. *The Atlas of World Hunger*. Chicago: University of Chicago Press, 2010.
Beck, Don Edward and Christopher C. Cowan. *Spiral Dynamics: Mastering Values, Leadership, and Change*. Malden, MA: Blackwell, 2006.
Beck, Lewis White, ed. *Kant: Selections*. New York: Scribner/Macmillan, 1988.

## Bibliography

Berry, Thomas. *The Sacred Universe: Earth, Spirituality, and Religion in the Twenty-First Century.* Edited by Mary Evelyn Tucker. New York: Columbia University Press, 2009.
———. *The Dream of the Earth.* San Francisco: Sierra Club, 1988.
Beversluis, Joel, ed. *Sourcebook of the World's Religions.* Novato, CA: New World, 2000.
Bloom, Allan. *Love and Friendship.* New York: Simon and Schuster, 1993.
Bloomfield, Harold and Sirah Vettese. *Lifemates: The Love Fitness Program for a Lasting Relationship.* New York: New American Library, 1989.
Bossidy, Larry and Ram Charan. *Execution: The Discipline of Getting Things Done.* New York: Crown Business, 2009.
Bowlby, John. *Attachment and Love: Vol. I.* New York: Basic, 1969.
Brander, Bruce. *Love that Works.* Philadelphia: Templeton Foundation, 2004.
Breasted, James Henry. *A History of Egypt: From the Earliest Times to the Persian Conquest.* New York: Scribner's, 1909.
Brier, Bob and Hoyt Hobbs. *The Daily Life of the Ancient Egyptians.* Westport, CT: Greenwood, 1999.
Bronfenbrenner, Urie. *The Ecology of Human Development: Experiments by Nature and Design.* Cambridge, MA: Harvard University Press, 1979.
Brown, Gordon. "Take Back the Future." *Newsweek,* May 5, 2011, 7–8.
Brown, Lester. *Plan B 4.0 Mobilizing to Save Civilization.* New York: Norton, 2009.
———. *World on the Edge: How to Prevent Environmental and Economic Collapse.* New York: Norton, 2011.
Browning, Elizabeth Barrett. *Sonnets from the Portuguese.* New York: Putnam, n.d.
Buber, Martin. *I and Thou,* 2nd ed. New York: Scribner's, 1958.
Burger, Julian. *The Gaia Atlas of First People.* London: Gaia, 1990.
Buss, David M. "Sex Differences in Human Mate Preferences: Evolutionary Hypotheses Tested in 87 Cultures" in *Behavior and Brain Sciences,* 12, 1989, 1–49.
Cacioppo, John T. and William Patrick. *Loneliness: Human Nature and the Need for Social Connection.* New York: Norton, 2008.
Carmichael, Liz. *Friendship: Interpreting Christian Love.* New York: T & T Clark, 2004.
Castenada, Carlos. *The Teachings of Don Juan: A Yaqui Way of Knowledge.* New York: Ballantine, 1968.
Chapman, Audrey R. and Bernard Spong, eds. *Religion and Reconciliation in South Africa* Philadelphia: Templeton Foundation, 2003.
Chapman, Gary. *Love As A Way of Life: Seven Keys to Transforming Every Aspect of Your Life.* Colorado Springs: WaterBrook, 2008.
———. *The Love Languages: How to Express Heartfelt Commitment to Your Mate.* Chicago: Northfield, 2004.
Chermack, Thomas J. *Scenario Planning in Organizations: How to Create, Use, and Assess Scenarios.* San Francisco: Berret-Koehler, 2011.
Childre, Doc, and Howard Martin. *The HeartMath Solution.* San Francisco: HarperSanFrancisco, 1999.
Chodron, Pema. *No Time to Lose: A Timely Guide to the Way of the Bodhisattva.* Boston: Shambhala, 2005.
Chopra, Deepak. *The Path to Love: Renewing the Power of Spirit in Your Life.* New York: Harmony, 1997.
Christakis, Nicholas A. and James H. Fowler. *Connected: The Surprising Power of Our Social Networks and How They Shape Our Lives.* New York: Little, Brown, 2009.

# Bibliography

Cicerio. *De Amicitia*. Loeb Classical Library. London: Heinemann, 1923, reprinted 1964.
Clark, Mary T. *Augustine of Hippo: Selected Writings*. New York: Paulist, 1984.
Cochrane, Charles Norris. *Christianity and Classical Culture*. Oxford: Oxford University Press, 1968.
Covey, Stephen R. *The Seven Habits of Highly Effective People*. New York: Free Press, 2004.
———. *Principle-Centered Leadership*. New York: Free Press, 1991.
———. *First Things First: To Live, to Love, to Learn, to Leave a Legacy*. New York: Simon and Schuster, 1994.
Coward, Harold and Daniel C. Maguire, eds. *Visions of a New Earth: Religious Perspectives on Population, Consumption, and Ecology*. Albany: State University of New York Press, 2000.
The Dalai Lama. *The Compassionate Life*. Boston: Wisdom, 2003.
———. *How to Expand Love: Widening the Circle of Loving Relationships*. New York: Atria, 2005.
———. *The Good Heart*. Boston: Wisdom, 1996.
——— and Howard C. Cutler, *The Art of Happiness: A Handbook for Living*. New York: Riverhead, 1998.
Daley, Herman E. and John B. Cobb Jr. *For the Common Good*. Boston: Beacon, 1989.
D'Arcy, M. C. *The Mind and Heart of Love: Lion and Unicorn in a Study of Eros and Agape*. New York: Holt, 1947.
Dawkins, Richard. *The God Delusion*. Boston: Houghton Mifflin, 2006.
———. *The Selfish Gene*, New Edition. Oxford: Oxford University Press, 1989.
De Burgh, W. E. *The Legacy of the Ancient World*. Baltimore: Penguin, 1963.
De Rougemont, Denis. *Love in the Western World*. Translated by Montgomery Belgian. Princeton: Princeton University Press, 1983.
Diamant, Anita with Howard Cooper. *Living the Jewish Life*. New York: HarperResource, 1991.
Dowd, Michael. *Thank God for Evolution*. New York: Plume, 2009.
Eagleman, David. *Incognito: The Secret Lives of the Brain*. New York: Pantheon, 2011.
Earth Charter. Earth Charter International Secretariat, San Jose, Costa Rica. http://earthcharteraction.org.
Emerson, Ralph Waldo, *On Love and Friendship*. Mount Vernon, NY: Pauper, n.d.
Epictetus. *Discourses of Epictetus*. In Whitney J. Oates, ed., *The Stoic and Epicurean Philosophers*. New York: Modern Library, 1940.
Erikson, Erik, H. *Identity: Youth and Crisis*. New York: Norton, 1968.
Ernst, Carl W. *The Teachings of Sufism*. Boston: Shambhala, 1999.
Esposito, John L. *Islam: The Straight Path*. Revised Third Edition. New York: Oxford University Press, 2005.
Ferguson, Duncan S. *Exploring the Spirituality of the World Religions*. New York: Continuum, 2010.
———. "The Way of Compassion: An Invitation." *Convergence* 1 (2006) 8–22.
Fisher, Helen. *Why We Love: The Nature and Chemistry of Romantic Love*. New York: Holt, 2004.
Fowler, James. *Stages of Faith: The Psychology of Human Development and the Quest for Meaning*. San Francisco: Harper and Row, 1981.
———. *Becoming Adult, Becoming Christian: Adult Development and Christian Faith*. San Francisco: Harper and Row, 1984.

## Bibliography

Freud, Sigmund. *A General Introduction to Psychoanalysis*. Translated by Joan Riviere. New York: Permabooks, 1958.

———. *The Future of An Illusion*. Translated by W. D. Robson-Scott. Garden City, NY: Anchor, 1964.

———. *Moses and Monotheism*. Translated by Katherine Jones. New York: Vintage, 1939.

———. *Sexuality and the Psychology of Love*. Translated by Philip Rieff. New York: Collier, 1963.

———. *Totem and Taboo*. Translated with an introduction by A. A. Brill. New York: Random House, 1946.

Fromm, Erich. *The Art of Loving*. New York: Bantam, 1962.

Gaylin, William. *Caring*. New York: Avon, 1976.

Gilbert, Paul. *The Compassionate Mind*. Oakland, CA: New Harbinger, 2009.

Gilligan, Carol. *In a Different Voice: Psychological Theory and Women's Development*. Cambridge, MA: Harvard University Press, 1982.

Gore, Al. *An Inconvenient Truth*. New York: Rodale, 2006.

Gottman, John M. and Nan Silver. *The Seven Principles of Making Marriage Work*. New York: Wiley, 1999.

Grant, Colin. *Altruism and Christian Ethics*. Cambridge: Cambridge University Press, 2001.

Greeley, Andrew M. and Mary G. Durkin, eds. *The Book of Love: A Treasury Inspired by the Greatest of Virtues*. New York: Forge, 2002.

Gustafson, James M. *Ethics from a Theocentric Perspective. Vol. One: Theology and Ethics. Vol. Two: Ethics and Theology*. Chicago: University of Chicago Press, 1981, 1984.

Hauerwas, Stanley. *The Peaceable Kingdom*. Notre Dame, IN: University Notre Dame Press, 1983.

Helmick, S. J., Raymond G. and Rodney L. Peterson, eds. *Forgiveness and Reconciliation*. Philadelphia: Templeton Foundation, 2001.

Heschel, Abraham Joshua. *God in Search of Man: A Philosophy of Judaism*. Northvale, NJ: Aronson, 1987.

Hoffman, Mary Ann. *All Kinds of Families*. New York: Little Brown, 2009.

Hunt, Mary E. *Fierce Tenderness: A Feminist Theology of Friendship*. New York: Crossroad, 1991.

Jackson, Timothy. *Christian Charity and Social Justice*. Princeton: Princeton University Press, 2003.

Johnson, Elizabeth. *She Who Is: The Mystery of God in Feminist Perspective*. New York: Crossroad, 1992.

Johnston, William, ed. *The Cloud of Unknowing*. Garden City, NY: Image, 1973.

Kavanaugh, John Francis. *Following Christ in a Consumer Society: The Spirituality of Cultural Resistance*. Maryknoll, NY: Orbis, 1982.

Kegan, Robert. *The Evolving Self: Problem and Process in Human Development*. Cambridge, MA: Harvard University Press, 1982.

Keller, Evelyn Fox. *The Mirage of Space between Nature and Nurture*. Durham, NC: Duke University Press, 2011.

King, Jr., Martin Luther. "Loving Your Enemies," "Letter from a Birmingham Jail," and "Declaration of Independence from the War in Vietnam" in the A. J. Muste Memorial Institute's Essay Series. New York, 1974.

## Bibliography

Kierkegaard, Soren. *Works of Love*. Translated by Howard and Edna Hong. New York: Harper Perennial, 1962.

Kohlberg, Lawrence. *The Philosophy of Moral Development*. New York: Harper and Row, 1981.

Korten, David C. *The Great Turning: From Empire to Earth Community*. San Francisco: Berrett-Koehler & Kumarian, 2006.

Kruger, Jeffrey. "Is God in Our Genes?" *Time*, October 25, 2004, 62–72.

Kubler-Ross, Elisabeth. *On Death and Dying*. New York: Macmillan, 1969.

Levinson, Daniel J. *The Seasons of a Man's Life*. New York: Knopf, 1978.

Levison, John R. *Filled with the Spirit*. Grand Rapids: Eerdmans, 2009.

Lewis, C. S. *The Four Loves*. London: Fontana, 1963.

Lewis, Thomas, et al. *A General Theory of Love*. New York: Vintage Books, 2000.

Lipman-Blumen, Jean. *The Connective Edge: Leading in an Interdependent World*. San Francisco: Jossey-Bass, 1996.

Love, Patricia and Steven Stonsy. *How to Improve Your Marriage Without Talking About It*. New York: Random House, 2007.

Lucretius. *On the Nature of Things*. In Whitney J. Oates, ed., *The Stoic and Epicurean Philosophers*. New York: Modern Library, 1940.

Luther, Martin. *Three Treatises: The Freedom of the Christian*. Translated by W. A. Lambert and revised by Harold Grimm. Philadelphia, PA: Muhlenberg, 1960.

Mahan, Brian J. *Forgetting Ourselves on Purpose: Vocation and the Ethics of Ambition*. San Francisco: Jossey-Bass, 2002.

Maji, Irshad. *The Trouble with Islam Today: A Muslim's Call for Reform in Her Faith*. New York: St. Martin's Griffin, 2005.

Marty, Martin E. with Jonathan Moore. *Politics, Religion and the Common Good: Advancing a Distinctly American Conversation about Religion's Role in Our Shared Life*. San Francisco: Jossey-Bass, 2000.

Maslow, Abraham. *The Farther Reaches of Human Nature*. Edited by Stuart Miller. New York: Viking, 1973.

McKibben, Bill. *Deep Economy: The Wealth of Communities and the Durable Future*. New York: Times, 2007.

Medina, John. *Brain Rules: 12 Principles for Surviving and Thriving at Work, Home, and School*. Seattle, WA: Pear, 2008.

Metaxas, Eric. *Bonhoeffer: Pastor, Martyr, Prophet, Spy*. Nashville: Thomas Nelson, 2010.

Meyer, Joyce. *The Love Revolution*. New York: Faith Words, 2009.

Meyers, Isabel with Peter B. Mayers. *Gifts Differing*. Palo Alto, CA: Consulting Psychologists, 1980.

Migliore, Daniel L. "The Love Commandment: An Opening for Christian-Muslim Dialogue." American Theological Society, April 4, 2008.

Mikulincer, Mario, et al. "Attachment, Caregiving, and Altruism: Boosting Attachment Security Increases Compassion and Helping." *Journal of Personality and Social Psychology* 89:5 (2005) 817–839.

Moltmann-Wendel, Elizabeth. *Rediscovering Friendship*, Translated by John Bowden. London: SCM, 2000.

Morgan, Douglas N. *Love: Plato, the Bible, and Freud*. Englewood Cliffs, NJ: Prentice-Hall, 1964.

Morgan, Peggy and Clive A. Lawton, eds. *Ethical Issues in Six Religious Traditions*. Edinburgh: Edinburgh University Press, 2008.

## Bibliography

Morris, Leon. *Testaments of Love: A Study of Love in the Bible.* Grand Rapids: Erdmanns, 1981.

Mortenson, Greg and David Oliver Relin. *Three Cups of Tea.* New York: Penguin, 2006.

Mount Jr., Eric. *Covenant Community and the Common Good: An Interpretation of Christian Ethics.* Cleveland: Pilgrim, 1999.

Murphy, Nancey and George F. R. Ellis. *On the Moral Nature of the Universe: Theology, Cosmology, and Ethics.* Minneapolis: Fortress, 1996.

Muslim Religious Leaders, "An Open Letter and Call from Muslim Religious Leaders to: His Holiness Pope Benedict, et al." Online: www.acommonword.com.

Nasr, Seyyed Hossein. *The Heart of Islam: Enduring Values for Humanity.* San Francisco: HarperSanFrancisco, 2004.

Nehring, Cristina. *A Vindication of Love: Reclaiming Romance for the Twenty-First Century.* New York: HarperCollins, 2009.

Neusner, Jacob and Bruce Chilton. *Altruism in World Religions.* Washington, DC: Georgetown University Press, 2005.

Newberg, Andrew and Mark Robert Waldman. *How God Changes Your Brain: Breakthrough Findings from a Leading Neuroscientist.* New York: Ballantine, 2010.

Nicholi Jr., Armand M. *The Question of God: C. S. Lewis and Sigmund Freud Debate God, Love, Sex, and the Meaning of Life.* New York: Free Press, 2002.

Niebuhr, Reinhold, *Moral Man and Immoral Society.* New York: Scribner's, 1932.

———. *The Nature and Destiny of Man.* New York: Charles Scribner's Sons, 1941.

Nielsen, Niles C., et al. *Religions of the World.* New York: St. Martin's Press, 1983.

Nitzberg, Rachel A., et al. "Attachment, Caregiving, and Altruism: Boosting Attachment Security Increases Compassion and Helping." *Journal of Personality and Social Psychology,* 89:5 (2005) 833.

Nomani, Asra Q. *Standing Alone: An American Woman's Struggle for the Soul of Islam.* San Francisco: HarperSanFrancisco, 2005.

Nygren, Anders. *Agape and Eros.* Translated by Philip S. Watson. London: SPCK, 1953.

Oates, Whitney J., edited with an introduction. *The Stoic and Epicurean Philosophers.* New York: Modern Library, 1940.

O'Connor, D. J. *Aquinas and Natural Law.* London: Macmillan, 1967.

O'Connor, Richard. *Undoing Depression.* New York: Little, Brown, 1997.

O'Donohue, John. *To Bless the Space Between Us.* New York: Doubleday, 2008.

Oord, Thomas Jay, *Defining Love: A Philosophical, Scientific, and Theological Engagement.* Grand Rapids: Brazos, 2010.

———. *Science of Love.* Philadelphia: Templeton Foundation Press, 2004.

Ovid. *The Art of Love.* Translated by Rolfe Humphries. Bloomington, IN: Indiana University Press, 1997.

Palmer, Helen. *Enneagram: Understand Yourself and the Others in Your Life.* San Francisco: HarperSanFrancisco, 1988.

Perls, Frederick. *Gestalt Therapy: Excitement and Growth in the Human Personality.* New York: Dell, 1951.

Parker, Helen. *The Enneagram: Understanding Yourself and Others in Your Life.* San Francisco: Harper SanFrancisco, 1988.

Peck, M. Scott. *The Road Less Traveled.* New York: Touchstone, 1978.

Pesso, Tana with Penor Rinpoche. *First Invite Love In: 40 Time-Tested Tools for Creating a More Compassionate Life.* Summerville, MA: Wisdom, 2010.

*Bibliography*

Peters, Thomas J. and Robert H. Waterman Jr., *In Search of Excellence: Lessons from America's Best-Run Companies*. Harper and Row, 1982.
Piaget, Jean. *The Construction of Reality in the Child*. New York: Basic Books, 1954.
———. *Origins of Intelligence in Children*. New York: Norton, 1963.
———. *The Moral Judgment of the Child*. New York: Free Press, 1963.
———. *Science of Education and the Psychology of the Child*. New York: Viking, 1969.
———. *The Equilibrium of Cognitive Structures: The Central Problem of Intellectual Development*. Chicago: University of Chicago Press, 1985.
Pinker, Steven. *The Better Angels of Our Nature: Why Violence Has Declined*. New York: Viking, 2011.
Plato. *Symposium*. In *The Dialogues of Plato*. Two volumes. Translated by B. Jowett. New York: Random House, 1937.
Post, Stephen G. *Unlimited Love: Altruism, Compassion, and Service*. Philadelphia: Templeton Foundation Press, 2003.
Post, Stephen, et al. *Altruism and Altruistic Love: Science, Philosophy, and Religion in Dialogue*. New York: Oxford University Press, 2002.
———, et al. *Research on Altruism & Love*. Philadelphia: Templeton Foundation, 2003.
Putnam, Robert D. *Bowling Alone: The Collapse and Revival of American Community*. New York: Simon and Schuster, 2000.
Ramadan, Tariq. *In the Footsteps of the Prophet: Lessons from the Life of Muhammad*. Oxford: Oxford University Press, 2007.
Rauf, Feisal Abdul. *What's Right with Islam: A New Vision for Muslims and the West*. New York: Viking, 2011.
Ravitch, Diane. *The Death and Life of the Great American School Systems: How Testing and Choice Are Undermining Education*. New York: Basic Books, 2010.
Rawls, John. *A Theory of Justice*. Cambridge, MA: Belknap, 1971.
Richo, David. *How to be an Adult in Relationships: The Five Keys to Mindful Loving*. Boston: Shambhala, 2002.
Rifkin, Jeremy. *The Empathic Civilization: The Race to Global Consciousness in a World in Crisis*. New York: Jeremy P. Tarcher/Penguin, 2009.
Robinson, George. *Essential Judaism*. New York: Pocket Books, 2001.
Rosenthal, Sheri A. *Toltec Wisdom*. New York: Alpha, 2005.
Runzo, Joseph and Nancy M. Martin, editors. *Ethics in the World Religions*. Oxford: One World, 2001.
Ruiz, Don Miguel. *The Mastery of Love*. San Rafael, CA: Amber-Allen, 1999.
Sachs, Jeffrey D., *Common Wealth: Economics for a Crowded World*. New York: Penguin, 2008.
———. *The End of Poverty: Economic Possibilities for Our Time*. New York: Penguin, 2005.
Sachs, Jonathan. *The Dignity of Difference: How to Avoid the Clash of Civilizations*. London: Continuum, 2002.
Sandel, Michael J. *Justice: What's the Right Thing to Do?* New York: Farrar, Straus and Giroux, 2009.
Scarf, Maggie. *Intimate Partners: Patterns in Love and Marriage*. New York: Ballantine, 1987.
Schiff, Stacy. *Cleopatra: A Life*. New York: Little, Brown, 2010.

*Bibliography*

Scioli, Anthony and Henry B. Biller. *Hope in the Age of Anxiety: A Guide to Understanding and Strengthening Our Most Important Virtue.* New York: Oxford University Press, 2009.
Sharot, Tali. "The Optimism Bias." *Time*, June 6, 2011, 40–46.
Sheehy, Gail. *Passages: Predictable Crises of Adult Life.* New York: Dutton, 1974.
Sider, Ronald J., *Rich Christians in an Age of Hunger.* Downers Grove, IL: InterVarsity, 1984.
Singer, Irving. *The Nature of Love.* Three volumes. Chicago: University of Chicago Press, 1984, 1987.
Skinner, B. F. *Beyond Freedom and Dignity.* New York: Knopf, 1971.
Slater, Lauren. "Love: The Chemical Reaction." *National Geographic*, February, 2006, 32–49.
Smith, David. *The Friendless American Male.* Ventura, CA: Regal, 1983.
Smith, Melinda and Jeanne Segal. The Holmes-Rahe Life Stress Test. In *Helpguide* (no date given), onlinewww.helpguide.org.
Smith, T. V., ed. *Philosophers Speak for Themselves: From Thales to Plato.* Chicago: The University of Chicago Press, 1956.
Snyder, C. R. and Shane J. Lopez, eds. *Handbook of Positive Psychology of Love.* Oxford: Oxford University Press, 2002.
Sorokin, Pitirim A., *The Ways and Powers of Love.* Philadelphia: Templeton Foundation, 2002.
———. *The Crisis of Our Age.* New York: Dutton, 1941.
St. Victor, Richard. *The Twelve Patriarchs: The Mystical Ark, Book Three of the Trinity.* Translated with introduction by G. A. Zinn. London: SPCK, 1979.
Stanley, J., ed. *The Standard Edition of the Complete Psychological Works of Sigmund Freud.* London: Hogarth, 1959.
Stein, Shifra and Aileene Neighbors, eds. *The Treasure of Love.* Kansas City, MO: Hallmark, 1975.
Sternberg, Robert J. and Michael Barnes, eds. *The Psychology of Love.* New Haven, CT: Yale University Press, 1988.
Sternberg, Robert J. and Karin Weis, eds. *The New Psychology of Love.* New Haven, CT: Yale University Press, 2006.
Sternberg, Robert J. *Cupid's Arrow: The Course of Love through Time.* Cambridge: Cambridge University Press, 1998.
———. *Love Is a Story: A New Theory of Relationships.* New York: Oxford University Press, 1998.
Stiglitz, Joseph E. *Globalization and Its Discontents.* New York: Norton, 2003.
Strachey, J., ed. *The Standard Edition of the Complete Psychological Works of Sigmund Freud.* London: Hargarth, 1959.
Stumpf, Samuel Enoch. *Socrates to Sartre: A History of Philosophy.* 4th Edition. New York: McGraw-Hill, 1988.
Templeton, John. *Agape Love.* Philadelphia: Templeton Foundation, 1999.
"Ten Vedic Restraints (Yamas)." Published by the Himalayan Academy, Kapa'a, Hawaii, 2009. www.himalayanacademy.com/basics.
Thich Nhat Hanh, *True Love: A Practice for Awakening the Heart.* Boston: Shambhala, 2006.
———. *Teachings on Love.* Berkeley, CA: Parallax, 1998.

## Bibliography

Tillich, Paul. *Systematic Theology.* Three volumes. Chicago: University of Chicago Press, 1964.

Toffler, Alvin. *Future Shock.* New York: Bantam, 1971.

———. *Power Shift: Knowledge, Wealth, and Violence at the Edge of the 21st Century.* New York: Bantam, 1990.

Tolle, Eckhart. *A New Earth: Awakening to Your Life's Purpose.* New York: Dutton, 2005.

———. *The Power of Now: A Guide to Spiritual Enlightenment.* Novato, CA: Namaste Publishing and New World Library, 1999.

Tolstoy, Leo. *Where Love Is, God Is Also.* Westwood, NJ: Revell, n.d.

Tone, Andrea. *The Age of Anxiety: A History of America's Affair with Tranquilizers.* New York: Basic Books, 2008.

Turkle, Sherry. *Alone Together: Why We Expect More from Technology and Less from Each Other.* New York: Basic Books, 2011.

Vacek, Edward. *Love, Human and Divine: The Heart of Christian Ethics.* Washington, DC: Georgetown University Press, 1994.

Viorst, Judith. *Necessary Losses: The Loves, Illusions, Dependencies and Impossible Expectations that All of Us Have to Give Up in Order to Grow.* New York: Fawcett, 1986.

Wagner, Walter H. *Opening the Qur'an: Introducing Islam's Holy Book.* Notre Dame, IN: Notre Dame University Press, 2008.

Wallis, Claudia. "The New Science of Happiness." *Time,* January 17, 2005, A1–A55.

Weiss, Robert S. *Loneliness: The Experience of Emotional and Social Isolation.* Cambridge, MA: The MIT Press, 1973.

Welch, Jack and Suzie Welch. *Winning: The Ultimate Business How-To Book.* New York: Harper Collins, 2005.

Welwood, John. *Perfect Love, Imperfect Relationships: Healing the Wound of the Heart.* Boston: Trumpeter, 2007.

Whitehead, Alfred North. *Process and Reality.* New York: Macmillan, 1929.

Williams, Daniel Day, *The Spirit and Forms of Love.* New York: University Press of America, 1981.

Wilson, Edward O. *On Human Nature.* Cambridge, MA: Harvard University Press, 1978.

Woolfolk, Anita. *Educational Psychology.* Eleventh Edition. Columbus, OH: Merrill, 2010.

Young-Bruel, Elisabeth. *Where Do We Fall When We Fall in Love.* New York: Other Press, 2003.

# Index

Abrahamic monotheistic religions, love in, 99–106
Academics, 64
acceptance, 205–6, 212–13
Ackerman, Diane, 58
action, 46
adequacy, 264
adult relationships, characteristics of, 204–13
affection, 207–8
*agape*, 33–34, 39, 43–46, 47, 67, 73, 82, 119, 180–82, 197, 263
    at foundation of Christian faith, 103–4
    as free gift of God, 69
    Nygren's exposition of, 69–70
*Agape and Eros* (Nygren), 69–70
aggression, 118
aging, 11–12
*ahimsa*, 93, 94, 260
Albert the Great, 67–68
Alper, Matthew, 140
altruism, 46–47, 178, 262
    conversion to, 168
    in human relationships, 143
    metaphorical, 144
    placing as highest standard of human behavior, 126
    study of, xi, 76–77
*Altruism and Altruistic Love* (Post el al.), 47
al-Wadud, 104
Alzheimer's disease, 139
ambivalence, 118
Ambrose, 64

Amen, Daniel G., 78, 140, 156–57, 171
Amen Clinics, 157, 158
*amicitia*, 68
Amini, Fari, 78
amygdala, 151, 173
ancient world, love in, 57–63
animals, protection of, 260–61
animists, 87
Antony, Mark, 57
anxiety, 22–23, 24, 117–18, 204
appraisal, 43, 59, 70
appreciation, 206–7
Aquinas, Thomas, 66–68, 83, 197, 248
*arête*, 84
Aristotle, 42–43, 58–59, 60–61, 65, 67, 83, 84, 85, 197, 200
*arjava*, 94
Armstrong, Karen, 184
*Art of Love, The* (Ovid), 62
Ashini, Daniel, 88
Asia, becoming the world's center of gravity, 8
*asteya*, 93
*ataxaria*, 86
Atharvaveda, 92
*atman*, 92
attachment, 84, 95, 176
attachment system, 77, 142
attachment theory, 55, 76
attention, 204–5
attraction, relationships of, 71–72
Augustine, 34, 35, 36, 64–66, 68, 69
Aurelius, Marcus, 62
authority, 126
autism, 139

## Index

autonomy, 123
awareness, mastery of, 89–90
Ayurveda, 92

Baer, Greg, 50
balance, 237, 250
beauty, 40, 60
Beck, Don, 239
Beech, Donna, 146
behavior
    explaining, 77, 114
    linked to brain functioning, 171–72
behavioral systems, 77, 142–43
belonging, 253
benevolence, 98
Beria, Raisa, 15
Bernstein, Richard, 263
Berry, Thomas, 129
bestowal, 43–44, 59, 70, 197
*Bhagavad Gita*, 94
biological sciences, studying love, 77
bio-reverence, 227
blessedness, 252
B-love, 75
*bodhichitta*, 96, 97
*bodhisattva*, 96, 176, 247
Bonhoeffer, Dietrich, 250
*brahmacharya*, 94
brain
    disorders of, treatment for, 158
    exercises for, 173–75
    health of, 153–55, 160, 169, 171, 206
    love originating in, 152–53
    structure of, 150–52, 157–58
brain model, 149–59
*Brain Rules* (Medina), 140, 153
brain science, 77–78, 139–40
Bronfenbrenner, Urie, 113–15, 122, 130, 131
Brown, Gordon, 111
Browning, Elizabeth Barrett, 54–55
Buddha, 168, 176, 247
Buddhism, 48, 91, 94–97, 173, 175–80
Buffalo Tiger, 88
Byron, George Gordon (Lord), 73

calling, 128, 245–46, 252–53
care, 47, 55
caregiving, 124, 142
*caritas*, 36, 67–68
Carmichael, Liz, 43
Castaneda, Carlos, 89
casual contact, 202
categorical imperative, 248–49
causality, 46
cave, Plato's allegory of, 40, 59, 60, 84
Center for Integrated Study of Spirituality and the Neurosciences, 172
change
    coping with, 16–17
    nature and pace of, 16
    need for, 165
    strategy for, 232–33
charity, 100–101, 106
"Charter for Compassion," 184, 267–68
Childre, Doc, 139, 146
China, 76
Chodron, Pema, 97
choice, 124
Chopra, Deepak, 183
Christianity, 101, 102–4, 179–82
Christology, 35–36
*chun tzu*, 98, 99
Churchill, Winston, 7
Cicero, 43, 64, 86
*City of God, The* (Augustine), 66
civilization, empathic, new vision for, 25
classes, economic, 61
Cleopatra, 57
climate change. *See* global warming
cognitive development, 120–22, 132
coherence, 147–48, 149, 169, 170
common good, 85, 86, 218–19
    covenant and, 219–20, 222–23, 227, 229, 232
    presence of, 221
"Common Word Between Us and You, A," 35n14, 104n38, 182–83
communication, 17, 192, 209–10, 214
community, 253
compassion, 47–48, 76, 94
    central to Buddhism, 175–80

# Index

commitment to, 184, 261–64
complexity of, 32
cultivating, steps for, 185–87
culture of, 241, 264–67
defined, 246
dimensions of, 261–64
life centered in, 112
pursuit of, 164
study of, xi
compassionate brain, 157
compassionate life, 96
compassionate love, 48
compassionate people, types of, 168
competency, adult, 124
*Confessions* (Augustine), 65
conflict, 5, 261
Confucianism, 91, 97–99
Confucius, 97–99, 247
conjunctive faith, 128–29
connection, 159, 209
conscience, 237
consciousness
　global, xi
　transmodern, 18–19
conservation, 226–27
consideration, 98
contemplation, 60
contemporary times, love in, 75
conventional moral reasoning, 125
conversation, 186
conversion, 59–60, 264–67
cooperation
　global, 9
　international, 4–5
Cortes, Hernando, 89
courtly love, 70–72, 73
covenant, 99–100, 219–20, 222–23, 227, 229, 232
Covey, Steven, 236
Cowan, Christopher, 239
craving, 95, 176
creation
　continuing development of, 34
　God's love of, 36
　story of, 34
crisis, language of, 111
criticism, 207

*Critique of Practical Reason, The* (Kant), 248

Dalai Lama, 4, 96, 177
Darwin, Charles, 77
Darwinian naturalism, 143–44
*daya*, 94
death, response to, 223
decision making, communal, 221
deconstruction, 18n24
deep limbic system, 158
deference, 98
*Defining Love* (Oord), 77
democracy, 259–60
depression, 23–24
desire. *See* eros
despair, 123
development, 8–9, 237
development crisis, 124, 127
*dharma*, 93, 95
*dhriti*, 94
dialogue, 174, 186
digital age, 16–18
directed memory, 159
disability, 23
discernment, 178, 245
*Discourses* (Epictetus), 62
discrimination, 259
distress, 21
divorce, response to, 222–23
D-love, 75
doubt, 123
Dowd, Michael, 139
dualism, 64
*dukkha*, 95, 176
Duplex Theory of Love, 75
duration, 211–12, 263
duty, 248–49
dyadic relationships, 141
dyads, 114, 131
dyads plus systems, 114, 131
dynamical evolutionary model, 141–42

Eagleman, David, 140
early fortunate, 168
earth, interdependency with, 88

## Index

ecological model, of human development, 113–15
ecology, 226–27, 255–58
economic justice, 258
economic policy, 259
economy
  global growth of, 8
  guiding globally, 9
  state of, 225–26
  urban-based, 8
education, 98, 229–30, 260
  access to, 12–14
  delivery of, 13–14
ego, 117
ego integrity, 123
Egypt, ancient, love in, 57–58
eightfold path, 176
electroencephalogram (EEG), 156
Emerson, Ralph Waldo, 201
emotional brain, 158
emotional health. *See* mental health
emotional maturity, cut-thru to, 170
emotional stress, 147
empathy, 48, 97, 119, 130, 166, 185, 208–9
enemies, 186
enlightenment, 91, 176, 177–78, 184, 247
*Enneads* (Plotinus), 64
enslavement, 58
environment
  affecting human development, 113–14, 130–31
  care for, 255–58
  changing, 113
  conservation of, 226–27
  influence of, 166, 206
  interaction with, leading to human development, 120
  supportiveness of, 159, 166–69
  sustainability of, 256–58
environmental crises, 8. *See also* global warming
environmental refugees, 6–7
Epictetus, 62
Epicurus, 85–86
epistemology, 59
*epithymia*, 41

equality, 259
equilibrium, 116, 117–18, 121, 169
Erikson, Erik, 122–24, 127, 129
*eros*, 39–41, 58, 60, 70, 75, 83, 84, 180, 196
ethical teaching, relating evolutionary biology to, 143
ethics, 59, 60, 126
  norms, 248–50
  principles, 253
*euonia*, 41n26
evil, problem of, 34–35, 64
evolution, 143, 184
evolutionary biology, 141–45
evolutionary development, understanding of, 159–60
evolutionary theory
  on early human history, 55–56
  on love, 77
excellence, 59, 237
exclusivity, 56
exercise, 153, 174
exosystems, 115, 131, 132
extensity, 262–63
extraversion, 194
extreme poverty, 14–15

fairness, 211
faith, 69, 174–75
faith development, 125, 127–30
Fall, the, 34
false friendship, 42, 85, 197
family, 132
  common good as goal for, 221
  relationships with, 98, 199–200
  settings for, 132–33
fear, 22, 89, 91, 184
feeling, 194
feelings, accuracy of, 73
Fetzer Foundation, xi n1
feudal system, 63
First Cause, 69
*First Invite Love In: 40 Time-Tested Tools for Creating a More Compassionate Life* (Pesso and Rinpoche), 178–79
first peoples, 87
Five Pillars, 106

# Index

forgiveness, 48–49, 210–11
forms, 59, 60, 84
*Foundations of the Metaphysics of Morals* (Kant), 248
*Four Books of Opinions (Sentences)*, 67
*Four Freedoms, The* (Ruiz), 89
Four Noble Truths, 95, 175–76
Four Passing Sights, 168
Fowler, James W., 125, 126–30
Francis of Assisi, 45, 119, 168, 205
freedom, 46, 237, 250–51
free will, 66
Freeze-Frame, 148
Freud, Sigmund, 73–74, 116–20, 124, 131
friendship, 41–43, 177, 196–97, 200–201. See also *philia*
   God extending to entire human family, 68
   love as, 58–59, 67, 68
   objects of, 68–69
   philosophies of, in ancient times, 86–87
   types of, 60
   value of, 86
*Friendship: Interpreting Christian Love* (Carmichael), 43
Fromm, Erich, 49, 74
frowning, 173
fulfillment, 124
functional MRI, 156
future, choice of, 254

Gandhi, Mohandas (Mahatma), 45, 94, 168–69, 233, 238, 260, 267
Gautama, Siddhartha, 176. See also Buddha
Gaylin, Willard, 47
*gemilut hassadim*, 101
gender equality, 259
generalized anxiety disorder (GAD), 22
*General Theory of Love, A* (Lewis, Amini, and Lannon), 78
generativity, 123
gentility, 98
Gestalt psychology, 130
Gilbert, Paul, 48

globalization, 111
global settings, 134
global warming, 4–l
God
   acting on behalf of people, 102
   as creator of the world, 34
   direct statements about, 103
   doing the will of, 253
   human connection to, 43
   image of, creating, 37, 47
   joining, as primary meaning of human life, 37–38
   kenotic style of, 34–35, 37
   kingdom of, 181
   as love, 33–34, 44, 103, 182
   love of, 35, 68, 105
   love for humankind, 102, 104–5
   person's perception of, linked to brain function, 172
   proving the existence of, 67, 69
   scientific interpretation of, 140
   triune nature of, 35
   union with, 43, 65
godly conduct, 94
Goethe, Johann Wolfgang von, 73
Golden Rule, 100, 103, 186, 247
good boy/good girl orientation, 126
goodness, 40
Gore, Al, 7
governance
   alternative strategies for, 238–40
   changes in, 19
   democratic forms of, 256
   humaneness in, 99
   participatory forms of, 241
grace, 66, 69, 87, 246
Great Work, 129
Greece, ancient, love in, 58–61, 84–86
growth, stages of, 60
guided imagery, 174
guilt, 123

Habitat for Humanity, 235
Haiti, poverty in, 15
happiness
   achieved in the supernatural realm, 65
   measure of, 135

## Index

Hatfield, Elaine, 76
healing, 70, 156
*Healing the Hardware of the Soul* (Amen), 156
health, 214. *See also* brain; heart; mental health; health care
health care, 11–12, 228–29
heart
　associated with love, 145–46
　change in, 135
　role of, in human flourishing, 78
　health of, 145–49, 169–70, 206
heart-brain connection, 146–48
*Heart Is a Lonely Hunter, The* (McCullers), 146
heart lock-in, 170–71
HeartMath, 146–49, 170–71
*HeartMath Solution, The* (Childre and Martin with Beech), 78, 139, 146
heart rate variability (HRV), 147
Heavenly Mandate, 99
Hebrew Bible, 101–2, 145
　compassion in, 246
　covenant in, 219–20
　story of, 99–100
*hesed*, 246
Hillel, 100, 247
Hinduism, 91, 92–94, 183, 247, 260
Holy Roman Empire, 63
homosexuality, 58
honesty, 94, 209–10
hope, 3, 76, 111–12
*Hortensius* (Cicero), 64
*How to Expand Love* (Dalai Lama), 177
Hsiao, 98
human development. *See also* humans
　crises in, 122–24
　ecological model of, 113–15, 130
　Erikson's approach to, 123
　Freud's approach to, 116–20
　models of, 115–30
　Piaget's approach to, 120–22
　shaped by interaction, 113
　social-cultural perspective on, 122
　stages in, 123
　theories of, 112

humans. *See also* human development
　complexity of, 119
　created in God's image, 37, 47
　developing meaning in their lives, 127
　in dyadic relationships, 141
　early life of, 55
　God extending friendship to, 68
　joining with God, as primary meaning of life, 37–38
　living in prison of fear, 89
　shifting understanding of, 255–56
　social nature of, 85
humility, 98, 186
hunger, 5

id, 117
idealization, 58
ideals, 59, 60, 84
identification, 117
identity, 123, 253
immaturity, blocking love and compassion, 124
impartiality, 46
improvement, continuous, 237
*Incognito: The Secret Lives of the Brain* (Eagleman), 140
income, adequacy of, 14
income gap, 7
independence, 128
indigenous wisdom traditions, 87–91, 227
individuality, 45, 221
individuative-reflective stage, 128
industry, 123
inferiority, 123
infidelity, 61, 63
infinite
　opening to, 90
　substituting for, 65–66
information technology, 16–18
initiative, 123
injustice, 100, 211, 233
inner coherence, 170
instincts, 116–17
integer person, 209
integrity, 169, 209–10
intensity, 261–62

intent, mastery of, 90
intention, 90
intentionality, 148
interconnectedness, 146
interdependence, 226
International Monetary Fund, 258
intimacy, 78, 123
introversion, 194
intuition, 194
intuitive-projective stage, 127–28
involvement, 251
irrationality, 58
Islam, 104–6, 182–83, 234, 247
isolation, 123

Jainism, 260
*jen*, 97, 98
Jesus
    drawing on the Hebrew Bible in his teachings, 102
    as model of love, 103–4
Johnston, William, 130
joy, 253
Judaism, 99–102
judgment, 46, 194
Jung, Carl, 193
justice, 63, 66, 85, 86, 100, 211, 230–32, 249, 256
    social and economic, 258
    understandings of, 231
*Justice: What's the Right Thing to Do?* (Sandel), 231

Kant, Immanuel, 248–49
karma, 176
*karuna*, 96
Keats, John, 73
kenosis, 34–35, 37
Kenrick, Douglas T., 77, 141
Kierkegaard, Søren, 34, 73
kindness, 98, 177–78
King, Martin Luther, Jr., 45, 233, 255
kingdom of God, 181
knowledge, 60
    increasing expansion of, 17–18
    obtaining happiness through, 62
    seeking, 186
Kohlberg, Lawrence, 125–26

*kshama*, 94

language, 122, 132, 174
Lannon, Richard, 78
laughter, 173
Lawrence, D.H., 74
leadership, style of, 236
learning, different methods of, 154, 155
Lewis, C.S., 41–42
Lewis, Thomas, 78
*li*, 97, 99
libido, 118
Lieberman, Debra, 76
life expectancy, 9
life partner, relationship with, 197–98
lifestyle, change in, 167
limbic brain, 150, 151, 152
limbic system, 157
Logos, becoming flesh in Jesus, 36–37
Lombard, Peter, 67
loneliness, 24–25, 198
love. *See also agape; eros; philia*; passionate love; romantic love
    in the Abrahamic monotheistic religions, 99–106
    as acceptable area for research, 76–77
    in ancient civilizations, 57–63
    Aquinas on, 67–68
    aspects of, 141–42
    Augustine on, 65–66
    biological understanding of, 77
    broader understanding of, 181–82
    centrality of, for Christianity, 179–82
    centrality of, to religious traditions, 83
    characteristics of, 33–34, 90–91, 104
    Christian tradition of, 67. *See also* Aquinas, Thomas; Augustine
    classical outlook on, 84
    cognates of, 46–49
    commitment to, 214
    complexity of, 32
    in contemporary times, 75

# Index

contributing to quality of life, 56–57
courtly, 70–72, 73
cultural variations in, 76
defined, 38–39, 49
development of, 109, 124
different forms of, within a family, 141, 142
disordering of, 66
double commandment of, 100, 103
Duplex Theory of, 75
elemental to human survival, 56
empowerment for, 175–87, 206
expanding the capacity for, 96
expressions of, 75
foundational New Testament teaching about, 103
friendship and, 41–43, 58–59, 67
given to others, 90–91
God as, 33–34, 44, 103, 182
of God, 35
growing capacity for, 138
heart associated with, 145–46
as ideal for life, 59
improving the capacity for, 159–60
in indigenous wisdom traditions, 87–91
Jesus as model of, 103–4
learning about, 164–65, 213
life centered in, 112
as Logos of the macroverse, 32
as mark of Christian life, 103
mastery of, 90
meaning of, 152
metaphysics of, 32–33, 38
in the Middle Ages, 63–72
modeling and teaching, 213
in modern times, 72–74
as motivation to solve global issues, 111–12
moving toward, 135–36
natural sciences research into, 77
objects of, 65–66, 68–69
originating in the brain, 152–53
for others, growing concern with, 87
phenomenology of, 75
power of, in spirituality, 183
practice of, 187
in primary relationships, 197–213
psychosocial, 261–64
self-giving and altruistic, features of, 44–45
as set of evolved decision biases, 141–42
as sexual attraction, 62
skills of, 165
in social and political situations, 97
social sciences research into, 75–77
stages of, 183
styles of, 75
as subject of inquiry and expression, xi, 74
as superior expression of excellence, 59
sustaining the spirit of, 213–14
in transcendental monist traditions, 91–99
types of, 39–46, 119
understanding, categories for, 58
understanding through the Hebrew Bible, 101–2
love songs, 72
love stories, 72
loving-kindness, 96, 101, 246
loyalty, 98
Lucretius, 61–62
*ludus*, 75
Luther, Martin, 68–70

macrosystems, 115, 131, 133–34
macroverse, 32n1, 34n11
magic, 58
Maimonides, Moses, 100
*maître*, 96
Major Depressive Disorder (MDD), 23–24
Mandela, Nelson, 233, 238
*mania*, 41
Manichaeism, 64
Marcuse, Herbert, 74
marriage, 56, 61–62, 63, 72, 183
counseling in, 212
postponing, 12–13
Martin, Howard, 139, 146

## Index

Maslow, Abraham, 75
masochism, 118
mate retention, 141, 142
mate selection, 142–43
maturity, 159, 160
    encouraging capacity for love and compassion, 124
    movement toward, 60, 112, 113, 120–21
    stages of, 60, 84
McCullers, Carson, 145–46
meaning, 253
Medina, John, 140, 153–54
meditation, 78, 159, 172–73, 174, 177–79, 185
*Meditations* (Marcus Aurelius), 62
Melasquez, Inti, 88
memes, 239–40
memory, 154, 158–59
mental health, 20–25, 78
mercy, 178, 246
Merton, Thomas, 169
mesosystems, 115, 131, 132
*metanoia*, 59
microsystems, 115, 131, 132
Middle Ages, love in, 63–72
Mikulincer, Mario, 77
Mill, John Stuart, 249
mindfulness, 185, 205, 206
mistrust, 123
*mitahara*, 94
moderate poverty, 14
moderation, 94
monastic communities, 169
monism, transcendental, 91–99
monotheism, radical, 35–36
moral development, 122, 125–26
moral transformation, 167
moral vision, 234–35
Moses, story of, 101–2
Muhammad
    love of, 105
    as model of compassion, 105
music, 173
Myers Briggs Inventory, 193–96
myth, 34n10
mythic-literal faith, 128

narcissism, 118
national settings, 133–34
natural law, 248
natural selection, 143
nature, as forming influence, 139
nature-nurture continuum, 113, 135, 138, 149
need
    exposure to, 167
    response to, 251–52
negative emotions, 148, 172–73
neocortex brain, 151, 152, 153, 154
Neo-Platonism, 64
Newberg, Andrew, 140, 172–75
*New Earth, A: Awakening to Your Life's Purpose* (Tolle), 184
*New Psychology of Love, The* (Sternberg and Weis), 77, 139
New Testament
    compassion in, 246–47
    covenant in, 219–20
Nhat Hanh, Thich, 96
*Nicomachean Ethics* (Aristotle), 42, 60
Nietzsche, Friedrich, 73
nirvana, 176
Noble Eight-fold Path, 95–96
noninjury, 93
nonstealing, 93
nonviolence, 259–60
Nygren, Anders, 69, 180

Obama, Barack, 10, 228, 235
Obama, Michelle, 11
Obama administration, 10, 12
obedience, 98
Oedipus complex, 74
*oikos*, 85
Oord, Thomas Jay, 50, 77
optimism, 76
other, recognition of, 186, 237
Ovid, 61–62

pain, 95
parenthood, postponing, 12–13
parents, caring for children, 55–56
participation, 167
passion, expression of, 72
passionate love, 61, 76

## Index

*Path of Love, The: Renewing the Power of Spirit in Your Life* (Chopra), 183
patience, 94, 102
peace, 253, 259–60
Peck, M. Scott, 50
perception, 194
perseverance, 211–12
Pesso, Tana, 178–79
*philia*, 39, 41–43, 60, 83, 84–85, 180, 196–97
Piaget, Jean, 115, 120–22, 124, 125
piety, filial, 98
Plato, 39–41, 58–60, 71, 84–85
Platonic love, 60
pleasure, 85–86
pleasure principle, 117
Plotinus, 64
Plutarch, 57
*polis*, 84, 85
political will, 237–38
population
    diversity of, 19–20
    increase in, 6, 7–8
positive emotions, 148, 171–72
positive feelings, 147–48
positive psychology, 76
positron-emission tomography (PET), 156
Post, Stephen G., 44–45, 49
post-conventional reasoning, 126
postmodernism, 18
*pothos*, 41
poverty, 14–16, 258
*Power of Now, The* (Tolle), 184
prayer, 159, 172–73
preconventional moral reasoning, 125
prefrontal cortex (PFC), 157
pre-modern times, 18
preoperational stage, 121
Presbyterian Church (U.S.A.), 252
presence, 204–5
present, emphasis on, 184
primary context, 132
projection, 118
prophet, role of, 36
protection, 55, 56
Proust, Marcel, 74

psychic health, 78
psychoanalysis, 116, 119–20
psychology, positive, 76
psychosexual development, 117–20
psychosocial love, 261–64
public good, serving, 102. *See also* common good
punishment-obedience orientation, 125
purchasing power, 14–15
purity, 94, 263
purpose, 253

quality of life, love contributing to, 56–57
quantitative EEG studies (QEEG), 156
Quran, 104–5

racial equality, 259
rationalism, 60
rationality, 86
rationalization, 118
Rawls, John, 249
reaction-formation, 118
reality
    Buddhist understanding of, 95
    holistic vision of, 87–88
    oneness of, 91
    partnering with the transcendent dimension of, 129
reality principle, 117
reciprocity, 177–78
reconciliation, 100, 210–11
Reed, Myrtle, 145
regeneration, capability for, 170–71
regional settings, 132–33
regression, 118
Reik, Theodore, 74
relationships
    adult, 203–13
    assessing, 193
    breakup in, 211–12
    committed, 183
    maintaining, 213–14
    primary, 192–93, 197–203
    widening, 177
relative poverty, 14
relaxation, 173

# Index

*ren*, 97, 98, 99
repression, 118, 131
reproduction, 56
reptilian brain, 150–51, 152, 154
resource display, 56
resource sharing, 56
respect, 97–99
responsibility, 221, 237
Richard of St. Victor, 36
Rifkin, Jeremy, 48
righteous behavior, 98
righteousness, 100
Rigveda, 92
Rinpoche, Penor, 178
*Road Less Traveled, The* (Peck), 50
Robinson, Edward Arlington, 3–4
role confusion, 123
Romanticism, 72–73
romantic love, 72–73, 139, 141
Rome, ancient, love in, 61–63, 86
*Romeo and Juliet* (Shakespeare), 72
Rousseau, Jean-Jacques, 73
*rta*, 93
Ruiz, Don Miguel, 88–91
rulers, 98–99
Rumi, Mawlana Jala al-Din, 106

Sachs, Jeffrey, 7–8, 9
sadism, 118
sadness, 23
sages, 98–99
salvation, 70, 87
Samaveda, 92
samsara, 176
Sandel, Michael J., 231
Sangha, 169
Santayana, George, 74
Sartre, Jean-Paul, 74
*satya*, 93
*satyagraha*, 94
*saucha*, 94
scholasticism, 67
Schweitzer, Albert, 168
second naiveté, 129
secrecy, 58
security, 55
self-awareness, 119–20, 196
self-centeredness, 250–51

self-compassion, 185
self-identification, 168, 221
self-interest, 86
self-love, 35, 68, 85, 90
self-mastery, 62, 63
self-worth, 207
Seneca, 86
senses, increasing power of, 58
sensing, 194
sensorimotor stage, 121
Seven Deadly Social Sins, 267
*Seven Habits of Highly Effective People, The* (Covey), 236
sexual feelings, 56, 61–62
sexuality, Freudian approach to, 118
sexual love, 71–72
sexual system, 142–43
Shakespeare, William, 72, 150
*shalom*, 100
shame, 123
shaping influences, 114–15, 131–34
Shaver, Phillip, 77
Shelley, Percy Bysshe, 73
*shema*, 102
*shu*, 97
Singer, Irving, 70–71
single photon emission computed tomography (SPECT), 156, 157
Skeptics, 64
sleep, 154
smiling, 173
social bonding, 159
social contract, 126, 219
social development, 122
social justice, 258
social order, 230–32
society, understood as extended family, 98
Society of the Missionaries of Charity, 238
sociobiology, 141–45
Socrates, 39–41
solidarity, 251
Sorokin, Pitirim, 44–45, 74, 75, 168–69, 261–64
*Spiral Dynamics* (Beck and Cowan), 239–40
spirituality, power of love in, 183

## Index

spouse, relationship with, 197–98
stability, 214
stage theory, 120–22, 127
stagnation, 123
steadfastness, 94
Sternberg, Robert J., 75
stimulation, 154, 155, 173
Stoicism, 62, 86
*storge*, 41, 75
strangers, relationships with, 202–3
stress, 20–22, 24, 147, 154–55, 204
subcultures, 132
sublimation, 118
sub-Saharan Africa, 7, 8, 14, 15
suffering, 46, 95, 175–77, 246
    empathy for, xi
    response to, 48
Sufism, 106
*Summa Theologica* (Aquinas), 248
superego, 117
support, mutual, 56
surrender, 184
sustainability, 9, 165, 256–58
*Symposium* (Plato), 39–41, 59
synthetic-conventional stage, 128
systems, transformative power of, 115

*tanha*, 95
Taoism, 97
tax policy, 259
*te*, 98–99, 99
technology, 16–18
Templeton Foundation series on Theology and the Sciences, 33n6
temporal lobes, 158
Ten Commandments, 102
Ten Vedic Restraints, 93–94
Teresa of Avila, 169
Teresa of Calcutta, Mother, 205, 238
thinking, 194
Thomas Aquinas. *See* Aquinas, Thomas
Three Great Jewels of Refuge, 176–77
*T'ien*, 97
*tikkum olam*, 101
Tolle, Eckhart, 183–84
Tolstoy, Leo, 73

Toltec people (Southern Mexico), 88–91
Torah, 99, 100, 101, 102
tranquility, 86, 92
transformation, 103, 168, 185–86
    mastery of, 90
    moral, 167
transmodern consciousness, 18–19
travel, 17
tribal outlook, 186
Trinity, God as, 35–36
trust, 123, 210
truth, personal search for, 87
truthfulness, 93
two-person systems, 114
*tzedakah*, 100

unanimity, 85
unconditional acceptance, 205–6
unconditional love, 102
unconscious, in the human psyche, 131
unconscious wishes, 117
understanding, human, shift in, 18–19
Underwood, Lynn, 48
undifferentiated faith, 127
UNESCO, 258
United Nations, 260
United States
    aging of, 11–12
    conditions in, 218–19, 220
    economy in, 225–26
    education in, 14, 229–30
    government in, mistrust of, 20
    health care in, 228–29
    justice in, 230–32
    limits of, 10
    new moral vision in, 234–35
    romantic love in, 76
universalizing faith, 129
universal law, 249
universe
    achieving harmony with, 92
    dualistic understanding of, 64
    as projection of God, 106
    structure of, 92–93
utilitarian ethics, 249
*Utilitarianism* (Mill), 249

values, 61, 253
  discerning, 158
  as focus of religious traditions, 205
  influencing understanding of love, 76
Vedas, 92
Venezuela, 15
violence
  religious, 182
  resorting to, 10
virtue, 62, 84, 86
vision, 155
visualization, 174
vocation, 128, 130, 252–53
Vygotsky, Lev Semenovich, 122n19

Waldman, Mark Robert, 140, 172–75
war, 5, 9–10
water
  access to, 6
  competition for, 5

wealth gap, 8, 9
well-being, scientific research into, 78–79
William IX, 72
William of Ockham, 69
William, Daniel Day, 45–46
Wilson, Edward O., 143
wishes, 117
women, discrimination against, 105n43
Woolman, John, 168
work, relationships at, 201–2
World Bank, 258

*Yama*, 93–94
yawning, 173
yogic breathing, 173

*Zakat*, 106
Zeno, 62

www.ingramcontent.com/pod-product-compliance
Lightning Source LLC
Chambersburg PA
CBHW032051220426
43664CB00008B/959